Social Stratification in Polynesia

THE AMERICAN ETHNOLOGICAL SOCIETY

Verne F. Ray, Editor

Social Stratification in Polynesia

By Marshall D. Sahlins

1958

UNIVERSITY OF WASHINGTON PRESS

Seattle

Lithographed in the United States of America

Acknowledgments

FOR CONSTRUCTIVE CRITICISM and suggestions made while I was writing this monograph, I wish to thank Professors Conrad Arensberg and Marvin Harris of Columbia University. I am especially grateful to Professor Morton H. Fried, also of Columbia, for encouragement at every stage of the research, and for seeing it through to conclusion and publication.

To Professor Leslie A. White of the University of Michigan I am indebted for the training which has led to the formulation of many of the hypotheses of this work. I thank Professor White for stimulation and guidance in the application of scientific methodology to the study of culture.

A grant from the Department of Anthropology of Columbia University to the American Ethnological Society defrayed a part of the costs of this publication. This grant I gratefully acknowledge.

It is impossible to exaggerate my debt to my wife, Barbara, who contributed not only her services in typing but also her confidence in the outcome of the research.

M. D. Sahlins

November 12, 1955
New York

v

Contents

FIGURES

Introduction

THIS IS A study of adaptive variation in culture. It attempts to relate differences in an aspect of the social systems of aboriginal Polynesia--stratification--to differences in the adaptation of the cultures to their environments. Technology is the subsystem of culture which articulates with environment; hence, the methodology of this study consists of relating variations in social stratification to variations in technological and environmental conditions. Stratification is viewed as an aspect of social structure functionally adjusted to the technological exploitation of the environment.

It is not claimed that the methodology or the concepts involved are new ones. The novelty of the present study is the attempt to explain social differentiation within a group of genetically related cultures. The Polynesian cultures derive from a common source; they are members of a single cultural genus that has filled in and adapted to a variety of local habitats. Since the environments and the techniques of adaptation vary, it can be expected that the social systems correspondingly vary. Specifically we show that social stratification varies both in degree and form according to ecological conditions.

The problem is not one of simple correlation between social stratification and ecological factors. There is a structural link between the technological base and the stratification superstratum. We shall find that certain elements of the economy, particularly the method of distributing food and other basic goods, bring ecology and social stratification into direct relationship.

A word of warning. Our explanation of variation in terms

of adaptation does not mean that such historical processes as diffusion are ignored. This study does not side with "internal development" as somehow opposed to diffusion. When considering cultural adaptation, this long-standing argument is unnecessary. A culture is at the same time a product of its traditions, including diffusionary influences, and its adaptation to its natural habitat. The actual process of adaptation depends, to a great extent, on the previous cultural form and the outside influences upon it. One cannot have a complete understanding of the differences between two cultures without knowledge of their previous forms as well as of their present adaptations. One could not explain the biological differences between primates and earthworms simply from the fact that primates took to the trees whereas earthworms took to the earth. Considering this, the choice of Polynesia as a laboratory for the study of cultural adaptation is a judicious one, for all Polynesian cultures have a great part of their history in common--tradition is almost a constant. Nevertheless, cognizance will be taken of the possibility that diffusion or some other historical process, perhaps nonadaptive, may have been operating differentially on features of social stratification in particular cases.

Social stratification may be divided into two aspects, the degree of stratification and the form of the stratification system. "Degree of stratification" refers to the complexity of the status system, i.e., the number of different kinds of ranks, and the extent to which they confer unequal privilege in economic, social and religious life.[1] "Form of stratification" refers to the social organization of the status system, that is, the sociological principles that determine rank differences. The treatment is divided into two parts following this division of the subject matter.

Variations in degree of stratification are considered first. "Degree of stratification" has an important implication for the evolution of political organization in primitive, kinship-based societies. It is common knowledge that societies at the lowest levels of culture are relatively unstratified, whereas stratification becomes more definite in more highly

---

1. The words "status" and "rank" will be used interchangeably because making a distinction between them does not clarify our problems.

developed cultures. Differences in degree of stratification may be built into the kinship structure of the society. As Paul Kirchhoff has shown, within some kin systems currently going under the term "clan" there is little status differentiation, while in other so-called "clans" differences in rank are closely associated with genealogical status.[2] However, kin societies can be classified by degree of stratification regardless of the type of clan. This type of classification is absolutely necessary if one aims to state a general theory of stratification, since there are many primitive societies which lack unilineal descent groups. Landtman, in attempting to explain the origins of social inequality, followed such a procedure.[3] Likewise in Polynesia it is possible to describe a gradient from more equalitarian to more stratified societies without direct reference to types of kin units. Furthermore, this series can be correlated with proportional changes in the technoenvironmental sphere.

A number of Polynesian cultures are classified below by degree of stratification. The relationship between stratification and certain ecological features, particularly technological productivity, is then tested. It is shown that, other factors being constant, the degree of stratification varies directly with productivity. This relationship appears to depend on the association between differences in rank and differences in function in the process of the distribution of goods. Everywhere in Polynesia, the chief is the agent of general, tribal-wide distribution. The chief derives prestige from his generosity. In turn, his prestige permits him to exercise control over social processes, such as production, upon which his functions of distribution rest. Consequently the greater the productivity, the greater the distributive activities of the chief, and the greater his powers.

We shall also consider the specific social organizations of stratification from the viewpoint of adaptive variation. Three types of social structure, each having a corresponding form of stratification, are distinguished in Polynesia. The first, called here the "ramage system," is based upon internally

---

2. Paul Kirchhoff, "The Principles of Clanship in Human Society," Davidson Anthropological Journal, I (1955), 1-11.

3. Gunnar Landtman, The Origin of the Inequality of the Social Classes (Chicago, 1938).

ranked, segmentary unilineal kin groups acting also as political units. The second is designated the "descent-line system" and is characterized by discrete, localized common
descent groups organized into territorial political entities.
Both ramage and descent-line systems are found mainly on
high or volcanic islands. The social systems of the atolls
tend to be distinctive in type. Elements of the two high-island systems may be found, but these are frequently combined into complex organizations of interlocking social
groups different from both ramage and descent-line structure. Generally each form of system is associated with a
particular set of ecological conditions. Ramage organization occurs with conditions of widely spread zones of highly
productive resources. Descent-line systems are found with
spatial concentration of highly productive resource zones.
Atoll organizations are related to low productivity and a
limited range of exploitative techniques.

This study is concerned with Polynesian cultures in the
ethnographic present, that is, at the time just prior to European influence. Any trait that can be attributed to European influence is excluded. Polynesia is defined as those islands usually considered by anthropologists to be Polynesian
in culture and language. This includes all the islands within
the triangle formed by Hawaii, New Zealand, and Easter Island, excluding Fiji, but including outliers located west of
the triangle, such as Tikopia and Ontong Java.

The major consideration in selecting cultures to be compared was the availability of ethnographical studies by com-
petent, trained observers. Hawaii and the Society Islands,
though lacking complete ethnographies, are included because
of their traditional importance. A second consideration was
the adequacy, for present purposes, of the ethnographic data. The islands of Niue and Tubuai are excluded because of
the paucity of information on economic and social organization. [4] The following are considered: Easter Island, Futuna,
Hawaii, Mangaia, Mangareva, Manihiki-Rakahanga, Marquesas, New Zealand, Ontong Java, Pukapuka, Samoa, So-

---

4. Edwin M. Loeb, History and Traditions of Niue (Bernice Pahau Bishop Museum Bulletin, No. 32 [1926]); Robert T. Aitken, Ethnology of Tubuai (Bernice Pahau Bishop
Museum Bulletin, No. 70 [1930]).

ciety Islands (primarily Tahiti), Tikopia, Tokelau, Tonga, Tongareva, and Uvea. Degree of social stratification is not treated for Manihiki-Rakahanga and Tongareva because the major sources lack specific information on economic processes, especially on distribution and production.[5] The New Zealand Maori are also excluded from such treatment because the most comprehensive reports treat Maori culture in generalized or "typical" terms, often failing to make clear the regional variation which existed. Corresponding to local conditions, Maori villages varied in their technological systems from pure hunting and gathering to rather intensive horticulture. The productivity differences connoted by this diversity of techniques are of first importance in evaluating the relationship between productivity and the degree of social stratification. It is therefore unsafe to proceed in the absence of specific information on specific Maori groups.

The sources utilized are primarily ethnographical. With the exception of the classic missionary accounts, such as those of Gill, Turner, Ellis, and a few others, original historical sources are rarely used. However, Williamson's exhaustive summary of these sources has been consulted.[6] Also, the ethnographic monographs usually summarize relevant historical materials.[7]

---

5. See Peter H. Buck, Ethnology of Tongareva (Bernice Pahau Bishop Museum Bulletin, No. 92 [1932]); Peter H. Buck, Ethnology of Manihiki and Rakahanga (Bernice Pahau Bishop Museum Bulletin, No. 99 [1932]).

6. Robert W. Williamson, The Social and Political Systems of Central Polynesia (Cambridge, Eng., 1924).

7. After the manuscript of this monograph had been completed, the author made an extended ethnographic study of the island of Moala in southeast Fiji investigating the same aspects of culture as those which are discussed in the present study. No attempt will be made here to generalize on the basis of these additional data, but it is of interest that no facts were encountered that would seriously challenge the major hypotheses developed here.

1. Social Stratification in Kinship Societies

VARIOUS DEGREES OF stratification can be distinguished among societies organized by kinship. There are some showing marked status distinctions, some in which equality characterizes most social relations, and a large range of intermediate types. A graduated series of different degrees of stratification could be determined for primitive societies. If the series were to be correlated with quantitative measures of significant ecological conditions, some general propositions relating these cultural phenomena might be stated. In this study we explore the possibility by consideration of adaptive variations in Polynesian stratification. The initial plan is to order Polynesian societies on a stratification gradient, and then to correlate the gradient with technoenvironmental differences, especially productivity differences. In this chapter we attempt to obtain criteria for placing Polynesian societies on a stratification gradient.

What is egalitarianism and what is stratification? Theoretically, an egalitarian society would be one in which every individual is of equal status, a society in which no one outranks anyone. But even the most primitive societies could not be described as egalitarian in this sense. There are differences in status carrying differential privilege in every human organization.

Although differences in status are regular features of human organization, the qualifications for status are not everywhere the same. In certain societies, e.g., Australian aboriginal communities, the only qualifications for higher status are those which every society uses to some extent, namely, age, sex, and personal characteristics. Aside from these

qualifications, there may be no others.[1] A society in which
the only principles of rank allocation are these universals
can be designated "egalitarian," first, because this society
is at the stratification minimum of organized human societies; second, because, given these qualifications, every individual has an equal chance to succeed to whatever statuses
may open. But a society unlike this, that is, one in which
statuses are fixed by a mechanism beyond the universals,
e. g., inheritance, can be called "stratified."

Societies vary in the degree to which they are stratified.
One society may be considered more stratified than another
if it has more status classes, restricted by principles other
than the universals, or if high rank bestows greater prerogatives in economic, social, political, and ceremonial activities. Criteria for estimating stratification in a kin society
are thus divisible into "structural," the degree of status differentiation, and "functional," the degree to which rank confers privilege.

In many primitive societies every person has a different
rank; the hierarchy is graduated by very small steps from
lowest to highest. However, in discussing the structure of
the ranking system, it is best to deal with broad groups or
categories of status, as these provide simple descriptive
generalizations. Frequently the natives themselves catego-
rize levels of status, and this may be an aid in determining
the structural criterion of degree of stratification. Such
groups of statuses might be and have been called "social
classes." However, in contrast to the social classes of market-dominated societies, status differences in kinship societies do not, as a rule, depend on differences in private

---

1. Other examples of societies of this type include pygmy
groups scattered from the Philippines to the African Congo,
the Sakai of Malaya, the Indians of the Great Basin region of
North America, the Ona, Yahgan, and other South American
marginal peoples, and the Bushmen of South Africa. With
minor modifications, slightly more advanced groups, even
lower horticulturalists and pastoralists, could be included,
such as Indians of the American Northeast, the Hottentots,
and many New Guinea peoples. See also Gunnar Landtman,
The Origin of the Inequality of the Social Classes (Chicago,
1938), chapter 1.

2

wealth. Status inequalities in primitive societies are not accompanied by entrepreneurial enterprise and the complete separation of producers from the factors of production. Social
relations of mastery and subordination are here not correlates of economic relations of owner and laborer. Modern
sociological definitions of class which stress occupational
standing, class antagonisms, differences of interest, and the
like are not applicable to societies of the primitive order. To
maintain a distinction, therefore, between what are really
different phenomena, categories of rank in kin societies will
be designated "status levels"; the term "social classes" will
be reserved for the social strata of market-dominated societies.

Functional criteria of stratification can be divided into
three broad categories: economic, sociopolitical, and ceremonial. The extent to which high rank is associated with control and privilege in production, distribution, and consumption is subsumed by the economic criterion. The sociopolitical criterion considers the powers bestowed by rank in the
regulation of interpersonal affairs, such as the authority to
apply sanctions to wrongdoers. Ceremonial inequality would
be manifest in differential access to the supernatural and in
distinctive ritual behavior.

The functional aspects of stratification are interrelated.
To a certain extent, the relationship is mutual and reciprocal. However, in many primitive societies, power, privilege,
and prestige appear to be generated primarily in the processes of goods distribution. Thus Thurnwald sees the distributive functions of primitive chiefs as the genesis of centralized political authority.[2] Almost universally, the chief is the
center of the tribal economy, concentrating goods made available by the various households and reallocating them for community activities. Malinowski writes: "I think that throughout
the world we would find that the relations between economics
and politics are of the same type. The chief, everywhere,
acts as a tribal banker, collecting food, storing it, and protecting it, and then using it for the benefit of the whole community."[3] The attribution of prestige and power to chiefly

2. Richard Thurnwald, Economics in Primitive Communities (Oxford, 1932), pp. 107, 180-81.
3. Bronislaw Malinowski, "Anthropology as the Basis of

3

generosity seems equally widespread. The essentials of the following statement, which refers particularly to the Trobriand Islanders, could be duplicated from all over the primitive world: "A man who owns a thing is naturally expected to share it, to distribute it, to be its trustee and dispenser. And the higher the rank the greater the obligation.... Thus the main symptom of being powerful is to be wealthy, and of wealth is to be generous."[4]

The chief's role as central distributive agent not only gives him the prestige by which he might extend his influence to other activities, it naturally demands that his powers be spread into other aspects of the economy and society. If there is separation on the basis of status between producers and regulators of general distribution, certain consequences would follow regarding the separation of such statuses in many other operations. First, there would be a tendency for the regulator of distribution to exert some authority over production itself--especially over productive activities which necessitate subsidization, such as communal labor or specialist labor. A degree of control of production implies a degree of control over the utilization of resources, or, in other words, some pre-eminent property rights. In turn, regulation of these economic processes necessitates the exercise of authority in interpersonal affairs; differences in social power emerge. Finally, all these differentials would probably be validated in ideology and ceremony. Sacredness and ritual superiority become attributes of high rank.

Ethnographic descriptions of Polynesian cultures clearly exemplify the posited relationship between the functional aspects of stratification.[5] There was specialization in the administration of distribution. Surplus production, i.e., food and other material goods not used by the producers, was periodically accumulated by certain members of the community and then periodically redistributed by them in support of communal and craft labor, religious ceremonies, and the like.

Social Science," in R. B. Cattell, et al., Human Affairs (London, 1937), pp. 232-33.

4. Bronislaw Malinowski, Argonauts of the Western Pacific (London, 1932), p. 97.

5. Annotated documentation on particular Polynesian societies may be found in the following chapters.

The distinction between producers and distributors corresponds precisely to that between nonchiefs and chiefs. The latter were focal points for the collection and redistribution of goods--a process Polanyi labels, "the redistributive form of economic integration."[6] As dispensers of food and other goods, and in reward of their logistic support of community enterprise, chiefs gained in prestige and extended their political and ceremonial prerogatives.

When it is recognized that the aspects of stratification are thus related, the hypothesis connecting stratification and productivity differences can be stated more explicitly than before. Degree of stratification is directly related to the surplus output of food producers. The greater the technological efficiency and surplus production, the greater will be the frequency and scope of distribution. Complexity of distribution will also be greater, for example, distribution to more kinds of specialists. Increase in scope, frequency, and complexity of distribution implies increasing status differentiation between distributor and producer. This differentiation will be manifest in other economic processes besides distribution, and in sociopolitical and ceremonial life. Therefore the hypothesis: other factors being constant, the degree of social stratification varies directly with productivity. It should be noted that other factors are rarely constant in culture. Although this does not necessarily affect the validity of the general statement, it may affect its applicability to specific cases. Comparisons within a group of historically related cultures, such as those in Polynesia, are therefore apt to be statistically more significant than cross-cultural comparisons.

The ethnographic accounts of Polynesian cultures do not treat social ranking according to the criteria we have outlined in this chapter; hence, it is necessary to give a detailed explanation of the procedure to be used to assess the degree of stratification in particular cultures.

Two or three categories of social standing, status levels, can be distinguished in most Polynesian societies. One cannot necessarily rely on the native's distinctions of social

6. Karl Polanyi, The Great Transformation (New York, 1944); see also Karl Polanyi, "Semantics of General Economic History" (mimeographed, rev. ed., 1953).

grade, nor even the ethnographer's--although both of these may provide valuable clues. Rather, an attempt is made to place all those who exercise comparable prerogatives on a comparable social level. For example, while an ethnographer might place a paramount chief in a class by himself, it is unnecessary from our point of view to segregate him from other chiefs relative to whom he is merely <u>primus</u> <u>inter</u> <u>pares</u>. In many societies considered, a scheme of social standing based on seniority of descent from a common ancestor pervades the entire group, so that every person has a different rank. The gradation between adjacent status levels is so subtle that both native and ethnographer have difficulty in determining where one category of rank leaves off and another begins. [7] Here the concept of status levels will be used to refer to extremes or to averages of social standing. As stated above, a society with a greater number of status levels than another can be considered more stratified. By definition, it must contain a more complex system of differential roles and privileges. Of course, where a group defined by egalitarian principles of status allocation, such as the elders of a community, has greater influence than hereditary high rank, a strong element of egalitarianism may be said to prevail.

The powers of those of high rank to determine the utilization of strategic resources must be considered. [8] The common form of Polynesian tenure may be termed "stewardship."[9] Plots of land, irrigation canals, and areas of ocean are usually corporate estates of groups of people, but title is particularly associated with the group head. All members of the group have customary rights of use; however, the head has the prerogatives of administering utilization, which he does in the best interests of the group as a whole. In a few Polynesian societies, each small kin group composed of a few households is an independent proprietary unit, the kindred head being subordinate to no higher authority in his prerogatives of management. In the majority of islands, how-

---

7. See chapter 8.

8. Hereafter, "strategic" is used with reference to things directly useful for materially sustaining life.

9. This is Drucker's terminology. Phillip Drucker, "Rank, Wealth and Kinship in Northwest Coast Society," <u>American Anthropologist</u>, XLI (1939), 55-65.

ever, the right of the head of the small kin group to control
use of a plot is subordinated to overriding claims of managership by persons of chiefly status. Thus chiefs may be stewards over a number of separate tracts, each having its own
manager. This system can be designated "overlapping stewardship" and, because of the differentiation by status involved, is considered a more stratified pattern than simple
stewardship. One of the rights of stewardship is that of placing a tabu on the use of a resource area. Such tabus have the
purpose of conserving the food supply against times of famine or for events requiring accumulation of large amounts of
food. There are variations in the powers of different statuses
to impose economic tabus and in the manner of enforcing
them. A supernatural sanction usually accompanies a tabu,
but breach of the prohibition in some societies brings secular punishment by persons of chiefly rank. The presence and
absence of powers of dispossession, especially of lower-
ranking stewards by higher ones, should be noted. The existence of lands held in an undifferentiated or communal manner
with free access to all members of the society may be considered an egalitarian trait.

Differences in supervision of production are implied by the
stewardship pattern of tenure, especially by the tabuing powers of stewards. Control of production, however, sometimes
takes more pronounced and direct forms in Polynesia. The
planting arrangements of individual households may be supervised by members of high status levels. Inspections may be
made and secular punishments imposed on those who neglect
their fields. As compared to supervision by household heads,
such arrangements may be considered indicative of greater
stratification. Furthermore, persons of high rank may also
control communal and craft production. They may be the only ones able to supply the food necessary to support such enterprises. The extent to which higher status confers the
right to regulate communal and craft production is an indication of degree of stratification.

Another type of status differential associated with production is the segregation of chiefs from subsistence activities
and their dependence upon the produce of other members of
the society. A society in which the higher status members
are divorced from production is taken to be more stratified
than one where such is not the case.

As indicated above, Polynesian chiefs function as central

7

agents in large-scale redistributions of food and other goods. All stewards, in fact, have this prerogative, but the higher the rank of the chief, the greater his distributive activities in terms of the amount of goods and people encompassed. The redistributive process provides the economic basis for the celebration of great religious ceremonies, including the rites of crisis in chiefly families, and for other community activities, such as warfare and communal labor. In many areas it also provides the mechanism for distributing food in famine periods. To engage in redistribution, chiefs must have call upon the goods produced in the households of the community. However, the sanctions behind this chiefly due vary. The degree to which chiefs use forceful confiscation or visit secular punishments on those who refuse to yield up goods is an index of stratification.

Throughout Polynesia rank confers differential prerogatives in the consumption of goods. A general feature is the reservation of choice foods for persons of high standing. The privilege to consume certain nonstrategic goods varies more widely from place to place. Some clothes, ornaments, mats, and the like may have only elite circulation and serve as insignia of high rank. The elaboration of insignia of rank is a measure of stratification.

Passing now to sociopolitical aspects of status, account is taken of observers' general statements regarding the degrees of "arbitrariness," "despotism," "equality," and "democracy" that characterize the social relations in particular islands. The vagueness and impressionistic nature of the terminology dictate that no great weight should be placed on such evidence. But sometimes valuable insights may be gained, especially if the impressions of a number of different observers of the same society show agreement. The actual power structure must be considered. How and from whom do important social decisions emanate? Where the low-standing persons are consulted on important matters, or where nonstratified status groups such as elders regulate sociopolitical affairs, the society is less stratified than one in which policies are laid down by the highest in rank.

The extent to which higher status allows physical force to be exercised with impunity in defense of one's rights is significant. Generally, collective kinship retaliation was the method of revenging injuries in Polynesia. Within this pattern, chiefs could usually muster the greatest body of sup-

porters, and hence inflict the greatest damage, as well as
evade punishment for injuries they committed against others.
But variations in these prerogatives of upper status members
occurred. The degree to which chiefs relied on supernatural
sanctions to enforce orders and avenge injuries is an index
of egalitarianism.

Important differences in stratification are revealed by tend-
encies toward intermarriage within the highest status level.
In all Polynesian societies, there was a preference, among
chiefs, for intrastatus marriages, those which consolidate
the economic, social, and ceremonial prerogatives of high
rank. In some societies this is rigidly enforced; close relatives are picked as mates, and marriage is not contracted
with those of low rank. In other societies, intrachiefly marriage is merely a loose preference, often ignored.

The high position of certain members of Polynesian island
communities is ceremonially indicated by the famous mana-
tabu complex which surrounds them. Chiefs are direct descendants of divinity; consequently, they are imbued with
certain sacred powers (mana). In many of the islands an elaborate system of tabus exists concerning touching these sacred
persons, touching their possessions, or otherwise violating
their sanctity. Such tabus are extensions of a general phenomenon of ceremonial prestige surrounding the head of every
family. The elaborateness of the tabu concerning members
of high status levels is a measure of the mana they possess
and hence may be used as a measure of stratification. Whether violations of these tabus are punished secularly or merely
supernaturally is also significant.

Other ceremonial indications of stratification are customs
of paying respect to chiefs, such as bowing and various forms
of obeisance postures, and addressing or referring to persons of different rank and their possessions by unique sets of
nouns and verbs. Sometimes high status is symbolized by exclusive participation in certain rituals, such as ceremonious
kava drinking. Finally, the extent to which the life-crisis
rites in high ranking families differ in kind and elaboration
from those generally found in the society is an index of degree of stratification.

In the following chapters fourteen Polynesian cultures are
examined in light of these criteria of stratification. The data
on each are not always complete but some information is usually to be found on every major aspect of stratification. Par-

ticular attention should be paid to the character of the evidence regarding certain crucial phenomena, such as the sanctions surrounding the personal and economic tabus of chiefs, punishments of wrongdoers, and the ability of the chief to kill and banish others. In many cases the data were gathered from informants long after the culture had ceased to exist as an ongoing, autonomous entity.[10] There is always the possibility, especially when dealing with sanctions, that the "ideal" culture rather than the actual workings of the society is described in the sources. Such a contingency could lead to serious misinterpretations. Consequently, whenever case materials are available on crucial points they are referred to in the discussion.

For convenience in handling the materials the cultures have been grouped into four major categories of stratification: Group I, Group IIa, Group IIb, and Group III, from more to less stratified. Finer discriminations are sometimes possible within a category as to which societies are most and which are least stratified. But because of the rough and qualitative nature of the criteria used to estimate the amount of stratification, more emphasis should be placed on the major groupings than on any finer discriminations. The two intermediate groups, IIa and IIb, are placed under the same Roman numeral since the amount of stratification is more nearly equivalent between societies in Group IIa and in Group IIb than between those in Groups I and IIa, or in Groups III and IIb. The following summary lists the societies contained in each group and the major characteristics of stratification of each group.

---

10. Hence the past tense is used in descriptions of the materials in chapters 2-5.

Group I. Hawaii, Tonga, Samoa, Tahiti

Structurally complex ranking systems, usually with three status levels; pre-eminent stewardship by high chiefs; severe punishments and dispossession of those who infringe chiefly decrees on land or sea use; control of communal production by high and middle levels; direct supervision of household production by chiefly and middle levels, including inspection and ability to apply secular sanctions for failure to plant; complex redistributive hierarchy of three levels; ability of chiefs to confiscate goods of others by force in some cases; divorce of upper level, and perhaps middle level, from subsistence production; large range of clothes, ornaments, etc., serving as insignia of rank; arbitrary despotism described in general statements by observers; control of socioregulatory processes by high chiefs; marked difference by status in ability to inflict secular punishments on wrongdoers including ability to kill or banish those who infringe chiefly rights; close-in marriages among chiefs strictly enforced; very complex mana-tabu system concerning upper status level; elaborate obeisance postures and other forms of respect including developed chiefs' languages and carrying of chiefs on litters, etc.; unique rites for all life crises of high chiefs, held on a spectacular scale.

Group IIa. Mangareva, Mangaia, Easter Island, Uvea

Two basic status levels with tendency to form third; pre-eminent stewardship by high chiefs; dispossession of lower status members from land possible; punishments for violation of economic tabus usually supernatural; control of communal and craft production by upper level; no direct regulation of household production; a two-level redistributive hierarchy; usually no ability of chiefs to confiscate goods by force; highest chiefs divorced from subsistence production; marked insignia of rank, but less elaborate than Group I; fair degree of arbitrary authority indicated by general statements of observers; control of socioregulatory process by chiefs; chiefs could punish those who infringed their rights severely in some cases, but more stringent limitations on this than in Group I; intrastatus marriage of chiefs not as rigidly enforced as in Group I; personal tabu system of chiefs not as elaborate as in Group I; obeisance postures not marked; special life-crisis rites often existed in chiefly families.

Group IIb. Marquesas, Tikopia, Futuna ·

Two status levels; highest rights of access to strategic resources usually held by upper status level; no dispossessions; economic tabus carrying supernatural sanction; communal production usually controlled by chiefs, craft production often so; no direct control over household production; chiefs often the foci of redistributions; except for the Marquesas, upper level not freed from subsistence production; few insignia of rank; limited chiefly authority indicated in general statements of observers; chiefs consult with elders on important de-

11

cisions; violent secular punishments inflicted by chiefs were few; chief's prerogatives supernaturally protected; only slight preference for intrachiefly marriages; nonelaborate personal tabu system of chiefs; few to no forms of obeisance; more difference in degree than kind in chiefly vs. nonchiefly crisis rites.

Group III. Pukapuka, Ontong Java, Tokelau

Two status levels; upper containing very few members; access to resources mainly vested in kin group heads; wide stewardship powers by chiefs not indicated; communal lands managed by community elders; violations of resource rights usually supernaturally punished; communal production usually initiated by community elders; craft production supported by kin groups; no chiefly supervision of household production; small role of chiefs in redistributions; distributive functions of elders relatively great, but most distributions were reciprocal exchanges between kin groups; insignia of rank almost nonexistent; in Tokelau only, chief did not produce own subsistence; general statements indicate lack of arbitrary powers on part of chiefs; elders and kin heads control socioregulatory procedures; status differences rarely manifest in punishments of wrongdoers; strong dependence on supernatural sanctions; a vague tendency toward marriage between parties with prestige; personal tabus concerning chiefs and respect forms compare favorably with Group IIb; only slight elaboration of chiefly life-crisis rites.

2. The Degree of Stratification in Hawaii, Tonga, Samoa, and the Society Islands

Hawaii

THE STRATIFICATION SYSTEM of aboriginal Hawaii can be divided into three status levels. [1] The first consists of "high chiefs" (alii) and their families, i.e., chiefs of islands and major districts of an island and their "retinues" of close relatives. The paramount chief (alii nui) of an island, which was usually the autonomous political unit, and his principal advisor (kalaimoku) were the most powerful members of this status level. A second level consisted of local "stewards" (konohiki), persons of intermediate rank who administered the great domains into which a chiefdom was divided. Persons of this status were distant relatives of the paramount chief, or were men of high descent in their locales, or both. The "commoners" (makaainana) formed the bulk of the population. They were frequently distant, inferior relatives of the chiefs and stewards.

The term kauwa, often used simply to indicate derogation,

---

1. Throughout the text all frequently occurring native terms are at first given in Polynesian transcription together with the English translation most frequently found in the sources. Thereafter, only the English language term will be used. Glottal stops are not indicated in the transcription of native terms because of frequent inconsistencies on this point in source materials. English terms are used to increase readability, but the author is merely following the usual translations or equivalents and cannot vouch for their accuracy.

perhaps refers to a fourth status level, an "outcaste" group. According to Malo, the status was inherited.[2] Bryan writes that it may have been formed by those who broke tabus, by conquered peoples, or by remnants of an aboriginal stock.[3] The economic and social significance of such a group is not recorded, but apparently they were few in number, were not a laboring class, did not act as servants, held land "given" them by their "masters," and were used for sacrificial offerings.[4]

Priests and craftsmen were not placed on separate status levels. The status of a priest or a craftsman was determined by his inherited rank, and this might vary from high to low.

The use of the lands throughout an entire island was managed by the paramount chief through his principal adviser. Other high chiefs managed districts of the island, men of intermediate status managed tracts of the districts, the commoners held small subdivisions of these tracts. Each manager was subordinate to the higher manager within whose domain he held stewardship prerogatives.[5] Thus, if a high chief declared a tabu on coconut harvesting in his district, his stewards controlling subdivisions of the district were obliged to honor the tabu. Each manager was considered the holder of the title to the land he managed. Prerogatives to the use of the sea within one and one-half miles from shore were held by the manager and the group bordering the sea.

2. David Malo, Hawaiian Antiquities (Bernice Pahau Bishop Museum Special Publication, No. 2 [1951]), p. 69.

3. Edwin H. Bryan, Jr., Ancient Hawaiian Life (Honolulu, 1950), p. 65.

4. Martha W. Beckwith, Kepelino's Traditions of Hawaii (Bernice Pahau Bishop Museum Bulletin, No. 95 [1932]), p. 144; this information suggests to me that kauwa was not a class of people but simply a derogatory term applied to sacrificial victims, especially.

5. Malo, Hawaiian Antiquities, p. 56; John H. Wise, "The History of Land Ownership in Hawaii," in E. S. C. Handy (ed.), Ancient Hawaiian Civilization (Honolulu, 1933), p. 88. Chiefs gave a few tracts in perpetuity to warriors, priests, and others for services rendered. See also Malo, Hawaiian Antiquities, 18n., pp. 194-95. Another few tracts were set aside for chiefly families themselves.

The paramount chief had the right to redistribute all lands upon his accession, but in practice severe tenure changes only took place as a result of warfare.[6] Usually, the larger stewardships were reallotted among the chief's close relatives (except the closest, for fear they might be tempted to revolt), but the tenure of commoners was rarely disturbed. The paramount chief could alienate the land of any manager and bestow it on someone else; he evidently did not appropriate it for himself. Anyone of higher status level could dispossess a commoner and replace him. Secreting "wealth," and failure of the woman of the household to produce mats were sufficient reasons for a commoner's dispossession.[7] Dispossession might also result from failure to contribute labor for irrigation-works construction, and from failure to make the household plot productive.[8] The frequency of dispossessions is not recorded.

The system of access to water used in irrigation was the same as that of access to land. The high chiefs and the local stewards supervised the allocation. The water allocated was proportional to the amount of labor supplied by any land manager in constructing the ditch, and to the acreage planted. Thus, the amount of water controlled by status levels was proportional to the amount of land controlled, and to the corresponding number of subordinate relatives. During the dry seasons, the high chiefs and men of local importance could adjust prearranged allotments. Any commoner who refused to contribute labor to the maintenance of ditches and dams could be deprived of water rights or lands.[9]

The high chiefs and local leaders of intermediate status initiated large enterprises such as ditch construction and repair, and cleaning of ditches. They also engaged craftsmen. Through their role in the redistributive network they could

---

6. Wise, "The History of Land Ownership in Hawaii," p. 82; Sanford B. Dole, "Evolution of Hawaiian Land Tenure," Hawaiian Historical Society Papers, III (1892), 6.

7. Malo, Hawaiian Antiquities, p. 74.

8. Antonio Perry, "Hawaiian Water Rights," Hawaiian Annual, XXXIX (1913), 93-94.

9. Ibid., p. 94; Emma M. Nakuina, "Ancient Hawaiian Water Rights," Hawaiian Annual, XX (1894), 82; Beckwith, Kepelino's Traditions of Hawaii, p. 173.

subsidize such activities. Commoners usually could not. The local stewards, as supervisors of construction and maintenance of irrigation works, formed a "primitive bureaucracy." They also directly supervised the production of the households under them, and made sure that the land was cultivated. [10]

Anyone of higher status could call upon those under him to contribute labor for communal enterprises. In this way, the command for labor for building irrigation works passed down the hierarchy of statuses to the commoner level, the major source of manpower. [11] Through the local stewards the paramount chief could also mobilize commoners and craftsmen for the production of houses, canoes, and religious structures for the chief. According to some sources, the demands for labor were fulfilled at regularized time intervals. It is unlikely that this was true before European contact; most probably, the demands occurred merely when necessary. [12] Malo states that a commoner could be put to death for refusing to comply with a demand for labor. [13] A refusal by a man of chiefly family to mobilize his labor force for the paramount chief was presumably tantamount to rebellion.

Although evidence is not entirely consistent, it appears that the high chiefs and their families did not engage in subsistence production. [14]

The three status levels were the focal points of the collection of larger and larger amounts of surplus food and manufactured goods and of their redistribution. A collection by a high chief necessitated prior collection by local stewards

---

10. E. S. Craighill Handy, "Government and Society," in E. S. C. Handy (ed.), Ancient Hawaiian Civilization (Honolulu, 1933), p. 34.

11. Terrace developments were large (up to three by one miles); their construction involved a great expenditure of labor. See E. S. Craighill Handy, The Hawaiian Planter (Bernice Pahau Bishop Museum Bulletin, No. 161 [1940]), pp. 36-37 and passim; Wendell Clark Bennett, Archaeology of Kauai (Bernice Pahau Bishop Museum Bulletin, No. 80 [1931]), passim.

12. See Handy, "Government and Society," p. 34.

13. Malo, Hawaiian Antiquities, p. 61.

14. Ibid., pp. 58, 63 f.; William E. Ellis, A Journal of a Tour around Hawaii (Boston, 1825), pp. 93, 396; Handy, "Government and Society," pp. 38.

from, in turn, the commoners. Distribution followed the same pattern. Most of the goods so collected reached the producers eventually, especially goods collected for feasts. Usually, a small share was taken out by high chiefs and local stewards in the process of collection. The magnitude of collection activities can be judged by Kepelino's account of the giving of gifts to chiefs. On formal occasions, calabashes of taro pudding (poi) presented to high chiefs numbered "perhaps not below 20,000 and the pigs 40,000."[15] Dogs, chicken, bananas, sea slugs, fish, and other items were also presented.

Goods were passed up the social hierarchy in connection with religious ceremonies that required offerings, and for festivities associated with life-crisis rites in chiefly families. The same was true of occasions when local stewards or chiefly families engaged specialists, when war parties were organized by the high chiefs, and when it was necessary to provide food for those engaged in communal labor. During Makahiki, the annual religious cycle of the god, Lono, there occurred mass ceremonial collections of goods involving entire islands. Most tabus on the use of land or its resources were placed by managers of the land so that it would be possible for goods to be amassed for purposes of redistribution. Such tabus were in the nature of conservation measures. This practice occurs generally in Polynesia.

Less regularized collections took the form of presents or gifts made to chiefly families and men of intermediate status by inferiors, whenever some item was plentiful. This was an obligation, but in no case was the amount of the obligation fixed; it probably varied with the current surplus. A high chief could seize foodstuffs from commoners if the latter did not contribute a "sufficient" amount.[16] The high chiefs had large storehouses to hold accumulated goods in preparation for redistribution.

In Hawaii, and generally in Polynesia, certain choice foods were reserved for the consumption of the high chiefs. The difference in food consumption, however, could not have been

---

15. Beckwith, Kepelino's Traditions of Hawaii, p. 148. Kepelino's excellent account of the manner of collection, but not distribution, is given by Beckwith.

16. Ellis, A Journal of a Tour around Hawaii, p. 398.

marked because the commoners were prosperous. [17] Indeed,
the obligation of the chiefs to redistribute accumulated food
insured an adequate quantity for all. The paramount chief's
counselors advised, "When the people brought presents of
food to the king [i.e., paramount chief]... it was a wise
thing for the king to invite all of the people to partake of the
food, that they might not go away fasting." The storehouses
controlled by the paramount chief were designed "as a means
of keeping the people contented, so they would not desert the
king [i.e., paramount chief]."[18] This slight difference in
food consumption was fairly constant throughout Polynesia
along with the chiefly redistributive ethic, and will not be
discussed in this comparative treatment.

The differences in the consumption of luxury goods are of
greater comparative significance. Often these goods were
distributed among members of the upper statuses exclusively, and therefore served as insignia of rank. The feathers
of certain birds were used only by the paramount and other
high chiefs as garment decorations. The high chiefs wore
special cloaks and battle regalia, feather-covered helmets,
whales' teeth, and other ornaments. They had staves of
office with bearers to carry them. The quality of housing
and the number of houses in one's establishment varied with
rank.

The native social system of the Hawaiian Islands has gained
notoriety for the marked social distinctions between statuses,
and for the personal despotism and authority of chiefs. An extreme but not uncommon view is expressed by von den Stein-
en: "A developed kingly despotism is characteristic of Hawaii.
The king is the sole ruler and possessor of power; his will
is law." ("... fur Hawaii ist charakteristisch eine ausge-
bildete Despotie des Konigs.... Der Konig ist der alleinige
Herrscher und Machthaber. Sein Wille ist Gesetz.")[19] Malo
repeatedly writes of the despotism of chiefs and of the life

---

17. Malo, Hawaiian Antiquities, p. 62.
18. Ibid., pp. 194-95.
19. (Editor's translation.) Diether von den Steinen, "Das
Stande-wesen der Polynesier in seiner wirtshaftlichen Bedeutung," Zeitschrift für vergleichende Rechtswissenschaft,
XLII (1926), 156.

and death powers that the paramount chief held over those of low rank.[20]

The administrative hierarchy in sociopolitical regulation was the same as the hierarchy operative in economic processes. Consequently, the various status levels exerted differing amounts of authority and power in the control of interpersonal affairs. The paramount chief probably consulted with other high chiefs to determine questions of peace and war. However, the decision evidently was made by the paramount chief and the kalaimoku before others were consulted.[21] Messengers were sent round the realm to inform the local stewards of the decision. They, in turn, mobilized the warriors. The assembled army was fed and led to battle by the high chiefs, but they did not necessarily lead in the actual battles.

According to Malo, chiefs did not adjudicate disputes.[22] But Ellis writes that the administrative structure formed the framework in which a hierarchy of chiefs acted as a series of courts of appeal to adjudicate disputes.[23] Both Handy and Perry report that high chiefs and local stewards settled altercations over water rights.[24] Case records are lacking.

Generally, assault, murder, and theft were punished by the collective action of the supporters of the injured party. The higher the status, the larger the musterable support. Consequently, punishment varied according to the status of the parties. Within this framework, coercive force was applied by the chief in punishing those who infringed his rights, especially if the transgressors were low in status. According to Ellis, Handy, Malo, and others, people were slain by a high chief if they violated his economic or personal tabus, stole from him, or committed adultery with his wife.[25] Malo,

---

20. Malo, Hawaiian Antiquities, pp. 34, 53, 57, 61; see also Ellis, A Journal of a Tour around Hawaii, p. 402.

21. Malo, Hawaiian Antiquities, p. 96.

22. Ibid., p. 58.

23. Ellis, A Journal of a Tour around Hawaii, p. 402.

24. Handy, The Hawaiian Planter, p. 34; Perry, "Hawaiian Water Rights," p. 95.

25. Ellis, A Journal of a Tour around Hawaii, pp. 401-02; Handy, "Government and Society," p. 34; see also Malo, Hawaiian Antiquities, passim.

19

who passed part of his life in aboriginal Hawaii, gives the
impression that violent punishments were frequent, but he
does not list specific cases. To take another example of the
role played by status differentials, it is stated that anyone
who discovered a man tampering with a dam could kill him
on sight, but if the offender were of high rank, the killing
caused considerable local "disturbance."[26] Fornander records an instance of a man of unstated rank stealing a pig
from a high chief of Oahu. The man was punished by being
forced to roast and eat the pig until he was "nearly suffocat-
ed with food." He was told that if he repeated the offense
"the law of the land . . . will punish you, viz., you will be
sacrificed as a malefactor. . . ." Fornander gives evidence
that chiefs did resort to the use of human sacrifices as a
means of eliminating those who fell from favor.[27]

In Hawaii, rebellion, assassination, and migration into
other domains were some of the mechanisms that limited
the tyrannical power of high chiefs and the local stewards.
Mechanisms of this sort which operated to inhibit tyranny
were a constant feature of Polynesian political life and will
not be considered in the comparative treatment of the islands.

The incest range was progressively narrowed toward the
top of the social hierarchy; hence, dispersal of economic,
social, and religious privileges was prevented. Care was
taken to select the nearest possible relative as a wife for a
high chief. Marriages with commoners were scrupulously
avoided. Brother-sister, or brother-halfsister marriages
were common among the paramounts.

The Polynesian tabus concerning approaching, touching, or
otherwise violating the sanctified chiefly personage, were
elaborate and rigidly enforced in Hawaii. Malo describes a
number of such tabus that surrounded the paramount chief.
The following is only a partial list: it was prohibited for a
man's shadow to fall on the paramount's house, back, robe,
or any possession; it was prohibited to pass through his
door, climb his stockade, to put out in a racing canoe before

---

26. Perry, "Hawaiian Water Rights," p. 95.
27. Abraham Fornander, An Account of the Polynesian
Race, Its Origin and Migrations and the Ancient History of
the Hawaiian People to the Times of Kamehameha I (London,
1880), II, 96, 269.

him, to put on his robe or his bark cloth; it was required that one kneel while he ate, not appear in his presence with a wet bark cloth, or mud on one's head. [28] In general, the commoner could not touch anything used by the paramount chief. Even the ground the chief walked on became charged with mana and was avoided by others. In the presence of the paramount, all had to prostrate themselves on the ground in a posture of extreme humility and obeisance. A paramount chief was preceded by heralds who warned of his coming so that the people could prepare themselves. Honorific terms were used in addressing all high chiefs. It is difficult to determine whether this was a "chief's language," a social dialect, such as was found elsewhere, particularly in Samoa and Tonga.

Malo indicates that death was the usual punishment for a breach of the personal tabu of a chief, but Ellis reports that death would not result if the delinquent had powerful "friends," another illustration of the role played by status differentials in the application of sanctions. [29] According to Kepelino's manuscript, many people, especially children, broke the requirement of prostrating oneself before the chief when "many of the chiefs traveled together." It became the function of the chief to spare the offender from the "executioner" who traveled with these parties. [30]

The paramount chief was the direct descendant of divinity. He had some priestly functions, including consecrating temples (heiau) and presiding over particular rites. Certain gods were worshiped only by high chiefs. Particularly spectacular ceremonial phenomena that distinguished high chiefs and their families from others were their life-crisis rites. There was a special ceremony to promote the conception of children among those of high rank, and special birth ceremonies, including consecration of males in the temples. Circumcision rites were elaborated in proportion to rank. There were three forms of the ceremony. One was for high chiefs, one for lesser chiefs, and one for the others. During a high chief's sickness, an entire island was practically immobi-

---

28. Malo, Hawaiian Antiquities, pp. 56-57.
29. Ellis, A Journal of a Tour around Hawaii, p. 389.
30. Beckwith, Kepelino's Traditions of Hawaii, pp. 138-40.

lized by tabus. No one was allowed to walk abroad, cook, or engage in other specified pursuits. The mourning ceremonies of chiefly families were presided over by high priests. Mutilations and other bizarre practices occurred that were absent at a commoner's death. [31] A paramount chief's corpse was defleshed and deified. Chiefs were buried in a flexed, commoners in an extended, position. [32]

Tonga

There were three status levels in Tongan society. The highest was that of the chiefs and their immediate relatives (eike). This included the heads of the great "lineages" (haa) and major lineage segments, and the three paramount chiefs of Tonga, the Tui Tonga, the Tui Haa Takalaua, and the Tui Kanokupolu. [33] The second level consisted of "chiefs' attendants" (matapule). The bulk of the society comprised the lowest level, the "commoners" (tua). The commoners were related to the chiefs and chiefs' attendants; they were lesser members of the same lineages.

The TT had executive aides (falefa) who were also chiefs.

---

31. Ellis, A Journal of a Tour around Hawaii, p. 151; Malo, Hawaiian Antiquities, pp. 100 f.
32. Additional principal sources consulted on Hawaii; M. K. Pukui (trans.), "The Canoe Making Profession of Ancient Times," Hawaiian Historical Society Papers, XX (1939), 27-37; William Alanson Bryan, Natural History of Hawaii, (Honolulu, 1915); Kenneth P. Emory, "Warfare," in E. S. Craighill Handy (ed.), Ancient Hawaiian Civilization (Honolulu, 1933); N. B. Emerson, "The Bird-Hunters of Ancient Hawaii," Hawaiian Annual, XXI (1895), 101-11; E. S. Craighill Handy, "Religion & Education," "Feasts and Holidays," and "Houses and Villages," in E. S. C. Handy (ed.), Ancient Hawaiian Civilization (Honolulu, 1933); E. S. Craighill Handy and M. Pukui, "The Hawaiian Family System," Journal of the Polynesian Society, LIX (1950), 170-90, 232-40; LX (1951), 66-79, 187-222; LXI (1952), 243-82; Jean Hobbs, "The Land Title in Hawaii," Hawaiian Historical Society Annual Report, XL (1931), 26-33.
33. Hereafter abbreviated as TT, THT, and TK, respectively.

22

The executives of the TK were petty chiefs, or perhaps attendants. The highest chiefs had a "retinue" or "court" composed of younger brothers and sisters, of illegitimate children of former high chiefs, and of executive aides. Mariner mentions the existence of a class of mua, intermediate between eike and matapule. But Gifford found no evidence of a significant level of this type, although he noted that offspring of chief-attendant unions were called mua. [34] Craftsmen came from all ranks except the highest, although certain crafts were restricted to certain statuses according to Mariner. [35] Priests came from all status levels. Gifford reports that there existed in aboriginal times a segment of the population lower than the commoners, known as the popula, which he translates as "slave" or "prisoner." This level was formed largely of war prisoners. [36] Its significance, if any, is not known.

The system of access to land and sea resources was similar in structure to the system that was found in Hawaii, with the exception that, since irrigation was not widely practiced in Tonga, chiefly control over water rights was minimal. The TT held a position and managership privileges comparable to that of the paramount chief in Hawaii. The THT and TK had administrative functions comparable to those of the chief adviser of the Hawaiian paramount chief. Lesser chiefs and attendants exercised land rights equivalent to those of konohiki (local stewards). Tua may be equated with makaainana (commoner). The TT could not dispossess other chiefs from the tracts (tofia) which they hereditarily managed. [37] But a member of a higher status level could remove a commoner living under him, or relocate a commoner's household on some other part of the tract. [38]

Members of the upper status largely controlled many types

34. Edward Winslow Gifford, Tongan Society, (Bernice Pahau Bishop Museum Bulletin, No. 61 [1929]), p. 109.
35. William Mariner, An Account of the Tongan Islands in the South Pacific Ocean (Edinburgh, 1827), II, 94.
36. Gifford, Tongan Society, p. 111.
37. Walpole as cited by Robert W. Williamson, The Social and Political Systems of Central Polynesia (Cambridge, Eng., 1924), III, 266.
38. Ibid.; Gifford, Tongan Society, pp. 127, 174.

of production. High-level chiefs had petty-chief emissaries who initiated and directed many types of communal production, the labor for which was supplied mainly by commoners. Some of these emissaries were "national" supervisors and were sent to various islands by the TT. Others were supervisors of lineage production and were subordinates of the lineage chiefs. Varieties of communal fishing and the construction of chiefly tombs, of large mounds used in connection with trapping pigeons, and of fortresses were under the direction of such supervisors. Household production was also under the supervision of these petty chiefs. They inspected the fields of each household to insure adequate production.[39] The inspectors also placed conservational tabus. They reported on the status of production to the higher chiefs. From these reports, sanctions were placed on those who broke the tabus or withheld surplus. The punishments were physical, not supernatural. "A commoner who broke the food tabus would be thrashed or possibly killed. The infraction was reported to Ata [a lineage chief] who determined the punishment and ordered someone to administer it. There seems to have been no fear of supernatural punishment."[40] The petty-chief emissaries were the Tongan counterpart of the "primitive bureaucracy" composed of local stewards in Hawaii. The direction of labor was divided among them; for example, some supervised the placing of tabus on lands, others supervised communal shellfish gathering.

An alternative method by which communal labor was directed was through a decree in council (fono). High chiefs would summon lesser chiefs and inform them of the project to be undertaken. The lesser chiefs would disperse, summon their followers to a council, and notify them of the proposed work. There were no discussions in councils, only decrees.

The Tongan system of redistribution was similar to the Hawaiian system. By decrees of councils and emissaries and through frequent gifts, especially of first fruits, foods and goods passed up and down the social hierarchy. Some of the

---

39. Gifford, Tongan Society, pp. 68 f., 98, 237; Williamson, The Social and Political Systems of Central Polynesia, I, 153.

40. Gifford, Tongan Society, p. 104; see also p. 342.

food was used to support communal and specialized production. Because chiefs and their attendants were focal points
of collection, they usually engaged specialists. However, if
the commoners were able to amass the necessary food, they
might subsidize craftsmen. There is evidence that chiefs
kept some of the accumulated food to feed their own households, so they were probably not involved in the actual production. [41] In a council described by Mariner, the chief of
the Vavau group urged all his chiefs to engage in agriculture,
and emphasized his own intention of doing so. [42] This indicates either that chiefs were not divorced from production
or that chiefs were rarely producers. The latter is more
probable since this was a period of extreme scarcity following prolonged war.

There is abundant evidence from early observers, cited by
Williamson, that the high chiefs had the power to confiscate,
with impunity, the goods of commoners. [43] La Billardiere
several times saw chiefs openly take possession of goods be-
longing to others, although "this did not affect the gaiety of
[the owner's] disposition." D'Entrecasteaux noted that
chiefs-pilfered inferiors at will. Veeson adds that exactions
were made even in times of scarcity for the benefit of the
chief's own household. Waldgreve and Young give confirmatory reports. More temperate, but not necessarily contradictory, statements are made by J. R. and G. Forster.
Forster wrote that the TT did not deprive others of "the in-
dispensable wants of nature." [44]

The events in Tonga that generated the collection and redistribution of food and other goods by chiefs were the same
as in Hawaii. In Tonga, as in Hawaii, there was a great annual religious ceremony that was accompanied by accumulation and dispensation of goods on a large scale. [45]

---

41. Ibid., p. 104.

42. Mariner, An Account of the Tongan Islands in the
South Pacific Ocean, I, 323-25.

43. Williamson, The Social and Political Systems of Central Polynesia, III, 118, 347 f.; see also Gifford, Tongan
Society, p. 127.

44. Williamson, The Social and Political Systems of Central Polynesia, III, 347.

45. Redistribution was the hallmark of chieftainship. This

Sumptuary consumption in Tonga was similar to that in Hawaii. Certain foods were restricted to chiefs, but as to commoners, "real poverty is not known among them."[46] Houses of chiefs differed structurally from those of the commoners. Chiefs and their attendants wore scented tapa loin cloths; commoners wore other materials. The combs of commoners and chiefs were distinct. Chiefs had special rest places or mounds, special tattoo designs, feather headdresses, whale's tooth ornaments, and guest houses. Besides, the TT had special portable houses erected wherever he went, wore a particular type of garland, ate coconuts with special implements, and had a unique method of hair trimming.

The arbitrary powers of Tongan chiefs have been eliminated by British rule; consequently, Gifford did not find much evidence of undue authority exercised by the chiefs.[47] However, most early accounts speak of despotic control.[48] Cook wrote that the TT's will generally prevailed, and reported an incident in which the TT, chancing on a party of fishermen, made them hand over their catch. Forster, as cited by Williamson, indicated that, "the obedience and submission with which the people revered their chiefs were evident proofs that their government, though perhaps not perfectly despotic, was far from being democratic." A member of Cook's party described an event in which the chief of Vavau,

---

is graphically illustrated in Mariner's account of the reaction of a Tongan chief upon being instructed in the nature of money: " 'Certainly money is much handier, and more convenient, but then, as it will not spoil by being kept, people will store it up, instead of sharing it out, as a chief ought to do, and thus become selfish; whereas, if provisions were the principal property of man, and it ought to be, as being both the most useful and the most necessary, he could not store it up, for it would spoil, and so he would be obliged either to exchange it away for something else useful, or share it out to his neighbors, and inferior chiefs and dependents, for nothing. ' " Mariner, An Account of the Tongan Islands in the South Pacific Ocean , I, 213-14.

46. Ibid., p. 230.
47. Gifford, Tongan Society, p. 123.
48. Williamson, The Social and Political Systems of Central Polynesia, III, 117 f.

26

wishing to see how a gun worked, asked that a man in a passing canoe be killed since he was only "a slave." Veeson reported that the chiefs held arbitrary powers, and the Duff missionaries were of the opinion that government "was evidently in a great measure aristocratic." According to these missionaries, the paramount chiefs had rights over the life and property of inferiors, "which the missionaries had seen exercised most despotically.[49] Waldgreve, Hale, Young, and West give confirmatory pictures of arbitrary authority. A French missionary of the mid-nineteenth century wrote that, "the chiefs determined the lives of their subjects, whom they could slay according to their caprice for faults which only deserved a slight reprimand."[50] Mariner records an incident in which a chief used the occasion of a council to have certain other chiefs who had been active against him in a recent uprising seized and killed.[51] Early accounts referred to by Gifford mention the TK cruelly severing a "servant's" arm.[52] "The launching of great vessels over the bodies of commoners was asserted by the chief Ata in reply to a leading question." Ata had heard the story elsewhere. According to another informant, "Takai the one-eyed chief of Pea, Tongatabu, on one occasion killed the first man of a crew that was tugging half-heartedly on the ropes by which a great stone slab was being moved from the weather shore to Pea."[53]

The administrative structure was based on the hierarchy of councils described above. The three statuses played three different roles in the regulation of interpersonal affairs. Chiefs initiated actions; lesser chiefs and attendants transmitted orders to commoners. Mobilization of warriors probably took place in the council framework, in as much as warriors were grouped for battle along the lines of the administrative hierarchy.

Evidence of the power of chiefs to adjudicate disputes is contradictory. Williamson describes a hierarchy of chiefly courts of appeal.[54] Gifford states to the contrary, that a system of

49. Ibid., p. 118.
50. Ibid., p. 119.
51. Mariner, An Account of the Tongan Islands in the South Pacific Ocean, I, 230-31.
52. Gifford, Tongan Society, p. 127.
53. Ibid., p. 323.
54. Williamson, The Social and Political Systems of Cen-

judges was lacking, although "a chief might settle a case [which concerned him?] and his armed followers execute his judgement. "[55]

Power differentials by status were apparent in the application of sanctions. Punishments varied in severity, usually in proportion to the status differences of the parties involved. Gifford notes that if a chief killed a commoner there was no vengeance; if a chief ordered a commoner to kill another chief, "it might or might not be done." According to one informant, murder of one commoner by another resulted in a blood feud which continued until the chief ordered it to cease. [56] Significant is Gifford's statement that: "Unlike commoners, few matapule were killed by chiefs for offenses. "[57] He adds that a chief would beat a man who seduced his daughter; if the daughter were raped, the culprit would either be killed or be forgiven. [58] No case material is given.

The socioeconomic privileges of the status levels were consolidated by intrastatus marriage. The TT either married into families of powerful chiefs, or else married a Samoan thus preventing the dispersal of his prerogatives. If a young chief married a commoner, the chief might be killed, although Gifford doubts that such killings often happened. [59] Cousin marriages were most frequent among chiefs; others married further out.

Ceremonially, the TT was to Tonga as the paramount chief was to a Hawaiian island. His sanctity was as great, and the tabu complex which surrounded him was equally elaborate. [60] Gifford repeatedly reports that tabus laid by chiefs carried no supernatural sanctions, the implication being that sanctions, if any, were secular. He seems to be referring primarily to economic tabus because he cites examples of supernatural punishments for breach of the personal tabus of chiefs. However, after describing some personal tabus pertaining to high chiefs,

---

tral Polynesia, II, 13-14.

55. Gifford, Tongan Society, p. 183.

56. Ibid.

57. Ibid., p. 141.

58. Ibid., pp. 184-85.

59. Ibid., pp. 112-13.

60. Ibid., pp. 71-75, 115 f., 342-45; Mariner, An Account of the Tongan Islands in the South Pacific Ocean, I, 85-86.

he states, "Breaches are subject to punishment by thrashing, often by the chief himself. The conception of a supernatural punishment does not seem to be entertained."[61] Aside from the usual restrictions regarding the touching of the TT's body and food, he was often carried about on a litter, and was greeted with a special salutation and institutionalized postures of humility and obeisance. A person who wished to see the TT first sat outside his house and spoke to an attendant who announced the visit to the TT. A "social dialect" was used for the TT and his high female relatives, another was used for other chiefs, and another for the people.

The tabus and ceremonial privileges of other high chiefs were slightly less elaborate than those of the TT. The ceremonial observation of crisis rites such as birth, marriage, and death varied in elaborateness according to the status of the person involved. This correlates with the differing role of commoners, attendants, and chiefs in the system of collection and distribution. The higher the status, the more people ruled, the greater was the surplus collected, and the greater the feast and ceremony. For example, special puberty rites were held for the TT's daughter; when a chief was ill, human sacrifices might be offered for his recovery; long and elaborate ceremonies followed the death of a chief during which the body was embalmed, females were strangled for burial with the body, and a special class of undertakers was assigned to the performance of various rites. [62]

Status was further symbolized by the order or precedence in serving kava to men of high rank at ceremonial occasions. Seating positions at such affairs indicated not only the fine gradations in rank but also the respective social positions of chiefs, attendants, and commoners. [63]

Samoa

The stratification system in aboriginal Samoa was divided into two status levels, those with titles (matai), and those without. Within the titled level there were various ranks, and two types of titles, chief (alii) and talking chief (tulafale).

---

61. Gifford, Tongan Society, p. 345.
62. Ibid., pp. 185 f.
63. For additional information on Tonga, see Ernest and

These two types of title were not ranked relative to each other but were found on all grades within the titled level. [64]
Each important chief had at least one talking chief of high rank, perhaps related to him, who acted as a sort of advisory executive. Only titled persons participated in the councils (fonos) which were found on village, district, and also higher levels of organization. The highest title in a village was chief of the village. He took the ranking position in the village council. The leading chiefs of a number of villages sat in councils of higher order. The highest-titled person in these councils was the district or island chief. In the villages, young and adult untitled males formed a distinct group (aumaga) that was led by the village chief's heir (manaia). Wives of titled men formed a group under the wife of the high chief, and unmarried women formed a group (aualuma) under the ceremonial maid of the village (taupo), who was a member of the village chief's household. The distinction between titled and nontitled individuals indicates a well-defined stratification system of at least two levels in Samoa.

A status-level distinction might be made between those with higher and those with lesser titles. The former were collectively known as pa'ia and had functions in district and other large governmental units. Men with the lesser titles only functioned in village life. [65] If this distinction is made, three rather than two levels are defined. [66]

Craftsmen were accorded respect, but they did not form a separate status level. Crafts were open both to titled and untitled persons.

Both individually, as heads of extended family groups, and more significantly, as a group in the village council, titled persons held the highest prerogatives of control of land and sea resources. Councils laid general tabus on the use of land.

Pearl Beaglehole, Pangai, Village in Tonga (Memoirs of the Polynesian Society, XVIII) (Wellington, N. Z., 1941).

64. Margaret Mead, The Social Organization of Manua, (Bernice Pahau Bishop Museum Bulletin, No. 76 [1930]), p. 33.

65. Felix M. Keesing, Modern Samoa (London, 1934), p. 53.

66. The analytical value of making such a distinction would certainly be much greater with regard to Western Samoa than to the more isolated and evidently, in some respects, less stratified Manua Archipelago.

Local councils supervised the production of the individual households and controlled both pig breeding and land cultivation. Council members according to Bülow made weekly inspections. If a family was not producing enough, it was ordered to do more planting. "The decisions of the assembly were binding."[67] Failure to comply with these decisions brought a fine of pigs, fowls, tapa, or forced labor on public works. According to Krämer the village council issued directives regarding the preparation of gardens, planting various crops, and care of domestic animals. A fine of five mats was placed on anyone who failed to comply, and failure to surrender the mats would result in slaughter of the offender's pigs.[68] This description of supervision by the council applies specifically to Western Samoa. Mead indicates that there was no such control in Manua, and that each household head directed the family production.[69]

The village councils also decided upon and initiated the tasks involving the organization of communal labor forces. They saw to it that food was collected to feed the laborers. Most specialized production was also instigated by titled persons, usually acting individually.

There was some differential access to tools of production, especially to fishing equipment.[70] Certain families (status unknown) controlled the use of certain fishing equipment utilized by large groups of individuals. Although this equipment could be borrowed, a present was expected in return. Every person "of any [?] status" had a bonito canoe. Pigeon netting was only done by higher-titled men, and these men probably controlled their own equipment.

The evidence is inconclusive as to whether or not titled men, even those of highest rank, were divorced from productive activities. Keesing writes that those with titles engaged mainly in ceremonial activities rather than in produc-

---

67. Cited by Williamson, The Social and Political Systems of Central Polynesia, III, 322-23.

68. Augustin Krämer, Die Samoa-Inseln (Stuttgart, 1902), I, 40 f.

69. Mead, The Social Organization of Manua, pp. 24, 71-72, 76.

70. Peter H. Buck, Samoan Material Culture (Bernice Pahau Bishop Museum Bulletin, No. 75 [1930]), pp. 522, 417, 544.

tion.[71] Mead notes that, because men of high rank were involved primarily in ceremonial affairs, the burdens of their younger relatives were onerous.[72] There is evidence that even those with the highest titles fished.[73] Turner says that the chiefs of villages, with few exceptions, worked as untitled men did in fishing, horticulture, and other productive activities.[74]

Titled persons acted, most often as a group in council, as the focal points of the system of goods redistribution. The council assessed the surplus goods of the individual households. These goods, plus the quantities of goods requisitioned from fines and communal productive activities, were used for redistributions. Any individual chief, as a village head, could call on those under him to supply him with their surplus so that he might engage a specialist or hold a large validating distribution upon his accession to a title.[75] The talking chiefs acted as executives in all distributions.

The usual restriction of certain foods for chiefly consumption was found in Samoa. Differences in nonstrategic consumption included the possession by high-titled persons of several houses including a guest house, the possession of fly flaps by titled persons, and possession of orators' staves by talking chiefs. High chiefs wore human hair ceremonial headdresses, had raised beds, and had houses raised on a number of terraces. Highest chiefs also had distinctive hair styles. The use of tapa as an article of dress was confined to a few females of high rank.[76] The possession of shark-teeth ornaments, and especially of many fine mats, provided an-

71. Keesing, Modern Samoa, p. 30.
72. Margaret Mead, "The Role of the Individual in Samoan Culture," Journal of the (Royal) Anthropological Institute, LVIII (1928), p. 485.
73. Buck, Samoan Material Culture, p. 517.
74. George Turner, Samoa (London, 1884), p. 175.
75. "Prestige comes through generous distribution, not the accumulation of wealth. The ceremonial life and such crises as birth, marriage, and death provide many appropriate occasions for such distribution." Keesing, Modern Samoa, p. 30.
76. Buck, Samoan Material Culture, p. 282.

other indication of status. Fine mats had a complicated, elite circulation. [77]

General statements about the amount of authority wielded by Samoan chiefs are apt to be misleading, because observers usually classify chiefs (alii) as a distinct high status, and contrast their power with the authority of the talking chief (tulafale). [78] However, when one considers the combined powers of all titled persons operating in councils, a picture of strong controls emerges. Thus, Krämer writes that while the power of the chief as opposed to the power of the talking chief varied from place to place, considered together, they had a great amount of authority. [79] There can be no doubt that the council of titled persons was the dominant and dominating political institution in Manua. Mead reports: "The village (fono) retained the right to levy fines for misdemeanors and crimes against the local society and in punishment of severe offense, the right to destroy a man's house, kill his pigs, cut down his breadfruit trees, and banish his entire family (tui paepae). These extreme measures have now been outlawed and it is difficult to be sure about details." [80] The titled man of Manua, in aboriginal days, is said to have had life and death powers over his household. However, this ". . . amounted to very little. If he administered summary capital punishment to an unfortunate member of his household, the village did not interfere. But if the offender escaped to another village, then the administration of justice was taken out of the matai's hands." [81] Mead notes that violation of the ceremonial pattern of silence in the entertainment festivities of one village was once punished by death. [82]

The administrative hierarchy was composed of a series of councils of title holders. The village councils contributed representatives to the higher-order councils that involved a number of villages or districts. In Manua, higher councils

77. Ibid.,pp. 317 f.; Turner, Samoa (London, 1884), p. 176.
78. Williamson, The Social and Political Systems of Central Polynesia, III, 99 f.
79. Krämer, Die Samoa-Inseln, I, 10 f., and passim.
80. Mead, The Social Organization of Manua, pp. 70-71.
81. Ibid., p. 40.
82. Ibid., p. 57.

were of virtually no importance, consequently, the chief of
the island group had no great power. In other areas, as
well, the villages were more or less autonomous, and high
councils were primarily concerned only with the nominations
of the highest chiefs or, more important, with conducting warfare. [83]

The village council exercised authority in economic matters, nominated candidates for titles, created titles, deposed title holders, settled disputes, imposed punishments,
regulated the conduct of the village in warfare, and held
ceremonies to avert various types of catastrophes. Decisions were not arrived at by vote, but by debate until unanim-
ity was reached. However, the decisions had already been
agreed upon through private discussion, and "everyone
knows beforehand more or less what will be said. "[84] The
balance of power in councils varied. The village chief may
have carried supreme veto power, the rights of final say
may have belonged to a particular title, or a small caucus
or set of chiefs may have held control. [85] In all councils, the
talking chiefs did most of the discussing. In some locales,
there were powerful talking chiefs who exerted considerable
authority in councils.

There are relatively many, though inconsistent, statements on the methods of applying sanctions to wrongdoers in
Samoa, but there is a dearth of case material. All of the evidence indicates that punishments varied with the status of
the parties involved. Much more physical force was exercised with impunity by titled persons than by untitled persons
in punishing offenses against themselves.

An untitled offender who injured another untitled individual
could have been punished forcibly by the injured man and his
kinsmen, or he could have expiated the offense by presenting

83. Keesing, Modern Samoa, p. 59; Turner, Samoa, pp.
180-81; Williamson, The Social and Political Systems of Central Polynesia, II, 448 f. , and passim.

84. E. Schultz, "The Most Important Principles of Samoan
Family Law, and the Laws of Inheritance," Journal of the
Polynesian Society, XX (1911), 45; see also Erich Schultz-
Ewerth and Leonhard Adam, "Samoa," Das Eingeborenenrecht
(Stuttgart, 1929-30), II, 667.

85. Mead, The Social Organization of Manua, p. 15.

gifts to the injured man and his party. [86] But certain offenses
were conceived to be crimes against the community, and
punishments for these were set by the council of titled persons. The council tried such offenses as adultery with a
wife of a high chief and seduction of the village ceremonial
maid. When untitled people committed murder, rape, or
adultery involving other untitled individuals, settlement was
a matter of private retaliation; but if such crimes were committed against titled people, the culprit could be drowned or
beaten to death by council command without further retaliation. The council also interfered when it was felt that private
retaliation had resulted in injustice, or when a prolonged
feud occurred that disorganized the village. The infringement of village regulations was punished by fines and hard
labor, or sometimes by destruction of property and banishment. The untitled men of the village acted as executors of
council punishments. [87] The "crimes against the village"
that Mead lists are: spreading scandal about one's village;
stirring up trouble with other villages; dishonoring the high
chief or any members of his household; failure to obey a village edict; outraging the village god (in one village only); giving defective or improper food in village collections; making
an insult in a council speech; incorrect distribution of kava;
making trouble between two titled persons. The village council also "took cognizance of" habitual theft, uncalled-for
cruelty by a titled man in his household, prolonged blood
feuds, and incest. According to Mead's informants, trials
took place in which both accused and plaintiff spoke. Orde -
als were administered and punishments were chosen by the
entire council. [88]
    Williamson's evidence, including reports from Ella, Elloy,
Turner, Bülow, Krämer, Brown, and Stair generally supports Mead's observations. Ella stated that although chiefs
adjudicated disputes their authority was little more than

-----

86. Ibid., pp. 169 f.; Turner, Samoa (London, 1884), p.
178; Williamson, The Social and Political Systems of Central
Polynesia, III, 2 f.; Reverend John B. Stair, Old Samoa
(London, 1897), pp. 91 f.; H. Ian Hogbin, Law and Order in
Polynesia (New York, 1934), pp. 292 f.
87. Mead, The Social Organization of Manua, p. 17.
88. Ibid., p. 169.

nominal. Elloy reported that the authority of chiefs was evident only when dealing with certain thefts, adultery, homicide, or insult in which chiefs were involved. [89] According
to Brown's account of council "trial" there was no recognized procedure and the accused was not allowed to be present unless he was a council member. [90] Williamson finds evidence that death was rarely inflicted by council decree. [91]

Stair distinguished two types of punishments, o le sala and
o le tua. [92] The former, decided upon and inflicted by the
council, included destruction of houses, domesticated animals, and plantations and sometimes seizure of personal
property, and banishment. The period of banishment, if any,
was not usually specified. One indication of differential
treatment by status is that, if the banished party were of
high rank, someone in the village would feel obliged to suggest that he be allowed to return, and he would do so. O le
tua was personal physical punishment. According to Stair,
it was inflicted by the whole district. Williamson points out
that "The evidence shows that various alternative punishments might follow the same offense, and that various offenses might be visited by the same punishment. "[93] This usually
is the case where rank is a consideration in punishment.

There was a marked emphasis on intrastatus marriages.
"A chief is careful to marry only in the family of a chief." [94]

The highest chiefs derived authority from their direct descent from the gods. This was reflected by the ceremonial
tabus that surrounded them. Most of these tabus referred to
contact with the chiefs' bodies or possessions, and were as
elaborate as those pertaining to the paramount chiefs of Hawaii or Tonga. [95] The only specific punishments listed by

89. Williamson, The Social and Political Systems of Central Polynesia, III, 2-3.
90. Ibid., p. 5.
91. Ibid., p. 11.
92. Stair, Old Samoa, pp. 91 f.
93. Williamson, The Social and Political Systems of Central Polynesia, III, 8.
94. Turner, Samoa, p. 175; see also Keesing, Modern
Samoa, pp. 53-54; Mead, The Social Organization of Manua, passim.
95. Mead, The Social Organization of Manua, pp. 113 f.,

Mead are supernaturally caused, but she writes that the high chief could dispense punishments for violations of his ceremonial tabus.[96]

The highest chiefs were carried in litters, greeted with elaborate prostration postures, had certain implements reserved for their own use, and had a great many ceremonial prerogatives. Samoa is famed for its "courtesy" or "chiefs' languages." These were particular sets of nouns and verbs used for speaking to or referring to a chief or his belongings on ceremonial occasions. Mead finds it difficult to determine if there were two or three distinct chiefs' languages. One was used for those with highest titles, and sometimes there were separate sets for talking chiefs. The order of precedence in serving kava on such occasions as council meetings, as well as position in the council house, indicated differences in rank among the titled individuals.

As in Hawaii and Tonga, the life-crisis ceremonies in Samoa that involved a titled person or a member of his family were much more elaborate than those involving untitled individuals.[97] For example, defloration ceremonies at marriages were usually dispensed with among poor families, but the ceremonial maid of the village, who was appointed by the village chief, had a defloration ceremony that was a village event. There were special death ceremonies and forms of interment, including mummification in western Samoa, for highest chiefs.[98]

Society Islands

Three nonegalitarian status levels can be distinguished: (1) the arii (chiefs), or ruling group, including their near patrilineal relatives (iatoai); (2) raatira, subchiefs under

---

176 f., and passim. Mead is of the opinion that the distinctively Polynesian tabu complex is attenuated in Manua. However, this does not necessarily imply that the complex was simple. See ibid., p. 119.

96. Ibid., p. 169.

97. Ibid., pp. 87 f.; Turner, Samoa, pp. 95 f.

98. For other principal sources used for information on Samoa, see Wilhelm von Bülow, "Der Landbesitz der Eingeboren auf der Insel Savaii," Globus, LXXXI (1902), 85-87;

the arii, probably only remotely related to them; (3) manahune (commoners), the great body of people.[99] A priest's
status was the same as his inherited secular status. Craftsmen also took the status assigned by birth. The hiva, body of
warriors or chief warrior, and other functionaries that
formed the "retinues" of paramount chiefs were close relatives of the chief they served.

The so-called slaves mentioned in the literature were arti-
sans whose families customarily had been craftsmen for a
chief. It was in that manner that they were attached to his
service, although they did not necessarily live with or near
him.[100]

The chiefs, subchiefs, and commoners fit into a system of
overlapping stewardship of land and sea resources as they
did in Hawaii and Tonga.[101] Each steward had tabuing powers over his section of land. The tabuing powers of the paramount chief extended over all of the polity. He had the right
to depose and banish a subchief, but the land and title con-

---

and Margaret Mead, Coming of Age in Samoa (New York,
1950).

99. Compare E. S. Craighill Handy, History and Culture in
the Society Islands (Bernice Pahau Bishop Museum Bulletin, No.
79 [1930]), p. 42. The scheme used here essentially agrees
with Handy's. See also Teuira Henry, Ancient Tahiti (Bernice
Pahau Bishop Museum Bulletin, No. 48 [1928]), p. 229. Ors-
mand's scheme, according to Henry, divides arii into two
groups. Our classification differs from Ellis' in that Ellis
groups manahune and raatira into one level and puts slaves and
menials into the third and lowest group. See William E. Ellis,
Polynesian Researches (2nd ed., London, 1853), III, 95. The
scheme used in this study appears to have the greatest functional
significance.

100. Handy, History and Culture in the Society Islands, p. 35.

101. Ibid., passim. At times Handy indicates that commoners' tenure of land was somehow different from that of
others. He speaks of them as having no "individual land
rights." There is ample evidence in other sources that they
had as much individual right as anyone else. They, of
course, did not exercise control or managership over tracts
as large as the sections controlled by the subchiefs or chiefs.

trolled were kept in the subchief's family.[102] Some tools of production, such as communal fishing equipment, were made at the instigation of chiefs and were under their control. Their permission had to be obtained before the equipment could be used.

The chiefs controlled production, especially communal and craft production. Subchiefs were intermediaries for the organizing and supplying of communal labor. They also subsidized craft production, but only the chiefs' specialists were more or less permanently attached to their service. No evidence was found that the subchiefs or chiefs supervised and inspected household production as they did in the other islands in Group I.

As in Hawaii and Tonga, large-scale redistribution was organized along status lines. Life-crisis rites in ruling families, the harvest of the first breadfruit crops, a number of tribal religious ceremonies, the commencement of communal labor, the equipping of war parties, and visits from the ariori (an entertainment group) were some of the occasions that necessitated large collections and distributions of food.[103]

Chiefs could make requisitions from subchiefs and commoners at will, and chiefs' "servants" could plunder food goods with impunity from subchiefs and "farmers."[104] "Nothing fostered tyranny and oppression in the rulers and reduced the population to a state of wretchedness so much as these unjust proceedings."[105] The paramount chief's servant could enter a person's house, seize cloth, kill pigs, take the

---

102. Williamson, The Social and Political Systems of Central Polynesia, III, 272. Williamson notes a case cited by Moerenhout that illustrates the forces that restrained the paramount chief from appropriating lands. In this example, the injured raatira (subchief), perhaps with a number of commoner relatives, fled to an enemy of the chief. At this, the chief promptly appeased the subchief with presents and the return of his land.

103. Henry, Ancient Tahiti, pp. 175-78.

104. Ellis, Polynesian Researches, III, 115-16, 129-30.

105. Ibid., p. 130. J. R. Forster, however, wrote that a return was made. See Williamson, The Social and Political Systems of Central Polynesia, III, 355.

last breadfruit, and pull up the houseposts for fire wood, while the owner, even if he were a subchief, would look on without saying a word. [106] Ellis notes that farmers, on pain of banishment or of being used as sacrificial victims, had to supply produce for chiefs if they stopped nearby while traveling. [107] Similar observations are made by Turnbull and early Spanish voyagers. The latter also confirm that anyone who neglected to render his surplus to the chiefs was banished or selected for sacrifice. [108] The distinction between bringing presents to the chiefs and raiding by the chiefs is not always clear. The arbitrary use of force through raiding was frequently required to enforce adherence to the custom of yielding surplus production, usually for redistribution, to the chiefs. [109]

The evidence indicates that chiefs and a good part of their households, and often subchiefs, derived a proportion of their subsistence from their role in distribution. Consequently, they were probably not producers themselves, at least not horticulturalists. [110] However, extreme exploitation was lacking; the redistributive ethic prevailed in Tahiti as it did elsewhere. [111]

Insignia of rank were many. Chiefs had very large guest houses, and their living quarters were larger and more elaborately ornamented than those of others. The rank of a chief was signalized by the size of his canoe and the way it was ornamented. The feathers of certain birds were used only by the highest chiefs. They were woven into girdles, head-

---

106. According to Williamson's sources, ibid. , pp. 354-55.

107. Ellis, Polynesian Researches, III, 95 f.

108. Williamson, The Social and Political Systems of Central Polynesia, III, 355.

109. Ibid. , p. 356.

110. Handy, History and Culture in the Society Islands, p. 43; Ellis, Polynesian Researches, III, 115 f. , 129.

111. Ellis notes that much of what the paramount chief accumulated was distributed the day it was received; indeed, promises were extorted by subchiefs and others from the high chief before goods even came. The result was "that more than was barely sufficient for his own use seldom remained in his possession." Ellis, Polynesian Researches, III, 128.

dresses, fans, and other regalia. Hibiscus mats were worn primarily by subchiefs. [112]

General characterizations of Society Island chieftainship made by early observers fall into two classes. Some stress the arbitrary powers of chiefs, others note that the subchiefs considerably checked such power, since they were supreme in their own domains. Ellis compares the arbitrary monarchy in the Society Islands to the despotism in Hawaii, although he finds that the different grades of society are more clearly defined in Hawaii. He differentiates both Hawaii and the Society Islands as more stratified than the societies of the Marquesas and New Zealand. [113] Absolute despotism of chiefs is reported by early Spanish voyagers and by Moerenhout. [114] Bougainville wrote that chiefs had life and death powers over commoners. [115] Cook, Lesson, Moerenhout, J. R. Forster, Salmon, and Ellis agree in stressing the powers of the subchiefs. [116] They enjoyed greater autonomy in their own subprovinces than the chief did over his entire polity. This was a great check on the despotism of the paramount chief and made it necessary for him to have the constant support of subchiefs. For example, if the chief decided on some action such as war, he summoned a council of the subchiefs. Here, the subchiefs could speak freely, and if they opposed war, [117] the whole council would end in chaos. [118] Banishment was a common punishment for treason,

---

112. Ibid., I, 186.

113. Ibid., III, 93-94.

114. Williamson, The Social and Political Systems of Central Polynesia, III, 125.

115. Ibid.

116. Ibid., pp. 122-25; Ellis, Polynesian Researches, III, 120, and passim.

117. Evidently, however, opposition was seldom expressed, at least pertaining to warfare, for Ellis also writes that peace or war was determined by the paramount and principal chiefs and the high priests, and that prayers, sacrifices, oracles, and councils were "only parts of the external machinery by which, as it regarded the mass of the population, these movements were decided." Ellis, Polynesian Researches, I, 278.

118. Ibid.

rebellion, or for not yielding surplus production; but if a sub-chief could muster support from other subchiefs for such actions, the paramount chief was powerless to act.[119] The result of this division of power, Ellis notes, was that "Their public measures were not distinguished by promptness or decision excepting when they wreaked vengeance upon the poor and helpless victims of their displeasure."[120]

Physical force could be exercised without fear of retaliation by chiefs against those who offended them. If the difference in status, and hence support, were slight, the injured party would either retaliate in kind, seek peaceful compensation, or use supernatural means to punish. Chiefs did not normally interfere with disputes that did not concern them, as Williamson indicates in a summary statement of "law" in the Society Islands: "It would seem, however, that the official system of administration of justice was put into motion in connection with offences against the chiefs rather as between the people themselves. It is stated that justice was not enforced by any law or regularly administered, though a chief did sometimes punish his immediate dependents for faults committed against each other, or even the dependents of other chiefs, if the offence was committed in his district; that there was no regular code of laws, and, except in cases of offences against the king or chiefs, rulers were seldom appealed to, that criminal punishment was unknown, except in the selection of obnoxious characters for occasional sacrifice; that the people obtained satisfaction with their own hands, whether justly or unjustly for every injury received."[121]

The "official system of administration of justice" that Williamson mentions consisted of the punishments meted out by the chief's body of warriors for failure to render surplus production to the ruling group, refusal to accept a "royal mandate," and refusal to provide a human sacrificial victim.[122] These punishments do not seem to have been specific

119. Ibid., III, 121-22; see also Handy, History and Culture in the Society Islands, p. 47.

120. Ellis, Polynesian Researches, III, 47.

121. Williamson, The Social and Political Systems of Central Polynesia, III, 17. (Emphasis M. D. S.)

122. See also ibid., pp. 16 f.

for specific offenses, but banishment, destruction of property, and death are mentioned by various writers.[123] In cases of theft, for example, instead of retaliation by restealing, the usual custom of most of the people, a chief could have "the culprit. . . banished from his house or lands, and reduced to a state of complete destitution."[124] Because very little case material has been found, it is difficult to estimate the frequency of application of such forceful sanctions. Williamson and Ellis mention a more informal method of punishing the offenders against the chiefs, viz., they were selected for human sacrifices that were held in conjunction with a variety of ceremonies, especially with chiefs' life-crisis rites.[125] In connection with justice, it is proper to mention the system of precepts (ture) that was passed down orally in the ruling families.[126] These precepts were moral statements, primarily concerned with the chief's duties to himself, his family, and his people, and secondly concerned with the duties of his people to him and to themselves. According to Handy, this is the beginning of law and represents "A phase of cultural evolution wholly different and entirely removed from that exemplified in the tribal life of the Marquesans and Maoris."[127] However, unlike early codes, these precepts refer primarily to the ruling group, not to dealings among people. Furthermore, they do not outline any system of law except for the implicit rule of lex talionis.

The prerogatives of the chiefly level were maintained by intrastatus marriages. According to Arii Taimai E, unequal marriages were impossible for chiefs because the family would not permit them, and illegitimate children were put to death if there was any chance that they might inherit a high

---

123. Ibid.; see also Ellis, Polynesian Researches, III, 122 f.

124. Williamson, The Social and Political Systems of Central Polynesia, III, 126.

125. See also William Smith, Journal of a Voyage in the Missionary Ship Duff to the Pacific Ocean in the Years 1796, 7, 8, 9, 1800, 1, 2, etc. (New York, 1813), p. 61.

126. Handy, History and Culture in the Society Islands, pp. 39 f.

127. Ibid., p. 40.

position.[128] However, it appears that such a child could be legitimatized by a ceremony which equalized the rank of the parents.[129]

The tabus protecting the persons, clothing, habitations, and other possessions of the high chiefs were as elaborate as on other Group I islands.[130] Everything the high chief touched, including the ground he walked on and houses he entered, became charged with mana. Consequently, the highest arii did not enter other people's houses lest they have to vacate, and he was carried around on the backs of special bearers. Honorific titles were applied to chiefs and to their equipment on ceremonial occasions. Special forms of address were used for each of the three status levels.[131] The drinking of kava was restricted to chiefs. Inferiors had to strip to the waist in the presence of highest chiefs. The sanctions regarding the breaking of the chief's tabu seem to have been mostly supernatural. However, Ellis states that those who stood over a paramount chief or passed a hand over the paramount chief's head were liable to be killed.[132]

The ceremonial distinction between statuses does not seem to have been constant. Ellis notes some striking contrasts. Sometimes the paramount chief ". . . was seen surrounded by the priests and invested with the insignia of royalty, and divinity itself; or appeared in public on the shoulders of his bearers, while the people expressed every indication of superstitious reverence and fear. At other times he might be seen on terms of the greatest familiarity with his attendants and domestics."[133] Whether or not this represents a breakdown of the system under European influence is hard to say. Another, more obvious explanation is that the "attendants" and "domestics" were close relatives of the chief and high in rank, so they were not as humble in their

---

128. Arii Taimai E, Tahiti, (New York, 1947), p. 37.

129. Ellis, Polynesian Researches, III, 98-99.

130. Handy, History and Culture in the Society Islands, pp. 36-38, 46; Ellis, Polynesian Researches, III, 106-07; Arii Taimai E, Tahiti, p. 7.

131. Handy, History and Culture in the Society Islands, p. 38.

132. Ellis, Polynesian Researches, III, 102.

133. Ibid., p. 114.

behavior toward him. Ellis also finds that "The difference between [the chiefs] and the common people was, in many respects, far greater than that which prevails between the rulers and the ruled in most civilized countries."[134]

Life-crisis rites in ruling families were different in degree of elaboration and different in form from those of others. Similarly, the life crises of subchiefs were more ceremoniously celebrated than those of commoners. Celebrations at the birth of the paramount chief's heir included human sacrifices, an elaborate birth feast, and seclusion of the mother and child for fourteen months. Even more feasts and more sacrifices followed. For the lesser chiefs' celebrations, pigs were substituted for human beings in sacrifices. The tabu placed on the land at the birth of the paramount chief's heir was so severe, "that all the people retired to the interior of the country where they could live in comfort, and build their cooking fires, without fear of dire punishment for infringing the tapu."[135] The ceremonies that occurred at the initiation, marriage, installation, and death of the highest chiefs were as spectacular and distinct as the birth rites.[136] The same was true of ceremonies that took place during illnesses of these persons.

Summary

Group I societies--Hawaii, Tonga, Samoa, and the Society Islands--had structurally complex systems of rank. Hawaii, Tonga, and Tahiti had three well-defined status levels, each with definite roles in economic and social life. Some question arises as to whether three or two status levels were operative in Samoa. Although the problem is difficult to resolve, there can be little doubt that the division of Samoan titled persons into chiefs and talking chiefs introduces another dimension of structural complexity into the ranking system.

Pre-eminent rights to control resources were held by the

---

134. Ibid., p. 101.

135. Handy, History and Culture in the Society Islands, p. 24.

136. Arii Taimai E, Tahiti, passim; Ellis, Polynesian Researches, I, 349-50, 411; III, 107 f., and passim; Henry, Ancient Tahiti, pp. 175-78, 186 f., 292 f., and passim.

45

upper status levels in each Group I society. These rights included prerogatives of managership over land and sea by means of general tabuing powers, powers to dispossess subordinates, and to inflict severe punishment, without retaliation, on those who infringed chiefly decrees regarding land use.

The higher status levels controlled communal and craft production. A significant feature, not found elsewhere in Polynesia, is the direct supervisory control exercised over the production of individual households. Supervision of household production included orders as to what was to be planted and the amount thereof, and inspection by functionaries of the chiefs to see that enough was planted. Sanctions of these directives were secular and applied with impunity by the chiefly level. Whether or not such a situation existed in the Society Islands was not discovered.

A complex redistributive hierarchy, with chiefs acting as focal points of collection and redistribution, and the middle status level acting as intermediaries, was characteristic of Group I stratification. The customary obligation of rendering surplus to chiefs was enforced by confiscation of goods, without reprisal in most cases. Prestige was not the only benefit that was derived from redistribution. Chiefs and their households were, to some extent, fed from surplus goods collected from others. The highest chiefs were generally divorced from subsistence production.

Differential consumption is also measured by the large range of objects that served as insignia of chiefly rank. There were marked status distinctions in dress, in house types, and in ornamentation.

Arbitrary exercise of physical force, control of socioregulatory processes by chiefs, and the differential applications of sanctions to wrongdoers according to status are all revealed in the evidence. Thus, in punishing offenses, private, continuing retaliations were the general rule where there was slight difference in status between the parties concerned; however, offenses against chiefs were punished severely and with impunity. Death, banishment, and destruction of property were not infrequently inflicted by chiefs.

Intrafamilial marriages in the upper status level are indicative of the social distinctions between chiefs and others. Marriage of high chiefs with members of lower status levels hardly occurred at all in Group I societies.

46

Ceremonial distinctions between ranks were well marked. The tabu and mana pattern regarding the high chiefs was extremely complex. Although the personal tabus of the chiefs intrinsically carried supernatural sanctions, in many cases there was no hesitation to inflict severe secular punishments on low-ranking violators.

The status of a chief was also symbolized by rituals such as elaborate postures of obeisance, the bearing of the highest chiefs on litters or on the backs of others, chiefs' languages, and exclusive participation in certain kava ceremonies.

The amount of ceremony celebrating the life cycle of the individual varied according to rank. Special forms of life-crisis rites, held on a spectacular scale, occurred in chiefly families.

In view of the degree of stratification in Group I societies, it is not accidental that of all the Polynesian societies affected by European influence, native secondary states under the rule of indigenous kings emerged only in Hawaii, Tahiti, and Tonga. Only Samoa, of Group I societies, failed to produce a native government, a fact that may be partially attributed to the localization of authority on a village level there.

Because of the lack of quantitative materials and the nature of the evidence, it is difficult to rank the particular Group I societies in a hierarchy of degree of stratification. The great power wielded by Hawaiian chiefs and local stewards in the supervision of water use, frequent and forceful sanctions applied by chiefs to those who infringed their personal and economic tabus, and the rigid prohibition of inter-status alliances in Hawaii that led to marriages between brother and sister, all appear to indicate that the Hawaiian organization was the most stratified. Samoa appears least stratified of the Group I societies. The lack of a clear-cut, three-status-level stratification system indicates variation in the direction of egalitarianism in Samoa. In Manua especially, chiefly powers were more limited than in the other societies considered so far.

3. The Degree of Stratification in Mangareva, Easter Island, Mangaia, and Uvea

Mangareva

THE STATUS LEVELS OF Mangareva are difficult to differentiate. Both Buck and Laval agree that the two basic grades of society were "nobles" and "commoners" (urumanu). But further analysis is difficult because of the proliferation of terms of rank in the literature. Togoiti, akariki, and momo-momo evidently refer to three grades of chief; and pakaora, ragatira, and tau refer to inferior urumanu, relatives of chiefs holding lands under them. Pakaora in particular denotes a person who was given a large share of conquered lands and became a steward of high order, although he was still a commoner. Members of groups defeated in warfare were called kio. Kio either took refuge with a powerful chief, perhaps a relative, occupied marginal, non-breadfruit-producing land, or they or their children were adopted into another group. They are usually referred to in the sources as "servants" or "menials" if they were attached to another household. [1]

Structurally, the status hierarchy appears to be composed of three levels, but functionally only the distinction between chief and nonchief is of great significance. The pakaora, as managers of relatively large plots, are comparable to the intermediate levels in Group I societies. However, pakaora

---

1. See pp. 175-78 , where a more complete analysis of these terms is undertaken.

had few roles or prerogatives, if any, beyond those held by other commoners. The subordinate position of those defeated in war and absorbed into other groups, and their supposed inferior social and economic privileges, would seem to place them as a distinct, low-standing group. However, definitive data are lacking. We do not know the fate of the offspring of such people and whether their lot differed substantially from that of commoners.

Neither craftsmen nor priests occupied or came from any particular hierarchical status level. The status of these specialists was dependent on their inherited position in the society.

The system of tenure of resources was identical in principle to the system that existed in Hawaii, Tonga, and Tahiti. The ten or twelve "tribal" chiefs were the supreme managers of large sections of the island. Those of lesser status were stewards of smaller sections. Certain of the commoners, probably those from groups defeated in war, did not cultivate but concentrated on fishing. Others were attached to houses of chiefs as menials. Buck frequently makes the possession of cultivable plots the differential between chiefs and commoners, the commoners having none.[2] However, even people of very low status (kio) are noted to have cultivated land, although their usufruct was subject to higher authority, and there is no doubt that commoner tau (often translated as farmers) inherited usufructuary rights in land plots.[3] Higher stewards could depose any of their underlings from stewardship over a section of land for refusing to yield surplus to chiefs, neglecting to produce crops, or for offending the higher stewards. The title was then bestowed on a near relative of the former holder--possibly the custom in all Polynesian dispossessions.[4]

Tabuing powers went with land stewardship. The punishment for breach of a conservation tabu was supernatural.

---

2. Peter H. Buck, Ethnology of Mangareva (Bernice Pahau Bishop Museum Bulletin, No. 157[1938]), passim.

3. Ibid., p. 163, and passim; see also Honoré Laval, Mangareva; L'Histoire Ancienne d'un Peuple Polynésien (Braine-le-Comte, 1938), pp. 223, 286 f.

4. Buck, Ethnology of Mangareva, p. 164.

Buck reports that "The institution of tapu applied sanctions generally in matters of a religious nature in which punishment was usually relegated to a supernatural agent." It is not clear in this passage whether the reference is to economic tabus or personal tabus of chiefs. However, on the same page, and referring specifically to tabus on breadfruit, Buck writes: "Signs representing tapu impressed thieves, who feared supernatural punishment if they infringed."[5]

Irrigation agriculture was practiced only on a small scale. Breadfruit rather than irrigated taro was the major crop, so the various rights regarding the use of water and ditches that were found in Hawaii were probably nonexistent in Mangareva.

The chiefs in this group of islands were the primary initiators of communal and craft production, just as they were in Group I societies. Household production, however, was supervised by household heads. There is no evidence of a duly constituted body of chiefs or inspectors who exercised direct control over the production of individual households.

The collection-redistribution functions of the upper status level in Group I societies were performed in Mangareva by tribal chiefs, but there were fewer intermediaries between producer and distributor than in Hawaii. The occasions of redistribution were similar to those in Group I: life-crisis rites in chiefly families, religious ceremonies accompanying communal labor, the compensation of specialists, and times of famine. Here, owing to the nature of the major crop, breadfruit, large collections were made at each seasonal harvest and stored by the chiefs. D'Urville reported that any one refusing to yield his surplus to the chiefs might be severely punished, even killed.[6] But chiefs did not have the power of seizing and confiscating the goods of others. "While the people accepted their hereditary rules as a matter of course, they would not suffer tyranny that took the form of forcibly taking their food."[7] Buck cites a case in which a chief was put to flight for taking the food of the peo-

---

5. Ibid., p. 161.
6. Cited by Robert W. Williamson, The Social and Political Systems of Central Polynesia (Cambridge, Eng., 1924), III, 360.
7. Buck, Ethnology of Mangareva, p. 159.

ple.[8] Caillot wrote that the "king" was not too greedy in his demands for goods. [9]

Whether or not members of the upper status level produced their own food is not decisively indicated. Laval writes that everyone worked at breadfruit harvest time. [10] However, the togoiti (chiefs), and perhaps members of victorious groups who were not togoiti, consumed some of the food they collected in the redistributive process. [11]

The usual reservation of certain foods for chiefs was found in Mangareva. Differential consumption of nonstrategic goods that served as insignia of rank was well marked. Chiefs had larger, better constructed houses than others; they had special stone benches, feather headdresses, staves of office, and whale-ivory breast ornaments. Chiefs used "private" canoe landings and pathways. The wearing of bark cloth was confined to members of victorious groups, including victorious commoners.

Coercive power at the chiefs' command was apparently used temperately for fear of revolt. Everywhere in Polynesia the possibility of revolt limited chiefly power, yet this point is curiously most emphasized in the Mangarevan data. For example, Caillot writes that the paramount chief declared war and peace, commanded canoes and armies, governed the nation, decreed laws, rendered justice, instituted feasts, and ordered human sacrifice, but was arbitrary only to a point because of the threat of deposition. [12] Métraux, commenting from Laval's data, finds that certain of the "seigneurs" were tyrannical but most "liked to conserve their tenants" ("aimaient a conserver leurs fermiers"). [13]

---

8. Ibid.

9. Cited by Williamson, The Social and Political Systems of Central Polynesia, III, 360.

10. Laval, Mangareva; L'Histoire Ancienne d'un Peuple Polynésien, pp. 261-62.

11. Buck, Ethnology of Mangareva, 164, and passim.

12. Williamson, The Social and Political Systems of Central Polynesia, III, 133; compare Buck, Ethnology of Mangareva, p. 160; see also Laval, Mangareva; L'Histoire Ancienne d'un Peuple Polynésien, passim. Williamson does not consider Caillot to be too trustworthy.

13. (Editor's translation.) Alfred Métraux, "Une Féodalité

Significant from a comparative point of view is Métraux's statement that, "The Mangarevans have not advanced the devotion to royal power to the same degree as their brothers in Hawaii or in Tonga, but their kings were surrounded by a mysterious air." ("Les Mangaréviens n'ont pas poussé la dévotion du pouvoir royal au même degré que leurs frères de Hawaii ou de Tonga, mais leurs rois étaient entourés d'un respect mystérieux.")[14]

Political powers were concentrated in the hands of chiefs (togoiti). They exerted authority in matters pertaining to offense and defense and to the regulation of interpersonal affairs. The chiefs played initiatory roles in the decisions regarding mobilization for war. For such important decisions, informal discussions were held among them.

The chiefs had some jurisdictional authority. They sent emissaries (vavao) or appeared in person to settle disputes over land boundaries. When the chief appeared himself, he attempted to fix the boundary by decree. "There were, however, obstinate individuals who did not submit to the dictation of their chief or submitted only reluctantly. These ran the risk of being put out of their establishment, unless the chief had some attachment for them." ("Il était cependant des individus entêtés qui ne cédaient pas à la voix de leur chef ou ne le faisent qu'à contrecoeur. Aussi ceux-là couraient le risque d'avoir à déménager, à moins que leur maître n'eut pour eux de l'attachement.")[15]

The predominant form of securing justice was retaliation. The murder of one commoner by another called for sorcery or a counterkilling. But if there were a great difference in status, the person of higher rank could often punish the offender severely and without fear of retaliation. Within unspecified limits, the killing of individuals by rulers was sanctioned by custom. The murder of "royalty" was avenged by a number of countermurders.[16] As in Hawaii and the Society Islands, the chiefs eliminated those who were offensive

Cannibale en Polynésie Française," Revue de Paris, V (1937), 641.

14. (Editor's translation.) Ibid., p. 648.

15. (Editor's translation.) Laval, Mangareva; L'Histoire Ancienne d'un Peuple Polynésien, p. 260.

16. Buck, Ethnology of Mangareva, p. 160.

to them by selecting them for human sacrifices.[17] According-
ing to Laval, a violator of the paramount chief's ceremonial
tabu was instantly speared to death.[18] In one legend, a chief
lanced a "cousin" who dared to address him with a kin term
rather than the chiefly title.[19] On the other hand, Laval
writes that high chiefs were given to committing suicide when
insulted, which hardly argues that their powers of retaliation were unlimited.[20]

There was a tendency toward intrastatus marriage. Chiefly families tried to form alliances with families of comparable rank, and marriages with commoners only occurred after long wrangling within the chief's family.[21] The exogamic
prohibition on first-cousin marriage was often broken by
chiefs.[22]

There were many tabus surrounding the paramount chief.
His person (especially his head), house, food, and utensils
were sacred. High chiefs (togoiti) were direct descendants
of divinity. Their heirs were born in sacred places, and fe-
tuses aborted by their wives were deified. There is no evidence that chiefs were carried on litters, that there was any
developed "chiefs' language," or that obeisant postures indicating extreme humility were assumed in their presence.

The life-crisis rites in chiefly families were much more
elaborate than those among nonchiefs. In chiefly families
the pregnant woman was secluded and guarded by priest-
esses, her body was specially painted, she had a hair cutting ceremony in the eighth month which included a whole
series of feasts and rituals, and the child was born on the
marae. The children of the paramount chief were secluded
in a special mountain nursery until adolescence and were

17. Ibid., pp. 154-55.

18. Laval, Mangareva; L'Histoire Ancienne d'un Peuple
Polynésien, p. 226; cf. Métraux, "Une Féodalité Cannibale
en Polynésie Française," p. 640.

19. Métraux, "Une Féodalité Cannibale en Polynésie
Française," p. 647.

20. Laval, Mangareva; L'Histoire Ancienne d'un Peuple
Polynésien, p. 226.

21. Ibid., pp. 239-40; see also Buck, Ethnology of Mangareva, pp. 130-32.

22. Buck, Ethnology of Mangareva, p. 132.

cared for by special attendants. Similarly, marriage and
death rites among chiefs took unique forms, including, for
example, human sacrifices at death. [23]

Easter Island

The basic status levels were, as in Mangareva, the chiefs
and the nonchiefs. Chiefs were heads of the ten large unilineal groups or "tribes." The secular paramount chieftainship
of the island was a spoil of war and went to a leader of the
militarily dominant tribe. He was called "the birdman." His
position was temporary. [24] Another tribal chief was the paramount religious leader, a priest-chief (ariki mau). This was
a stable, inherited position.
   The fate of groups defeated in war (kio) is not altogether

---

   23. Also consulted: S. Percy Smith, "Notes on the Mangareva or Gambier Group of Islands, Eastern Polynesia,"
Journal of the Polynesian Society, XXVII (1918), 115-31.
   Ambiguity is characteristic of the literature relating to
the stratification system of Mangareva. This is true of the
reports of early observers and, unfortunately, of scientific
observers. Terms such as rent, landlord, tax, tribute, king,
estate, and contract belie the essential kinship organization.
Meek has commented on the lack of reliability of reports on
land tenure wherein "English terms such as 'rent' or 'lease'
have been employed to denote practices which bear only a
superficial resemblance to those denoted by these terms.
The gifts given to chiefs as administrators have been assumed to be 'rent' and the chiefs to be 'landlords.'" C. K.
Meek, Land, Law and Custom in the Colonies (London, 1946),
pp. 11-12.
   The major ethnographic works on Mangareva are perme-
ated with such obvious distortions, and the misconceptions
they cause have been perpetuated in interpretive analyses.
Similar errors are evident in ethnographies of other Polynesian islands and frequently have led to the mistaken application of the term "feudal" to these kin-organized societies
(see, for example, the title of Métraux's article cited
above).
   24. For a more complete discussion of the birdman see
below pp. 169-71.

clear. They seem to have served their conquerors by cultivating land and rendering "tribute." This category was not stable. The defeated either were absorbed into other groups or regained their independent status.

Priests came from the tribe which supplied the paramount religious leader. The so-called "servants" of the paramount religious leader were high-ranking relatives.[25]

The system of tenure of land and sea resources consisted of a pattern of overlapping stewardship. The tribal chiefs were the paramount managers of major divisions of lands and seas, but there were few intermediate stewards between them and heads of ordinary households. The paramount religious leader had supreme tabuing powers. Perennially, he placed a conservational tabu on crops before they were harvested. The tabu had to be lifted before harvesting could begin. Roussel writes: "Alas for the man who dared to violate the tapu. Often he was deprived of his property and possibly of his life."[26] Defeated people could be expelled from their lands and given a portion of the conqueror's land to cultivate, or left on their lands only to have the conquerors appropriate a large measure of the goods they produced.[27] It is not known if commoners could be freely dispossessed.

Large-scale enterprises of various types, including the transportation of the famous large stone heads, were initiated by members of the chiefly status level. Evidently most craft production was stimulated by chiefs. Production of individual households was supervised by household heads. There was no direct chiefly supervision of household production.

There is little direct evidence that the paramount religious leader and the birdman were focal points of accumulation

---

25. Alfred Métraux, "The Kings of Easter Island," Journal of the Polynesian Society, XLVI (1937), 49.

26. Ibid., pp. 54-55.

27. Alfred Métraux, Ethnology of Easter Island (Bernice Pahau Bishop Museum Bulletin, No. 160 [1940]), pp. 120-21, 139, 149. The treatment of defeated persons varied considerably. In another, more miserable state, described in legends, they hid in caves or were pursued to uninhabitable lands where they were left to a grubbing existence until the fortunes of war changed. (Ibid., p. 139.)

and redistribution. The religious leader distributed certain fish brought to him in the form of first fruits and gifts to "important old men," but who these were is not known. There is little information as to what became of many of the goods the religious leader received. The birdmen were entitled to the largest share of feasts, but the disposition of the share is not clear.[28] It can be supposed from comparative data that these members of the upper status level were acting as focal points in accumulation and redistribution in most cases. It is more certain that this is so of other members of the upper status level, the heads of major kinship groups. The occasions of these chiefly distributory activities were similar in nature to redistribution elsewhere in Polynesia. The customary obligation to give surplus production to the chiefs was not enforced by confiscation. However, the birdman and his followers, during periods of his reign, are reported to have ranged about the island, plundering and appropriating food at will.[29]

Some upper-status members probably were exempt from subsistence production. The birdmen evidently depended to a large extent on plunder and the obligations of others to provide sustenance. The paramount religious leader had "servants," relatives attached to his household, one class of which cultivated his food. But even he fished and made fishing equipment.[30] Métraux believes there was a class of professional warriors (matatoa) distinct from the tribal chiefs, who did no work.[31] Thomson, however, states to the contrary that there were no professional warriors, that every man was a soldier, and that the tribal chiefs led the tribes to battle.[32]

The usual restrictions of certain types of food to the chiefs were present on Easter Island. Certain ornaments such as crescent-shaped breast ornaments, served as insignia of

---

28. Ibid. , pp. 132, 238.
29. Ibid. , p. 131; see also Williamson, The Social and Political Systems of Central Polynesia, III, 383-84.
30. Métraux, Ethnology of Easter Island, p. 131.
31. Ibid. , p. 338, and passim.
32. William J. Thomson, "Te Pito Te Henua, or Easter Island," United States National Museum, Annual Report (1889), pp. 475-76.

high rank. The paramount chief's attire included six of these, a yellow tapa cloak, and a feather headdress. Métraux writes that "The dress of the king [ariki mau] was not very different from that of any wealthy man."[33] "Wealthy" in this case might refer to other chiefs, as chiefs in general wore, for example, feather headdresses.[34] The length of one's cloak was proportional to one's status. The high chiefs had staves and standards of office.

General statements by early observers about the amount of power wielded by chiefs are apt to be misleading because native political controls disintegrated shortly after European contact.[35] In early aboriginal times, the paramount religious leader had both secular and sacred power. Later his temporal power declined.[36] Williamson thinks that the bird-man's secular powers are underemphasized, and missionary accounts seem to support this theory.[37] The extent of his power is indicated by the report that the houses of those who did not contribute to the birdman's maintenance were burnt.[38] Thomson writes that "The ancient government . . . was an arbitrary monarchy."[39] Geisler and Gana reported that the paramount religious leader had despotic powers, but both sources are considered unreliable by Métraux.[40] One French missionary reported--evidently after the population had been decimated by disease and slave raids--that Easter Island government was a specimen of anarchy.[41] Métraux concludes that the government was decentralized and localized in the hands of the tribal chiefs.[42]

33. Métraux, "The Kings of Easter Island," p. 50.
34. Thomson, "Te Pito Te Henua, or Easter Island," p. 472.
35. Métraux, "The Kings of Easter Island," p. 43.
36. Ibid.; Métraux, Ethnology of Easter Island, passim.
37. Williamson, The Social and Political Systems of Central Polynesia, I, 405-6; see also Métraux, Ethnology of Easter Island, p. 338.
38. Mrs. Scoresby Routledge, The Mystery of Easter Island (London, 1919), p. 264.
39. Thomson, "Te Pito Te Henua, or Easter Island," p. 472.
40. Métraux, "The Kings of Easter Island," pp. 58-59.
41. Cited by Williamson, The Social and Political Systems of Central Polynesia, III, 136.
42. Métraux, "The Kings of Easter Island," p. 43.

Chiefs had few jurisdictional powers. [43] Private retaliation by kin groups was the predominant method of punishment. Severe physical sanctions were applied with impunity by chiefs, since they could muster the largest bodies of supporters. For example, chiefs could kill their wives for committing adultery, but others would merely thrash theirs. [44] However, Thomson writes that thieves caught in the act were beaten, and if the guilt were fixed with certainty, the weak could retaliate against the strong by summoning the entire community. [45] Other observers cited by Métraux give further information relating to the influence of status considerations on the punishment of theft. [46] One tells about a chief who broke a young boy's leg for stealing a chicken from the chief. Another writes that if something were stolen from a chief, he could do nothing more than scream in anger. Supernatural means were often relied upon for revenging murder. [47] The only known punishments for breaking the paramount leader's personal tabus were supernatural. [48] Breaking an economic tabu was physically punished. Human sacrificial victims were often those who displeased the paramount priest-chief. [49]

The paramount priest-chief married within certain subbranches of his family. It is not known if other chiefs also practiced intrastatus, near-relative marriage.

The paramount religious leader was surrounded by numerous tabus. All the objects used by him were sacred. The body of the ariki mau was also sacred. In fact, his head was so sacred that his hair could not be cut. [50] Although Routledge says that others were surrounded by the same tabu, Métraux argues that they were probably "noble" relatives of

---

43. Thomson, "Te Pito Te Henua, or Easter Island," p. 473.

44. Métraux, Ethnology of Easter Island, p. 114.

45. Thomson, "Te Pito Te Henua, or Easter Island," p. 465.

46. Métraux, Ethnology of Easter Island, p. 146.

47. Ibid., p. 147.

48. Ibid., p. 131.

49. Ibid., p. 329; see also Thomson, "Te Pito Te Henua, or Easter Island," p. 473.

50. Métraux, Ethnology of Easter Island, p. 132.

the paramount leader. [51] No one could see the paramount priest-chief or his son eat or sleep except the kinsmen who served them. Similarly, the birdman was so sacred that he did not bathe himself, he remained in seclusion a good part of his term, he had his food prepared in a special oven by a special attendant, and he did not have his hair or nails cut.

There were no elaborate forms for paying respect to high chiefs, and the paramount priestly leader was given no great homage. [52] According to one legend, he was carried in a litter, but this is the only hint of such a custom in Easter Island. [53]

It is not known that chiefly families practiced special forms and elaborations of life-crisis rites. Métraux's long discussion of the life cycle of the individual, culled from many sources, does not mention any differences in the rites that could be correlated with status. [54] It is known, however, that birdmen were given special burial feasts and were buried in a special interment terrace (ahu). [55]

Mangaia

There were two basic status levels in Mangaia, chiefs and nonchiefs. The upper level included the two high priest-chiefs, and chiefs (pava), and subchiefs (kairanga) of the large, unilineal kin units or "tribes." The leader of the tribe militarily dominant at the moment was acknowledged secular leader of all Mangaia, the "Temporal Lord of Mangaia." [56] His occupancy lasted only as long as the ascendancy of his group. The mass of the people formed the lower status level. Those who were defeated in war either were pushed out of their lands, eventually perishing; took inferior lands with the hope that they would eventually regain their lands through war or the beneficence of the conquerors; or were absorbed by adoption into the tribes of their wives or mothers.

51. Métraux, "The Kings of Easter Island," p. 48.
52. Thomson, "Te Pito Te Henua, or Easter Island," p. 473.
53. Métraux, Ethnology of Easter Island, p. 131.
54. Ibid., pp. 97-119.
55. Ibid., p. 339.
56. Hereafter abbreviated TLM.

Priests other than the two priest-chiefs retained their secular status. Craftsmanship was not a status occupation.

Each tribal chief was the supreme steward of land and sea in his own district. The Mangaian system of tenure was similar to management systems in other islands. Defeated peoples, as indicated, either were ceded land by the conquering tribe or by relatives or were pushed into marginal lands. Conquered people might at any time be ejected from lands given them by others.[57] However, no evidence was found that ordinary commoners could be dispossessed by their chiefs. Aboriginally, there was a chiefly official, "The Ruler of Food," who in times of peace could place tabus on water and land resources throughout the island. Since 1800, this has been carried out on a district-wide scale only.[58] Punishments for breaking these economic tabus are discussed below.

In a general discussion of Cook Island tenure, Buck notes that the chief who ruled over a land area controlled the irrigation channel therein and the distribution of water. He could refuse water to anyone who had not rendered the customary surplus production to the chief.[59] This might refer primarily to Rarotonga where irrigation was more widespread than it was in Mangaia.

Communal and craft production were largely controlled by chiefs as a corollary of their control of redistribution.

Chiefs may have been divorced from production; it is reported that "commoner" relatives performed menial tasks in chiefly households.[60] The priest-chiefs and their families were fed by daily contributions of food from the community.[61] There was no bureaucratic control of household production. The family head supervised familial production.[62]

The upper status-level members directed the accumula-

---

57. William Wyatt Gill, From Darkness to Light in Polynesia (London, 1894), pp. 101-2.

58. Peter H. Buck, Mangaian Society (Bernice Pahau Bishop Museum Bulletin, No. 122 [1934]), pp. 141-43.

59. Peter H. Buck, Arts and Crafts of the Cook Islands (Bernice Pahau Bishop Museum Bulletin, No. 179 [1944]), p. 250.

60. Buck, Mangaian Society, pp. 111, 130.

61. Gill, From Darkness to Light in Polynesia, p. 117.

62. Buck, Mangaian Society, p. 129.

tion and redistribution of large masses of foods and other goods. Because there was no intermediate status level in Mangaia, the process of collection and redistribution was not as elaborate as it was in the Group I Islands. The occasions for these activities were similar to those elsewhere. There is no evidence of forceful confiscations of goods by chiefs.

Certain foods were for chiefly consumption only. Feather pouches, feather headdresses, certain types of bark cloth, a particular kind of plaited belt, phallic ear ornaments, and human-hair armlets and anklets were insignia of rank worn by various chiefs.

The administrative hierarchy in Mangaia corresponded to the system of land managership and to the roles of the respective statuses in distribution. The tribal subchiefs formed an informal council that aided the chief of the tribe in directing most affairs, for example, preparations for war. The TLM evidently exerted the major share of his authority, in aboriginal days, only over districts he had conquered. If there were trouble in other districts, the TLM merely visited them and exhorted the local chiefs to preserve the peace. High priests, through oracular proceedings, were able to exercise authority in some instances. Buck tells how two priests who were acting as mediums saved sections of other tribes by decreeing banishment rather than death. [63] In general, priests "were wise enough to follow the feelings and desires of their group when making known the wishes of the gods." [64]

Wrongdoers were punished by retaliation, but reprisals varied with the status of the parties concerned because of the usual differences in support. Most thefts were committed by members of defeated tribes. Consequently, the holder of the plot dealt harshly with thieves, spearing them if he could. Gill records a number of such cases. [65] Buck interestingly points out that "Because of the severity of the punishment, it is evident that the thieves were of the con-

---

63. Ibid., p. 152.
64. Ibid., p. 119.
65. William Wyatt Gill, Life in the Southern Isles (London, 1876, passim; see also Gill, From Darkness to Light in Polynesia, passim.

quered tribe or men of no standing, and that the land holders, on the other hand, belonged to the party in power. Capital punishment under these circumstances could be summa-
rily inflicted without leading to reprisals."[66] A case of
theft reported to have been aboriginal by both Gill and Buck
succinctly delimits the chief's role and power in punishing
offenders. One chief's taro gardens were raided with impunity by his own people because a close relative of the chief
had been stealing from their gardens. This so enraged the
chief that he slew his kinsman. However, he did nothing to
recoup his own losses.[67]

The punishment for committing adultery "depended on the
possibility of its application."[68] A commoner was unable to
redress such an injury against a powerful chief. Even a
lesser chief could not retaliate directly. Buck tells about an
offended husband who attempted to regain his wife by sham-
ing the adulterer, who was the TLM.[69] When the status of
the parties was more or less equivalent, movable goods of
the offender could have been confiscated by the wronged husband. Even land could be appropriated "if the injured husband felt his tribe strong enough to withstand the war that
was bound to follow."[70]

Punishment for murder followed the same pattern. "If the
family of the murderer was weak and had no status, it was
useless for them to withstand a powerful family seeking
vengeance. . . . If . . . the positions were reversed it was
equally useless for a weak family to seek redress. . . . If
both families were powerful, the only recourse was war."[71]

Although the chiefs were able to punish severely and without fear of retaliation in some instances, it is interesting
that "Punishment for infringement of tapus was supposed to
be brought about automatically by the gods. The gods sometimes acted slowly. . . . Sometimes the gods, if left to
themselves, acted not at all."[72] Buck does not differentiate

---

66. Buck, Mangaian Society, p. 153.
67. Ibid.; see also Gill, Life in the Southern Isles, pp. 47-49.
68. Buck, Mangaian Society, p. 154.
69. Ibid.
70. Ibid.
71. Ibid., pp. 155-56.
72. Ibid., p. 152.

between personal and economic tabus here, but in either case, infringement was an offense against a member of the chiefly level. Ironically in the only documented case of physical punishment of tabu transgression, the TLM was slain by a tribal priest for wearing a scarlet flower in a sacred area.[73] The case comes from native historical traditions.

Human sacrifices were made to insure peace after battle and, under desperate conditions, to insure victory in battle. The victims often came from subjugated tribes; hence, sacrifice does not seem to have been used as a means of punishing their own underlings who were offensive to the chiefs.

According to Buck, social status was the first consideration for marriage, and it can be inferred that the chiefly families maintained their prerogatives through intermarriages.[74] It is not known if any interstatus marriages were permitted.

Although only **meager** data on differing socioceremonial activities and privileges are available, they indicate some marked distinctions in this aspect of stratification. The concentration of socioceremonial prerogatives, privileges, and obligations seems to have been heaviest with respect to the two high priests. As long as they did not meddle in secular affairs their persons were sacred and inviolable. This was especially true when they were performing sacred functions at their temples (marae). At such times they were given marked obeisance, even by the TLM, whose sacredness was less than that of an officiating priest-chief. The latter officiated at the installation of the TLM--an island-wide affair attended with much ceremony and human sacrifices--and at the installation of the Ruler of the Food. Because of their sacredness, the priest-chiefs were not tattooed and were not permitted to dance.

Life-crisis rites in chiefly families were more elaborate than those in nonchiefly families. For example: the birth of children of rank was "a social occasion" and was celebrated by special ceremonial forms; children of chiefs were secluded in youth so that they would develop fair, fat bodies; among the masses, living together constituted marriage, but there were marriage ceremonies for the ranking families;

---

73. Ibid.
74. Ibid., p. 90

for some months after the death of a person of chiefly blood elaborate death rituals were held. [75]

Uvea

There were two distinguishable status levels in Uvea: (1) the titled members of the island community including the paramount chief, his six or seven councilors (or "ministers" as they are termed in the literature), and the chiefs of the various villages; (2) the remainder of the population. Burrows believes that the village chiefs were only on the border of true chieftainship as they were called "village elders" (matua fenua) as often as "village chiefs" (aliki fenua). [76] Indeed, relative age, as opposed to seniority of descent, was apparently a factor of some importance as a qualification for title. [77] However, another egalitarian characteristic of the stratification system, the participation of all adult males in village councils, is somewhat negated by the fact that in these councils there was no vote; the titled village chief did most of the talking; the others merely concurred.

Status differences in rights to administer strategic resources occurred with respect to village taro lands. These belonged to the villages but they were allotted to households by the village council which was dominated by the village chief. It is said that villages on the main island collectively owned the reef islets that were opposite them, but the administration of these islets is not recorded. Except for taro fields and certain lands not claimed by anyone in particular, all land was independently held by small kinship groups or lineages, and the lineage head who managed the land did not necessarily hold a chiefly title. Chiefly lineages were larger than untitled lineages; and presumably the lands of a

---

75. Ibid., pp. 84 f.

76. Edwin G. Burrows, "Breed and Border in Polynesia," American Anthropologist, XLI (1939), 11.

77. "The role of seniority [by age] in inheritance of property and titles shows that authority tends to increase with age, although by the rules of descent young men may outrank their elders within the lineage." Edwin G. Burrows, Ethnology of Uvea (Bernice Pahau Bishop Museum Bulletin, No. 145 [1937]), p. 58. See also p. 72.

chiefly lineage would be larger in extent. [78] Burrows does
not indicate a pattern of overlapping stewardship, although,
according to Bataillon, in aboriginal times the paramount
chief could tabu resources throughout the island. [79] The
sanctions for such tabus are not known.

The titled members of the community, in their capacities
in councils, initiated communal enterprises. Bataillon's
statement that the paramount chief had the right to draft labor probably refers to the fact that some communal projects
were decided by the high council of the island. [80] Craftsmen
were engaged by both chiefs and nonchiefs, but because the
chiefs were the foci of collection and redistribution (see below), it may be inferred that they more frequently supported
craft production. Household production was directly supervised by the household head. There was no direct chiefly
supervision of household production. [81]

Large-scale accumulations and redistributions of food and
other goods were initiated by members of the chiefly level
in connection with life-crisis rites in their families, religious ceremonies, communal labor, and the like. The contribution of each family was fixed by councils, usually the
village council, but how this was done is not clear. Bataillon
and Mangaret wrote that high chiefs had command over the
people's resources and could take what they pleased. [82]
Whether or not the high chiefs ever engaged in subsistence
production is not known.

There was very little differential consumption of strategic
goods. Certain foods considered choice went to chiefs. Soft
mat kilts, walking sticks, and special sitting mats were insignia of chiefly rank, but each of these items could be used
by untitled individuals, especially elders, an indication of
egalitarianism. [83] The houses of the chiefs were not differ-

78. Ibid. , p. 65.
79. Cited by Burrows, ibid. , p. 76.
80. Ibid.
81. Ibid. , p. 68
82. Cited by S. Percy Smith, "Uea, or Wallis Island, and
Its People," Journal of the Polynesian Society, I (1909), 113;
Williamson, The Social and Political Systems of Central Polynesia, III, 362.
83. Burrows, Ethnology of Uvea, p. 73.

ent from those of others except that they were raised, according to Mangaret. But Burrows is not satisfied that such houses were restricted to chiefs. [84] He writes that platform houses were numerous on the shore, where the platform was needed to keep the floor dry. [85]

General statements about the power of chiefs in Uvea indicate a fair degree of political development. Burrows found the chiefly hierarchy more elaborate and marked by greater subservience to chiefs than in Futuna, where he also did field work. [86] Some statements indicate extreme despotism: "In the old days the power of chiefs was so absolute that commoners were little better off than slaves. . . . That some chiefs had little regard for the lives of their subjects is shown by the use of a man's body to illuminate a birth feast, and in the flexed bodies found at the feet of the kings at Atuvalu--probably bodies of commoners buried alive with their lords, as in Tonga."[87] Bataillon makes similar statements. [88] Burrows writes that the exercise of such power by the paramount chief depended on his personality and on the state of the island. [89] One of the rulers cited as wielding extraordinary power was a queen who ruled after the period of European contact. (She died in 1893.)[90] Early missionary accounts speak of the paramount chief as a "vacillating character."[91]

Councils, under their presiding chiefs, formed the administrative structure of the society. Disregarding the district council, which is presently found but is almost certainly a result of acculturation, [92] there were two types: (1) the council of the paramount chief and his "ministers," all of whom were ranked relative to each other and all of whom were members of the upper status level; (2) the village council

---

84. Ibid.
85. Ibid.
86. Burrows, "Breed and Border in Polynesia," pp. 11-12.
87. Burrows, Ethnology of Uvea, p. 69.
88. Cited by Smith, "Uea, or Wallis Island, and Its People," p. 112; see also Burrows, Ethnology of Uvea, p. 76.
89. Burrows, Ethnology of Uvea, p. 76.
90. Ibid., p. 77.
91. Cited by Burrows, ibid.
92. Ibid., p. 78.

composed of the village chief and all adult males. These bodies decided questions relating to public works, to festivals, and even to disputes. When the council of the paramount chief decided on a course of action, the edict was communicated by members of the paramount chief's family to the lower-order councils. The so-called "ministers" had certain functions in addition to participating in the paramount chief's council. For example, one of these councilors acted as a director of offensive and defensive activities, with one of the village chiefs serving as the actual battle leader.

It is reported that councils had jurisdictional authority. They heard and adjudicated complaints and imposed fines of food, bark cloth, mats, and labor.[93] Burrows writes that chiefs adjudicated disputes over land "on the basis of the chief's knowledge of traditional history and genealogies."[94] Each village reputedly had a "policeman" (tangata fekau) who reported offenses to the village council. Imposition of fines, adjudication by council and by chiefs, and existence of police, however, may have developed after European contact. The only available cases involving these procedures are clearly postcontact.[95] The method of enforcing decisions is not described.

According to Burrows, "An old Uvean custom, now abandoned through European influence, was the laying waste of whole villages for misdeeds of one inhabitant."[96] In one example, an entire village was evacuated when a man killed his wife, because the people expected to be descended upon. A missionary entreated the paramount chief not to destroy the village and, after three days of "prayers and supplications," won out.[97]

Collective retaliation, another method of punishment, probably existed before European influence. Status was a factor. Mondon wrote of a murder that no one dared punish because chiefs were the culprits.[98] However, Henequel's

93. Ibid., pp. 78-79.
94. Ibid., p. 69.
95. Ibid., pp. 68, 78-79.
96. Ibid., p. 79.
97. Ibid., from Bataillon.
98. Cited in ibid., p. 70.

transcription of native historical traditions "tells of chiefs, even kings, suffering death for various misdeeds, but factional rivalry had much to do with such vengeance."[99]

The only evidence discovered regarding sanctions for violations of tabu indicates supernatural punishment.[100]

Whether or not there was a preference for intrastatus marriage has not been recorded.

The tabu complex surrounding the paramount chief was not elaborate. According to Mangaret, things used by the chiefs could not be touched, and one had to avoid looking at the paramount chief when speaking to him.[101] One sat down when receiving orders from a superior or when the high chief passed; however, these forms of respect also characterized filial behavior.[102] There was a "chief's language" consisting of special terms of address and a few other expressions.[103] Kava had to be presented to people of high rank when they were visited, and a dry coconut leaf was worn by the caller. Status was also symbolized by participation of chiefs in ceremonial kava servings.

Birth celebrations of the first-born in chiefly families were more elaborate than those in other families, and the death rites of the three highest chiefs included special ceremonial forms. Aside from these, no differences were indicated between chiefs and nonchiefs in Burrows' discussion of the life cycle.

Summary

Group IIa societies, Mangareva, Easter Island, Mangaia, and Uvea, had stratification systems structurally divisible into two status levels. In Mangareva, Easter Island, and Mangaia, there was a tendency to form a third and lowest level composed of peoples who were defeated in war. In Man-

---

99. Ibid.

100. Ibid., p. 86.

101. Cited in ibid., p. 73.

102. Ibid.

103. Ibid., p. 74. Samoan chiefs' languages were more elaborate. See also Margaret Mead, The Social Organization of Manua (Bernice Pahau Bishop Museum Bulletin, No. 76 [1930]), pp. 114-16.

gareva, the tendency toward a third level was also manifest
in the distinction between pakaora (inferior relatives of
chiefs) who were high-order land managers, and those who
held smaller plots. Economic and social processes under
the chiefs' directions can be expected to have been less intricate in Group IIa than in Group I, since the status systems
were less complex. The chain of command was shorter.

As in Group I, pre-eminent rights to administer resources
were held by the upper status levels. These rights included
prerogatives of dispossessing lesser-order stewards in
Mangareva and Easter Island and of dispossessing defeated
peoples from assigned lands in Mangaia. The right of dispossession apparently did not prevail in Uvea. Some evidence suggests that Mangaian chiefs could deprive underlings
of access to irrigation waters. General tabuing powers were
an aspect of chiefly control over land and sea. Sanctions for
transgressing economic tabus were supernatural in nature,
with the exception of Easter Island where there were secular punishments.

The chiefs controlled communal production, and usually
craft production. In contrast to Group I societies, there was
no direct chiefly control over the production of individual
households in the sense of directing planting and of inspect-
ing to insure adequate cultivation.

A redistributive hierarchy of two levels with chiefs acting
as focal points of collection and redistribution was characteristic of Group IIa societies. The customary obligation to
give surplus to chiefs was not enforced by forceful confiscations. Possible exceptions were Uvea, where one source reports that chiefs could take goods, and Easter Island, where
the birdman practiced institutionalized plundering. Highest
chiefs were supported by contributions of food, and they usually did not engage in subsistence production.

Insignia of rank were marked but evidently were not as
numerous as in Group I societies.

Chiefs exercised control of socioregulatory processes.
General statements by observers indicate that a fair degree
of arbitrary authority was wielded by chiefs. Differences in
status resulted in differential applications of sanctions to
wrongdoers. Within this pattern, the chief could punish severely in certain cases. But there were more stringent limitations on the chiefs' ability to inflict secular punishments
on offenders in Group IIa societies than in Group I societies.

This is exemplified by the frequent occurrence of suicides among chiefs in Mangareva resulting from insults to them, the lack of ability of the Mangaian chief to control raiding of his taro plot as the expression of his people's feelings of injustice at the hands of one of the chief's near kin, by the retaliation of the "weak" against the "strong" in Easter Island in certain cases, and by the general predominance of supernatural sanctions for punishment of breaches of the chief's personal tabu.

A preference for intrastatus marriage existed among the chiefly levels. In no case was this preference as rigidly enforced as it was in the Group I societies.

Ceremonial distinctions between statuses were fairly well marked. The personal tabu system surrounding the high chiefs was marked by fewer types of prohibitions than comparable systems in Group I societies. With the exception of Mangareva, supernatural punishments followed tabu breaches of this kind. Obeisant postures in the presence of chiefs were not marked except in Uvea where one sat down in the high chief's presence, and in Mangaia where high priest-chiefs were treated with reverence when they were officiating at their temples. Chiefs were not ceremonially carried. A courtesy language was present in Uvea, but it was less elaborate than the ones that existed in Samoa and in Tonga.

There were often special life-crisis rites in chiefly families. These rites were not as elaborate or as different in form from commoners' rites as those of chiefs in the Group I societies.

Mangareva appears to have been the most stratified of the Group IIa societies. Apparently there was a greater tendency toward the development of a third status level there. Secular, severe punishments were applied to those who refused to render surplus production to chiefs, and to those who broke the personal tabu of the high chief. Chiefly life-crisis rites were most elaborate in Mangareva. Some aspects of the Uvean stratification system indicate that Uvea was less stratified than Mangareva, Mangaia, and Easter Island. There was a lack of any tendency toward a third status level; a greater amount of prestige given to elders, as may be seen in the fact that insignia of chiefly rank were also worn by elders; and a small amount of control over familial lands exerted by chiefs. However, respectful behavior toward chiefs was more marked in Uvea than in other Group IIa islands, and it may be that the above indications of less stratification are due to poor data.

4. The Degree of Stratification in Marquesas, Tikopia, and Futuna

Marquesas

THE RANKING SYSTEM in Marquesas was relatively undifferentiated. Each of the many so-called "tribes" was an autonomous sociopolitical unit. The paramount chief (hakaiki), the tribal priest, the heads of a few high-ranking families, and the households of these men formed the chiefly level. The remainder of the population comprised the lower status level (mata-ei-nana). The practice of priestly or craft occupations did not affect status as assigned by birth. The tribal priest was a close relative, usually a younger brother, of the high chief.

Access to land and sea resources was of the overlapping stewardship type. The chief was the supreme steward, and every household head was also the steward of his family's lands. There was evidently no intermediate level of stewardship. The chief had general tabuing powers. Violations of tabus on resources generally brought supernatural punishment. [1] Des Vergnes reported that the chief did not have the right to dispossess those under him and never did so. [2]

---

1. E. S. Craighill Handy, The Native Cultures in the Marquesas (Bernice Pahau Bishop Museum Bulletin, No. 9 [1923]), p. 59. Some secular sanctions may be implied by Handy when he mentions that the chiefs' councilors ("administrative tahunas") also enforced the tabus.
2. As cited by Robert W. Williamson, The Social and Po-

Handy, however, writes that chiefs could alienate land.[3] Linton states that the chief "was hesitant to take a garden from even the lowliest native for fear of retaliation through magic."[4] These contradictory statements may reflect regional variations in Marquesan customs. Because of their combined polygynous-polyandrous marriages, chiefs generally had more manpower in their households.[5] Therefore, they probably used more land and produced more strategic goods than other people. However, this did not confer material advantages because many of the goods produced were distributed among the people in feasts that were sponsored by the chiefs.

Chiefs held the highest prerogatives regarding the use of large canoes and deep-sea fishing nets. Their permission had to be obtained before the equipment could be used, and the user had to present the chief with a gift of a share of the produce.

The chief initiated large-scale productive activities, including the harvesting of the first breadfruit crop. Craft production was largely stimulated by chiefs, but anyone who could raise the necessary goods could engage craftsmen. Chiefs were exempted, at least to some extent, from subsistence production, being supported by goods that were reserved from tribal collections and by fields cultivated by members of their households.[6] There was no direct supervision of household production by the chief. Each household head determined the planting arrangements of his family.

As elsewhere, the paramount chief received surplus food and other goods and used them for general distributions and for subsidizing craft production. Tribal storage pits of breadfruit were under the chief's control. The first breadfruit crop was stored in these pits. The occasions for redistribu-

litical Systems of Central Polynesia (Cambridge, Eng., 1924), III, 296-97.

3. Handy, The Native Culture in the Marquesas, p. 57.

4. Ralph Linton, "Marquesan Culture," in Ralph Linton and A. Kardiner, The Individual and His Society (New York, 1939), p. 139.

5. Ibid., pp. 152, 156-57.

6. Handy, The Native Culture in the Marquesas, pp. 47-48, 59, and passim.

tion of these and other goods were similar in nature to those on other islands. Radiquet wrote that chiefs could take what they pleased from "commoners."[7] Evidence from other sources indicates that the chief's right to surplus production was not arbitrarily enforced. Stewart and Vincendon Dumoulin reported that a chief could not levy a "tax." If he wanted something, he had to ask for it as a gift or barter for it.[8]

In the Marquesas, as in other islands, certain foods were reserved for members of the chiefly level. Insignia of chiefly rank consisted of a certain type of staff and a pandanus fan. The size of one's house platform was proportional to one's status. The quality of a chief's clothing might have been better than that of others' although not different in kind. Bennett, in 1840, saw no "badges of dignity" worn on ordinary occasions.[9]

General observations of travelers, missionaries, and ethnographers indicate that the power wielded by Marquesan chiefs was extremely limited. Early accounts agree almost unanimously on this.[10] The Duff missionaries found the Marquesan chiefs to have less authority than the Tahitian chiefs. Krusenstern wrote that the people of Nukuhiva did not regard the "king" a tyrant. He observed of the chief of one tribe that "the people laughed at his orders, and should he venture to strike anyone, he would infallibly meet with a like return."[11] Langsdorff "saw nothing like a form of government, and the most important man in the valley did not seem to have the power of a chief. His commands were laughed at, and he was not able to keep the crowd from the visitor's ship. All the chiefs seen by him had less power over their subjects than a village mayor over his peasants."[12] Porter found a "perfect democracy," having no chiefs, only patriarchs. Stewart observed that the well-organized "monarchies" of Hawaii and Tahiti were not present in the Marquesas. Jardin and des Vergnes gave similar reports. Melville's

---

7. As cited in Williamson, The Social and Political Systems of Central Polynesia, III, 359.
   8. Ibid.
   9. Ibid., p. 130.
   10. Ibid., pp. 129 f.
   11. Ibid., p. 130.
   12. Ibid.

experience illustrates the relatively limited importance of
chiefly power: "Mehevi was in fact the greatest of the chiefs
--the head of his clan--the sovereign of the valley; and the
simplicity of the social institutions of the people could not
have been more completely proved than by the fact, that after having been several weeks in the valley, and almost in
daily intercourse with Mehevi, I should have remained until
the time of the festival ignorant of his regal character."[13]
Mathias asserted that in former days the chief might have
those who were disobedient put to death.[14]

Modern scientists and observers agree with the consensus
of early accounts. Handy calls Marquesan government "pa-
triarchal-communism"; the chief's position relative to the
people was comparable to that of the father in a family.[15]
Burrows and von den Steinen also comment on the relatively
small importance of status differentials.[16] Rollin writes of
the native polity: "It was the democratic communistic regime,
a small uncivilized republic in which each was the protector
of his own rights and his own judge." "C'était la régime
communiste démocratique, une petite république 'en sauvage'
dans laquelle chacun était le protecteur de ses droits et son
propre justicier."[17]

---

13. Herman Melville, Typee (New York, 1931), p. 252.
Since the completion of this monograph, it has come to the author's attention that Melville's Typee is not entirely an autobio-
graphical record but leans heavily on the journals of the explor-
ers Stewart and Porter. However, according to C. R. Anderson, who discovered this fact, the ethnography embodied in
Melville's novel is, except for a few minor details, accurate--
or at least it was taken from the journals of Stewart and Porter
without distortion. See Charles Robert Anderson, Melville
in the South Seas (New York, 1939), Chapters V-VIII.

14. As cited by Williamson, The Social and Political Systems of Central Polynesia, III, 130.

15. Handy, The Native Culture in the Marquesas, p. 45.

16. Edwin G. Burrows, "Breed and Border in Polynesia,"
American Anthropologist, XLI (1939), 5; see also Diether von
den Steinen, "Das Stande-wesen der Polynesier in seiner
Wirtschaftlichen Bedeutung," Zeitschrift für Vergleichende
Rechtswissenschaft, XLII (1926), 195.

17. Louis Rollin, Les Iles Marquises (Paris, 1929), pp. 80-81.

In all sociopolitical matters in which the chief played some role, he was aided by an informal council composed of important, usually aged (an egalitarian qualification) members of the group, including household heads, important warriors, and the so-called political experts (political tahuna). Linton describes a typical meeting of the chief and the elders in which ". . . questions would be thrashed out, and at the end of the evening the point would be settled. An agreement would be reached without anyone, even the chief, putting forward a vigorous opinion."[18]

Evidence from early accounts indicates that chiefs had no jurisdictional powers, and that the injured persons personally settled disputes and avenged murder, theft, and other wrongs.[19] Linton, however, states that the chief interfered in disputes by indicating which side he favored. The other side usually withdrew.[20] But according to Linton, this was all that the chief could do. He had no power to compel the disputants to follow his suggestion.

Sorcery, ridicule, and retaliation were methods by which injured parties wreaked vengeance on offenders. But there were status differences in the application of sanctions. For example, according to Mathias, an injured party could retrieve a stolen article and take even more, but a chief could kill the thief.[21] Handy, however, reports that "stealing within a tribe was very rare . . . killing was more so."[22] The punishment for breaking the personal tabus of chiefs and others was usually supernatural, sometimes physical.[23]

Chiefs tended to marry women of high status, and on some northern islands, chiefs never married women of low rank. But generally, a chief could marry a woman of low status and neither he nor his offspring would lose standing.[24]

---

18. Linton, "Marquesan Culture," p. 161.
19. Williamson, The Social and Political Systems of Central Polynesia, III, 25.
20. Linton, "Marquesan Culture," p. 160.
21. Williamson, The Social and Political Systems of Central Polynesia, III, 26.
22. Handy, The Native Culture in the Marquesas, p. 57.
23. Ibid., pp. 52, 56-57, 263.
24. Ibid., p. 50. Handy notes the striking contrast with Hawaii and Tahiti.

The body of the chief, especially his head, was tabu, and on Ua Pou and Nukuhiva, his house and personal possessions were also inviolable. But, according to Handy, the mana-tabu complex of the chief was not elaborate. This was especially true in the southern Marquesas. "The sanctity of male children in general . . . was merely exaggerated in the case of male chiefs. The head being the most <u>tapu</u> of all parts of the body, for chiefs in particular but likewise for every first-born, many precautions were taken to prevent anything profane from passing over it or touching it. The persons of both chiefs and chieftesses were regarded as <u>tapu</u> in Nukuhiva and Ua Pou, but, apparently, in the southern section of the group chiefs and people concerned themselves little about it."[25] There was actually no distinctive tabu concerned with the chief that might not also be associated with any first-born male.[26] Few of the Polynesian forms of paying respect to chiefs were present. Only high-ranking individuals drank kava, but there were no exaggerated obeisant postures and no "chiefs' language." Bennett reported that he saw no ceremonies of respect being paid to chiefs.[27]

Life-crisis rites in chiefly families were mostly exaggerated forms of those occurring generally in the society.[28] "No rites were practised exclusively for chiefs or their families--as far as I could discover. The rites which might be performed for anyone, particularly for first-born sons, were more elaborate for chiefs than for others simply because their wealth was greater than that of others. . . . Any wealthy man could celebrate any event in exactly the same way as the chief, if he had the wherewithal".[29] A few distinctive rites for members of chiefly rank are found in Handy's evidence, such as a presentation rite for chiefly children on the northern island of Nukuhiva.[30]

---

25. Ibid., p. 51.   26. Ibid., p. 52.
27. Cited by Williamson, The Social and Political Systems of Central Polynesia, III, 130.
28. Compare Handy, The Native Culture in the Marquesas, pp. 71 f.
29. Ibid., p. 53. "Wealthy" means the ability to accumulate goods for distribution, probably from one's own labor and solicitations from kinsmen.
30. Ibid., p. 93. For additional principal sources for

Tikopia

The structure of the ranking system was simple in Tikopia. Two nonegalitarian status levels can be distinguished: (1) the four chiefs (ariki) and their immediate families including close collateral relatives (paito ariki); (2) the nonchiefs, the remainder of the populace. Close collateral relatives of the chief were distinguished from other members of the paito ariki as maru. The nonchiefs can be divided into (a) those families headed by ritual elders and (b) those not so headed. This last distinction is most significant in ceremonial, rather than political or economic, organization. Craftsmen usually came from the nonchiefly level.

The significance of the chief in economic processes has been well summarized by Firth: "The chief has been shown to be the most important single human factor in the economic life of the Tikopia. Not only does he play a part as a producer within his immediate household, but by initiative and example he gives direction to the productive work of the community; he is titular owner of the most valuable property of the members of his clan; he imposes far-reaching restrictions on production and consumption and in many important activities he acts as a focal point in the processes of exchange and distribution."[31]

The four chiefs held the highest privileges of land administration in a system of overlapping tenure. They exercised

---

this section, see also R. H. Drioult-Gerard, La Civilisation des Iles Marquises (Paris, 1940); and Ralph Linton, The Material Culture of the Marquesas Islands (Bernice Pahau Bishop Museum Memoir, Vol. VIII, No. 5 [1923]).

Most of our materials refer to Nukahiva and Hiva Oa. There are indications that some of the Marquesan islands, as Ua Pou, had a more highly stratified organization than that generally described here. See Handy, "The Native Culture in the Marquesas," pp. 30-31. It is noteworthy in this respect that irrigation agriculture was more widespread in Ua Pou. See Ralph Linton, Archaeology of the Marquesas (Bernice Pahau Bishop Museum Bulletin, No. 23 [1935]), p. 101.

31. Raymond Firth, Primitive Polynesian Economy (New York, 1950), p. 231.

the usual prerogatives, such as placing general tabus on land use. Firth notes that in times of land shortage men of rank attempted to enlarge their resources at the expense of others. He cites a case in which a chief "resorted to an orchard of his clansfolk . . . they deserted it because they were afraid that if they persisted in taking food from it he would bewitch them."[32] Firth also reports, however, that "A person . . . who systematically exploited the best land of others, would gradually incur opprobrium which would hamper his activities in other directions where cooperation was essential. Even in the case of a chief this tends to be an important factor."[33] In actuality, some commoners had "considerably" more land than some chiefs.[34] Inequalities in land use were, furthermore, remedied by the Tikopian custom, unique in Polynesia, by which persons wishing to plant nontree crops on unused land of another group could do so without prior permission. In the operation of this custom, a chief did not override the claims of others. Firth describes a situation in which a good piece of taro ground held by a man was rushed by others who began to plant on it. One of the chiefs "was rather piqued" because he had meant to ask for a plot but didn't, and had to be content without one.[35]

The interior lake was considered the property of the four chiefs, especially of chief Kafika, who had the highest status among them. However, anyone could use the lake freely if he sent his chief a part of the catch. Fishing resources on the sea were evidently not held in overlapping stewardship, but were free to all; portions of the reef were used by the local and adjoining population.

Large ocean-going canoes used for deep-sea fishing (sacred canoes) were owned by chiefs. Some commoners owned canoes identical to these but they were not consecrated.[36] The chiefs' canoes were borrowed freely by others. Firth writes: ". . . the conventions of the society do not allow material goods to be withheld from production for any long

---

32. Ibid., p. 164; compare p. 58; see also Raymond Firth, We, the Tikopia (London, 1936), pp. 361, 383-84.
33. Firth, We, the Tikopia, p. 404.
34. Firth, Primitive Polynesian Economy, p. 53.
35. Firth, We, the Tikopia, p. 379.
36. Firth, Primitive Polynesian Economy, p. 117.

time when they are required by other individuals, nor the possession of them to be used as a bargaining instrument to secure an abnormal rate of return."[37]

In theory all canoes, nets, houses, and all other types of goods were considered by the people to be the property of the chief, even though the persons who built and used them had "full rights of use."[38] This is an extension of the pattern of overlapping stewardship tenure of land to all objects held by the group. As Firth describes the phenomenon, "in the last resort their [the people's] interest in it [a good] will give way to his [the chief's]."[39] An important distinction should be made between this ideological extension of stewardship in other things, which confers no actual managerial power for the chief, and the stewardship over land. It is possible that the "over-all stewardship" phenomenon occurred generally in Polynesia, but because sophisticated field workers appeared on the scene long after cultural decay set in, the custom is not fully reported. Tikopia was studied prior to such decay.

The chiefs initiated communal productive activities and subsidized much of the craft specialization. A chief could not force a nonchief to engage in communal labor. "Even in the case of an enterprise sponsored by a chief, there are sometimes too few workers."[40] The chief's people "are not constrained to assist him in any absolute sense."[41] A number of examples may be found in the literature. Once when the people were late at the rethatching of his canoe house, the chief merely complained. "On another occasion at the ritual of yam planting at Kafika the Ariki Kafika arrived at the cultivation at the agreed time before sunrise, but nearly all his party were so late that most of the planting was over before they came. He was very angry and whooped loudly twice to show his disapproval. They

---

37. Ibid., p. 148

38. Raymond Firth, The Work of the Gods in Tikopia (London, 1940), p. 23; see also Firth, We, the Tikopia, passim; and Firth, Primitive Polynesian Economy, passim.

39. Firth, The Work of the Gods in Tikopia, p. 23.

40. Firth, Primitive Polynesian Economy, p. 142.

41. Ibid., p. 196.

were ashamed, though they later joked with him about it. "[42]

There was no duly constituted agency to regulate production in nonchiefly households. The method by which a chief instigated production in other households was to work furiously on his own cultivation. This would activate others to work on theirs as the implication was that some ceremony requiring their contributions would soon be forthcoming. [43] It can be inferred that chiefs were not exempt from subsistence production. [44] However, they usually did not carry burdens and did not participate in the heaviest manual labor in group activities.

The chiefs were the foci of accumulations and redistributions of goods. The collections and distributions took place for events similar in nature to those occurring elsewhere in Polynesia. Goods were often given to the chiefs in the form of presents. There was no secular sanction enforcing the customary obligation to give goods to them, and there were no forceful confiscations by them. "Failure to assist the chief in production or to give him customary tribute incurs his displeasure and grumbling, but involves no direct material sanctions against the defaulter, and is not backed up by any consensus of popular approval. "[45] The differences in consumption between chief and nonchief were often a matter of quantity rather than quality. Prestige goods were held by most families and therefore were not insignia of rank. "To some extent chiefs and their immediate relatives require and get choicer food, build somewhat larger houses and have finer mats and ornaments. But in most of their ordinary meals they eat exactly the same provisions as other people, they wear barkcloth of the same quality and their house furniture is of the same simplicity. The interior of a chief's house is no richer in appointments, no more sumptuous than that of a commoner, though there may be more things in it. "[46] Titled men may have had three or four houses in different parts of the island, which were evidently more than commoners had.

---

42. Ibid.; see also Firth, The Work of the Gods in Tikopia, p. 336.
43. Firth, Primitive Polynesian Economy, p. 199.
44. Ibid., p. 191.   45. Ibid., p. 232.
46. Ibid., p. 34; see also p. 244.

81

Firth makes several statements to the effect that chiefs exerted considerable authority in the regulation of interpersonal affairs. He writes that they held life and death powers over their people "in the last resort," and that their orders were "implicitly obeyed."[47] He also reports that authority was absolute only in theory,[48] and that "the forms of executive authority are vaguely defined and come into operation only to cope with major breaches of the law, such as incest or direct insult to the chief."[49] It should be noted that in making any important decision the chief consulted with other men in his "clan," especially with the "ritual elders."

The chief's power to adjudicate disputes was limited. Firth refers to the chief's intervention as "the crystallization of public opinion."[50] In quarrels within families and most quarrels over land, his opinion was not a judgment and was not necessarily taken.[51] If quarrels occurred near the house of a chief, the house of his relative, or the house of a ritual elder, the owner could admonish or strike the disturber of the peace if the latter were a commoner.[52] If a dispute concerning the use of land arose in his "clan" and there was no prospect of immediate settlement, the chief intervened either by ordering both parties off the land, or by ordering both parties to plant in it.[53] On one occasion, when two close relatives of a chief intervened in a land dispute, the disgruntled party decided to migrate. The chief overruled his relatives and reinstated the offended party.[54] In another case, the chief did not explicitly interfere in a boundary dispute, but his presence on the scene had a quieting effect. According to Firth, in such disputes the chief could send both parties away and announce his intention to confiscate the

---

47. Firth, Primitive Polynesian Economy, pp. 230-31; Firth, We, the Tikopia, p. 381.

48. Firth, We, the Tikopia, p. 384.

49. Firth, Primitive Polynesian Economy, p. 232.

50. Ibid., p. 235.

51. Raymond Firth, "Authority and Public Opinion in Tikopia," in M. Fortes, Social Structure (Oxford, 1949), pp. 173-74.

52. Ibid., p. 174.

53. Firth, We, the Tikopia, p. 384.

54. Firth, Primitive Polynesian Economy, pp. 188-89.

land if they were both under his jurisdiction and the quarrel threatened to become serious. "Even the warning of such a possibility is usually enough to induce the rival claimants to compose their differences."[55] But if the disputants were of different clans, the feud could smoulder even if the chief were involved, and no settlement would be reached.[56]

Differential punishments for social misconduct were correlated with status differences. For example, if a commoner struck a chief, he would probably have to "expiate his offense by going off to sea. The reverse can occur with impunity."[57] Chiefs were wary of commoners who began to usurp authority by accumulating and redistributing goods. In such a case, "According to precedent in Tikopia history, they [the chiefs] would probably take an opportunity to seize his [the commoner's] goods or to kill him."[58]

The chief took no action in apprehending thieves and was in the same position as anyone else with regard to punishing them: "I have heard the Ariki Kafika, premier chief of the community, shriek and curse like an ordinary man [when his cultivations were raided]--and with as little effect."[59] Confronting the thief and demanding compensation, and ridiculing and bewitching him were the general means of obtaining satisfaction.

Firth gives several cases in which chiefs' tabus on certain resources were violated. One chief became extremely angry and dispatched a man to order the offenders to the woods. They fled to the woods but only until the chief became calm again.[60] It was said that, if frequent violations of this type occurred, the chief would banish the offender to the sea. Actually, most offenses and insults to the chief could be atoned for by crawling up to him, exhibiting marked obeisance, and offering a compensatory gift of food and goods. Once, when a nearby village violated a chief's decree that no one should indulge in jubilance because his son was ill,

55. Firth, We, the Tikopia, p. 397.
56. Ibid.
57. Ibid., p. 35.
58. Firth, Primitive Polynesian Economy, p. 243.
59. Firth, "Authority and Public Opinion in Tikopia," p. 176.
60. Ibid., p. 179.

the chief ordered the village to migrate. Everyone prepared to go, but there was an implicit understanding that they would not actually have to leave. They did not.[61] Actual banishment was rare, although one who offended against the social order might banish himself.

Other examples could be cited to illustrate the lack of coercive power of the chief. In Tikopia, most types of misconduct were punished supernaturally, even infringements of the chief's personal or economic tabus.[62]

Firth writes that in former times there was a preference for intrastatus marriage, but at the time of his study interstatus marriages occurred freely.[63] Some survival of the older custom remains. For example, men of rank desire virgins for wives, and daughters of chiefs theoretically are tabu in premarital sexual relations. Chief Tafua attributed the infusion of commoner blood into chiefly families to the chiefly preference for "beauties."[64]

Chiefs were representatives of the gods. They had power (mana) over the fertility of the land and played a central role in kava rites and a number of religious ceremonies. Unlike other men, the chiefs neither cooked nor carried burdens. However "The system of personal tapu is not highly developed in Tikopia--there is nothing approaching the complexity of Maori regulations, for example--and in its field of operation it appears to be largely a function of the kinship situation."[65] The personal tabu of the chiefs did not differ from the tabu surrounding the head men of ordinary households. For example, the tabu on touching the chief's head

---

61. Ibid., p. 184.

62. Firth, We, the Tikopia, pp. 153, 395-96, and passim; Firth, "Authority and Public Opinion in Tikopia"; and Firth, Primitive Polynesian Economy, pp. 188-89, 203, 207, 211, 235, 270.

63. Firth, We, the Tikopia, pp. 88, 358.

64. Ibid., p. 514. This situation contrasts sharply with that described by Rivers' informant, a native pastor originally from Uvea, who reports that chiefs never married nonchiefs and, if a commoner violated a woman of chiefly family, he was banished or killed. See W. H. R. Rivers, The History of Melanesian Society (Cambridge, Eng., 1914), II, 305.

65. Firth, We, the Tikopia, p. 183.

referred primarily to his sons, not to the general population. The difference between chiefs and commoners in this respect was the strictness with which the tabu was obeyed.[66]

In ordinary affairs there were no elaborate forms of respect paid to chiefs. Chiefs and commoners "mingle freely, exchanges take place between them on a basis of general reciprocity, there is no 'chief's language' as in Samoa or Java, kinship terms are used between them. . . . "[67] A group of people might have paid homage to a chief by raising him above their heads, but the only stated occasion was a case in which the chief, reluctant to pass a sentence, was held in the air by his subjects until he yielded and passed the sentence that they desired--banishment.[68]

The life-crisis rites in chiefly families were more elaborate than those practiced generally in the society. The childhood and adolescence of children of chiefs, of children of near relatives of chiefs, and of children of wealthy elders were periodically marked by feasts. The initiation ceremonies of boys of rank lasted longer and were on a larger scale than other initiations, although the form of the ceremony was not unique. Families of rank gave large feasts at marriages; but commoner families might also have done so.[69]

Futuna

The population of Futuna was divided into two status levels,

---

66. Ibid., pp. 183-84.

67. Ibid., p. 358. This conflicts with one of Rivers' informants who reported that people crawled up to chiefs on their hands and knees. See W. H. R. Rivers, The History of Melanesian Society, II, 305. Such behavior did occur if an atonement or a request of a chief was being made, but not otherwise. See Firth, The Work of the Gods in Tikopia, p. 203.

68. Firth, "Authority and Public Opinion in Tikopia," p. 185.

69. For additional principal sources of information on Tikopia, see also Raymond Firth, "Report on Research in Tikopia," Oceania, I (1930-31), 105-17; Raymond Firth, "Totemism in Polynesia," Oceania (1930-31), 291-321, 377-98.

those who were titled, and those who were not. The island was divided into "districts," and the upper or titled level consisted of the chiefs of these districts and their attendants, the district distributor of food, and the village chiefs. The rest of the population was untitled.

Councils, rather than individuals, were the major forces in economic and social life. The highest political bodies were the two district councils. Each was presided over by the paramount district chief and was composed of some district functionaries and the village chiefs. Another council on the village level was presided over by the village chief. Theoretically, it was open to all male members of the village, but, in practice, only elders attended. The village councils were discussion groups, the chiefs not exerting exclusive authority. The village council thus tends to be an egalitarian body.

Control of land resources was mainly vested in kinship groups regardless of whether or not they were headed by chiefs. Heads of kinship units were the stewards of the kinship land, but they had no power of alienation or allotment without the consent of the group. Small amounts of cultivated land in the mountains and large fish nets were held and used communally by villages. The district chief, evidently after consulting with the titled members of the district, could place general tabus on food stuffs.[70] According to Smith, "no one dared violate [the tabu] on pain of the anger of the gods."[71]

Each household head supervised production in his own household. Village communal enterprises were usually instigated by the village council. Sometimes villages performed tasks assigned to them by the district council of chiefs. Specialists were often employed in connection with village tasks and were engaged by the village council. Canoe builders were supported by the man who wanted the canoe built, not necessarily by a chief. Not even the paramount district chiefs were exempt from tilling the soil and cooking.[72]

---

70. Edwin G. Burrows, Ethnology of Futuna, (Bernice Pahau Bishop Museum Bulletin, No. 138 [1936]), p. 97.

71. S. Percy Smith, "Futuna, or Horne Island and Its People," Journal of the Polynesian Society, I (2nd. ed.; 1909), 40.

72. Burrows, Ethnology of Futuna, p. 43.

Village and district councils often collected and redistributed surplus foods and other goods for ceremonies and feeding workers engaged in communal labor or labor for the community. Sometimes the household heads met in the village council and decided what contributions were to be made; sometimes the village chief ordered the allotments. "Householders will complain if the levy seems too large."[73] Food stuffs and manufactured goods collected as fines were also used for such distributions. Often one village was designated to provide most of the food for district-wide feasts. The chiefs, acting as individuals, exercised some claim on the resources of their villages for use in feasts in certain life-crisis rites that involved the upper status, and for entertaining visitors. Chiefs probably could not force contributions for such occasions.

Burrows finds few insignia of rank, but earlier sources mention crowns of white feathers, a coconut-leaf necklace, a white tapa bracelet, and staves as distinctive accoutrements of various types of chiefs.[74]

General statements by early observers indicate that chiefs had relatively limited power. According to Williamson, Mangaret held that Futuna is more properly considered a "republic" than a "monarchy."[75] Bourdin reported that the "king" was strictly obeyed, but he did not usually interfere in local matters.[76] One of the French missionaries wrote that the power of the old men (the village council?) was stronger than that of the "king" and the chiefs.[77] According to Boisse, "the two kings had little more than the title; each Futuna head of the family was really perfectly independent, but the decisions of the old people were generally submitted to."[78]

The power structure is an indication of the relatively non-stratified character of the society. The elders in the village

---

73. Ibid., p. 100.

74. Ibid., pp. 90-91; Smith, "Futuna, or Horne Island and Its People," p. 41.

75. Williamson, Social and Political Systems of Central Polynesia, III, 134-35.

76. Ibid., p. 135.

77. Ibid.

78. Ibid.

council, which assigned communal work and designated household contributions to feasts, were "prominent in official discussions."[79] In one village council observed by Burrows, the council fined the chief and a fellow villager for quarreling.[80] Whether such an event could occur under aboriginal circumstances is not known.

The village and district councils meted out punishments in cases of theft, sexual misconduct, and fighting. Severe cases went to the district council (or to the French, in Burrows' time), less severe cases to the village council. Punishments were labor or fines of food stuffs and other goods which were used in communal distributions. Burrows writes that in aboriginal times mutilation or the death penalty may have been imposed by councils on culprits, but, if so, such powers were abrogated by the French.[81] On the other hand, French occupation probably strengthened the authority of councils in certain matters. Burrows suggests that council adjudication was a development from a less definite aboriginal regulatory pattern under French acculturation.[82]

Possibly another post-European development is the existence of one or two policemen (ofisa) in each village. The title suggests acculturation. One informant said that ofisa existed in aboriginal times as guards over the taro gardens. Missionary sources disagree as to the aboriginal presence of the position, although one missionary is cited as having created it.[83]

Raiding parties are described as an aboriginal method of punishment of an offense against the village. The offender was supposed to prepare pigs for "the whole population" on pain of having his house and gardens destroyed. Differential status and backing could be expected to be manifest here with regard to submission, but Servant reported that resistance "is so rare that not a single example can be cited."[84]

There is no direct evidence on whether or not intrastatus marriage was preferred.

---

79. Burrows, Ethnology of Futuna, p. 67.
80. Ibid., p. 101.
81. Ibid., p. 98.
82. Ibid., p. 101.
83. Ibid.

Information on the personal tabu complex surrounding the high chiefs is meagre. The degree to which the prohibitions were elaborated is not known. In Burrows' time, failure to behave with appropriate respect was punished supernaturally.[85] Schouten and Lemaire describe marked forms of paying respect to superiors; however, it was to the visiting Europeans that most of the homage was shown.[86] To what extent such respect and obeisance were typical of Futuna life is not known. Removing one's headpiece when passing a high chief is practiced today. Chiefs were not carried. Polite forms of speech, consisting of several repetitions of everything said, were customary when addressing superiors. But this form of respect was not exclusively given to chiefs. Status was clearly demarcated in the ritual kava circles in which only chiefs and their ceremonial attendants participated.

Some life-crisis rites were more ceremoniously celebrated in chiefly families than they were in other families. Although there is no evidence of distinctive chiefly ceremonies at birth or puberty, there were a special death ceremony and special mourning rituals for the paramount chief.

Summary

Group IIb societies, Marquesas, Tikopia, and Futuna, had stratification systems containing two structural levels. There was no tendency to from a third level, and the upper level had few members compared to Group I and IIa societies.

The highest rights of resource administration were held by the chief in the Marquesas and Tikopia. In Futuna the prerogatives to manage land were divided between the village chief and the elders of the community. Prerogatives did not usually include the right to dispossess underlings. High chiefs generally had the power to place widespread tabus. The sanctions for transgressing economic tabus were usually supernatural. Some secular punishments obtained in the Marquesas.

---

84. Ibid., p. 98 (quoted by Burrows).
85. Ibid., p. 91.
86. Cited by Burrows, ibid., pp. 90-91.

The chiefs controlled communal production in the Marquesas and Tikopia. In Futuna some communal production was controlled by chiefs, some by the village council composed of a chief and elders. Craft production could be supported by anyone although probably chiefs most often engaged specialists. There was no direct chiefly control over the production of individual households.

The chiefs were foci of large-scale collections and redistributions of goods. They did not forcefully confiscate the goods of others. Chiefs were not exempt from subsistence activities, except in the Marquesas. Insignia of status were few. In Tikopia quantity rather than quality of valued possessions distinguished chiefs.

General statements by both early and late observers indicate that the chiefs' powers in interpersonal affairs were limited. The chiefs usually held informal consultations with elders of the community before important decisions were reached. In Futuna these consultations were institutionalized in the form of a council, and the village elders exerted a great amount of authority. Differences in status sometimes conferred the right on the upper level to punish offenders severely. However, violent secular punishments inflicted by chiefs were rare, perhaps most frequent in the Marquesas. Breaches of the chief's personal tabus were punished supernaturally. Indeed, sanctions were predominately supernatural throughout the Group IIb societies. Violence anywhere in the society was infrequent.

There was a slight preference for chiefly endogamy but a chief's standing was not lowered by marrying a commoner. In Tikopia, at least, marriages of chiefs with nonchiefly women were the rule.

The personal tabu system of the high chiefs was usually unelaborated. The prohibitions were similar to those which surrounded the head of any household in Tikopia and the Marquesas. In Tikopia, in fact, the tabu of the chief was primarily respected in his own household. With the possible exception of Futuna, obeisant postures and elaborate forms of paying respect were minimal.

Life-crisis rites in chiefly families were often more elaborate than in nonchiefly families, but others could indulge by amassing the goods requisite for the ceremonies. This fact and the nonchief's privilege of subsidizing craftsmen indicate that the chief's redistributive functions were not

90

much greater than those of some who were not chiefs. Differences by status in the life-crisis rites were more of degree than of form.

It is difficult to rate the Group IIa societies on a gradient of stratification. The application of one criterion results in one sequence; of another criterion, a different sequence. However, the important role played by the elders of Futuna in the regulation of economic and social affairs indicates that this society was the least stratified. Some aspects of Marquesan stratification suggest greater development than Tikopia, viz., the occasional use of secular punishments for violations of the Marquesan chief's personal and economic tabus, and the exempting of chiefs from at least some subsistence production. In the northern Marquesas one also finds a more rigid preference for intrachiefly marriage and more elaborate personal tabus concerning chiefs.

5. The Degree of Stratification in Pukapuka, Ontong Java, and Tokelau

Pukapuka

THE STRATIFICATION SYSTEM of Pukapuka was divided into two levels: (1) the chiefs (aliki) and subchiefs (langatila) who were heads and subheads of kinship groups and villages; (2) the remainder of the population. The Beagleholes note that the upper status level did not have the major control of economic and regulatory processes. The concentration of power rested with the elders (tupele) of the island society. [1] Entrance into the group of elders was open to all men of advanced years in Pukapuka. This group was especially important in the regulation of island affairs, but almost all adults participated in the regulation of village affairs. The society thus had a definite egalitarian emphasis. The relative importance in community life of age distinctions and ordinary kinship groups as opposed to the status levels will be discussed below.

The chiefs did not exercise stewardship over land. The head of the family group was the sole administrator of his family's land. [2] These heads often belonged to the lower status level. Each village had prior rights to certain reefs and fishing grounds. The village chief did not have supreme control over these fishing resources. Each village controlled communal taro beds and reserve lands. The former were

---

1. Ernest and Pearl Beaglehole, Ethnology of Pukapuka (Bernice Pahau Bishop Museum Bulletin No. 150 [1938]), pp. 233-34.
2. Ibid., p. 43.

divided into three sections, one each for men, women, and children. As a result, each household held an amount proportionate to its size. [3] Communal taro beds and reserve lands of each village were watched over by guards who prevented trespassing, placed tabus on the land, and reported thefts. The guards were in two cases the adult males of the village, twenty-five serving at a time. In the third Pukapukan village the guarding was done by the elders. Decisions regarding the use of the communal lands were made at village meetings at which the elders and guards discussed the issues. Canoes and similar objects were controlled by kinship groups with the eldest male as nominal owner. Certain fish weirs were controlled by the village as a whole.

Most production was undertaken by, and regulated entirely within, households. Certain activities were carried out on a communal, village, or island-wide scale, or by age groups in the community. [4] Deep-sea fishing in fleets was done by an age group of young adult males under the direction of the elders. The village guards also fished as a group at the end of their term, and organized the care of village taro beds. When an abundant supply of food was accumulated on the reserve lands, the tabus were lifted and a communal gathering of supplies was held under the direction of the guards. The decision for this and other actions involving village production rested with the village council of chiefs and the adult males. Specialists were engaged and supported by both chiefs and nonchiefs. Chiefs were not supported by any kinship group other than their own; they did not receive "tribute" from other households. [5] It is not known whether or not they engaged in subsistence activities.

Reciprocal exchanges between kinship groups and individuals appear to have been the most common sort of transactions, [6] although some redistributive activities also took place. On the village level, redistribution was arranged by the councils of the chiefs and adult males, each household contributing according to its ability. For island-wide collections and redistributions, the chiefs and elders handled the arrangements and determined village contributions. The fo-

---

3. Ibid., p. 41.
4. Compare ibid., pp. 36, 48-49, 67-68, and passim.
5. Ibid., p. 246.   6. Ibid., pp. 90-91.

cal points and initiators of accumulation and redistribution were not, in the main, members of the upper status level.

The elders were supported by taro given to them by members of their own lineages and by deep-sea fish received from the young men. On the whole, there is little evidence of differential consumption of strategic resources between the different nonegalitarian status levels. Chiefs might have been given certain portions of deep-sea fish as emblems of their status, but it was only the elders who ordinarily posessed deep-sea fish while other persons had none. The chiefs had bathing and resting places reserved for their use but goods serving as insignia of rank were practically nonexistent. The chiefs' houses were the same size as were those of anyone else. Valued luxury goods were owned by untitled as well as chiefly kinship groups.[7]

General statements by the Beagleholes indicate a limited development of power differentials by interited status in Pukapuka.[8] They find Pukapuka more egalitarian then certain western Polynesian islands, particularly Samoa and Tonga.[9]

The adult males, the chiefs, the subchiefs, and the elders were organized into a number of councils which regulated interpersonal affairs. There were village meetings attended by all adult males including chiefs and subchiefs, meetings of the elders, and meetings of the chiefs. The village councils discussed village affairs and settled intravillage disputes and matters concerning the reserves. The elders discussed island affairs, and the guards and elders of each village discussed matters concerning the village taro beds. The chiefs discussed island and interkin group ("lineage") matters.

The workings of these councils, as remembered by the Beagleholes' informants, were as follows: The paramount chief called the minor chiefs together to ratify decisions of the group of elders. "Whether or not this approval was nominal depended on the prestige and power of the high chief."[10]

_____

7. Ibid.
8. See ibid., pp. 234, and passim.
9. Ibid., p. 414.
10. Ibid., p. 245.

The final veto was held by the wola, who was an elder in liaison with the high chief. The paramount chief sent a representative to meetings of the elders, but he did not himself attend. The village men controlled village affairs in council; the local chief had no coercive authority in village meetings. [11] The entire island populace was called together to discuss divisions of reserve lands, or realignment of their boundaries. The Beagleholes compare the power of the chiefs to the power of the elders in the following terms: "In island affairs, the chiefs and sub-chiefs were advisory and executive officers, but the real balance of power, in theory at any rate, seems to have been with the old men. . . . When the high chief or his executive . . . was an outstanding personality, he might assume for himself many of the powers that ordinarily lay with the old men; these powers would revert to the old men on the chief's death. "[12]

Physical punishment was infrequently used in Pukapuka. "Sanctions invoked to deal with most antisocial conduct were not secular, but depended on punishment, usually sickness, sent to the wrongdoer by the gods. "[13] Those who stole from the reserves and those who murdered were usually so punished. During periods of famine, however, the guards were empowered to kill those caught thieving from the reserves, and if the gods delayed too long in punishing those who committed willful homicide, group action ensued and the murderer was killed. [14]

There was also a system of fines for thieves caught in the reserves by the guards. This may have had an aboriginal basis, but certainly the police authority of the guards was increased through French influence. [15] Theft from an individual was settled either by retaliation, atonement by relatives of the thief, or by a wrestling match. Insult by slander could also have been settled by a wrestling match. [16] Insult to a chief was punishable by sickness. There is no evidence of variation in ability to punish physically that might be corre-

---

11. Ibid., pp. 245-46.
12. Ibid., p. 24.
13. Ibid., p. 246.
14. Ibid.
15. Ibid., p. 248.
16. Pukapukan wrestling matches usually ended in a draw.

lated with status. Apparently, a chief was not able to invoke
more severe sanctions than any other party.

According to the Beagleholes, "The mate for a chiefly
family was chosen from a family wealthy in talo and coconut
trees."[17] "Wealthy family" might mean chiefly family.

The Beagleholes' informants believed that aboriginally
chiefs "were approached at any time without ceremony or violation of tapu" but the majority said they were sacred from
the time of succession, although not tabu in boyhood.[18] The
chief entered his house through a special door. He ate with
his family, but his old clothes and mats were thrown away
because they had become tabu through contact with his body.

Although there was no developed chief's language, there
were certain forms of respect given to chiefs.[19] A special
salutation was used in greeting a chief or one of his family;[20] when he finished bathing he was carried out of the water; he was given the right of way on paths. The chief had
certain priestly functions. He was ceremonially installed.
He had a "sacred maid" who remained a virgin all her life
and was symbolic of the status of the chief and his lineage.
He also had an attendant (toa) who was his executor and
speaker.

Crisis rites were sometimes more elaborate in chiefly
families than they were in nonchiefly families. More rarely
they were different in form. A family that "ranks in status
and wealth" distributed food to more people at birth feasts
than a nonranking family and held such feasts at every child's
birth, whereas others only celebrated first births.[21] Similarly the scale of chiefly marriage celebrations was larger
although the rites themselves were not unique. Procedures
following the death of a chief included special rites.[22] Such
customs as seclusion of youths to promote fairness of skin
and obesity were not, however, restricted to children of
chiefs.[23]

---

17. E. and P. Beaglehole, Ethnology of Pukapuka, p. 296.
18. Ibid., p. 236.   19. Ibid., p. 237.
20. A variant of this was used between commoners when
they were being extremely polite.
21. E. and P. Beaglehole, Ethnology of Pukapuka, p. 275.
22. Ibid., pp. 302 f.
23. Ibid., pp. 282-83. For an additional principal source

In Ontong Java, the stratification system was simple. Each of the two "tribes" that existed on the atoll had a number of priest-chiefs (maakua) who were the oldest male members of particular kinship groups--patrilocal extended families--in which the title passed. The leaders were ranked among themselves. Three of the eight leaders in the Luangiua tribe were major leaders. They appointed officers who presided over ceremonial redistributions. One priest-chief was considered the senior of the eight. Thus there were two status levels, the priest-chiefs, and the remainder of the population.

In the nineteenth century, there arose a secular supreme leader whom Hogbin is pleased to call "king." Evidence is later presented that this position, and especially the authority wielded through it, were European-influenced. [24]

Access to most of the land and sea resources was controlled by kinship groups. Managership over lands of this category did not go beyond the kin group; the priest-chiefs were not supreme stewards of land. Hogbin differentiates "poor families" from "wealthy families" in that the former only held land on the islet on which the village of the tribe was located, while the latter owned outlying islets as well. How this land differential arose is difficult to envision from Hogbin's materials, but it seems possible that it is related to the depopulation that had occurred by his time and the possible reduction and regrouping of joint families and villages. [25] The village in which the tribe centered communally held two or three nearby islets as reserve lands. A system of guards, appointed by the priest-chiefs from the adult males and under the direction of a member of a priest-chief's family, guarded these islets to prevent trespassing.

---

of information used for this section, see Gordon MacGregor, Notes on the Ethnology of Pukapuka (Bernice Pahau Bishop Museum Occasional Papers, Vol. XI, No. 6 [1935]).

24. Some aspects of the maakua system also do not appear to be aboriginal. See pp. 226-30.

25. See H. Ian Hogbin, "The Problem of Depopulation in Melanesia as Applied to Ontong Java," Journal of the Polynesian Society, XXXIX (1930).

Permission of the head guard had to be obtained before the lands could be entered. [26] The communal lands were utilized in certain religious ceremonies during which the priest-chiefs, evidently as a function of their paramount roles in these ceremonies, directed the exploitation of the reserves.

The patrilocal extended family groups and groupings of matrilineal kin were the major production units. Their own headmen exclusively directed their economic undertakings.[27] Specialists were contracted for by kinship groups. In canoe making, at least, the builder was probably a member of the canoe crew, which in turn was composed of males of a patrilocal joint family. [28] The limited communal production, such as exploitation of the village reserves, was directed by the priest-chiefs.

Extrafamilial distributions of food and other goods were mostly reciprocal exchanges between kin units. [29] Activities involving the collection and redistribution of food and other goods by a third party were infrequent and occurred mainly in connection with the annual tribal religious rite, the sanga. At this ceremony, the priest-chiefs, through appointed relatives, presided over the redistribution of food taken from the reserve lands. At times the term "redistribution" is inappropriate. Although coconuts taken from reserve lands were brought to one place, each collector kept a separate pile and took home those remaining after the priests and guards had taken a share. [30]

From distributions of this kind, and from offerings to the tribal gods made at the sanga, the priest-chiefs derived some of their subsistence. However, they probably did not receive sufficient food to last all year, and it is likely that they engaged in productive activities themselves.

There was very little differential consumption by status. Ordinarily priests were not distinguished by dress or other

26. H. Ian Hogbin, Law and Order in Polynesia (New York, 1934), p. 211.

27. Ibid., pp. 130-32.

28. Ibid., pp. 96, 287.

29. Ibid., pp. 196 f.; see also H. Ian Hogbin, "Tribal Ceremonies at Ontong Java (Solomon Islands), Journal of the (Royal) Anthropological Institute, LXI (1931), passim.

30. Hogbin, Law and Order in Polynesia, p. 187.

insignia of rank from others. During tribal ceremonies, however, they wore regalia consisting of a pandanus-leaf necklace, a fan, a mat, and a staff.

The priest-chiefs did not wield great authority in secular affairs. Hogbin, referring to the head priest-chief, notes that "this latter title [there was no actual title] was an empty one, for he had no authority to back it up beyond his own personality."[31] In Hogbin's opinion, the limited development of stratification in Ontong Java is not typically Polynesian.[32]

The village guard, and hence the priests, had some say in how one who stole reserve foods was to be punished. This was the only organized sanction in Ontong Java, according to Hogbin.[33] Otherwise, punishments were brought about supernaturally or were inflicted through private retaliation by kin groups. Murder within the patrilineal kin groups, incest, and other "sins" were supernaturally punished.[34] In the course of private retaliations, differential ability to inflict punishment according to the respective statuses of the parties involved was occasionally manifest. In one case of interfamilial adultery reported by Hogbin in which the two men concerned were from equally "powerful" families, the guilty one was killed, and no retaliation or compensation followed.[35] In another case, the guilty man was from a "weak" group. He was killed by the husband who was from a "strong" group, and no retaliation or compensation was made. But in a third instance, a father dissuaded his son from killing an adulterer who was a leader. Later the leader made a payment of goods. Also, fights occurred between families of equal strength over adultery. Sometimes, however, the husband merely released his wife.[36] Private retaliation also operated in punishment for thefts. In one case, a thief was killed. Thieves were usually from "poor" families.[37] Sorcery was an alternate to violence in punishment of both adultery and theft.[38]

---

31. H. Ian Hogbin, "The Social Organization of Ontong Java," Oceania, I (1930-31), 423.
32. Ibid., p. 425.
33. Hogbin, Law and Order in Polynesia, p. 211.
34. Ibid., pp. 143 f. A number of examples are cited.
35. Ibid., pp. 211-12.   37. Ibid., p. 215.
36. Ibid., pp. 212-14.   38. Ibid., pp. 216 f.

After the so-called "kingship" was established, one of the
late kings, Uila, exerted considerable authority in settling
disputes and regulating interpersonal affairs in general.[39]
He "reigned" from 1878 to 1905, a period marked by strong
European influence in Ontong Java.[40] The judicial functions
of Uila cannot be considered aboriginal.

A tendency toward intrastatus marriage may be inferred
from Hogbin's statement that "Wealthy parents as a rule prefer their children to marry someone of their own social
standing, and with this end in view they themselves often ar-
range the marriages."[41]

There was some development of ceremonial differences
between the priest-chiefs and the populace. During the tribal
ceremonies the former were generally sacred and inviolable.
The fertility of the land was vested in them. When a priest
became ill, he was expected to commit suicide so that he
would not endanger this fertility. When a priest-chief died,
the entire tribe gathered for the rites. A certain ceremonial prestige, however, was held by the heads of all joint
families as representatives of the family founder. The
priests were supremely sacred only when they wore their
regalia, i. e. , during tribal ceremonies. At other times,
they were no more sacred than any other headman.[42]

Tokelau

There were two status levels in Tokelau. The high chief
and the high priest (usually the son of the former's sister) on

39. Ibid. , pp. 225 f.
40. See below pp. 229-30. Hogbin remarks, "Even after
the kings had been in power for several decades, order was
maintained chiefly by a belief in the supernatural." Hogbin,
"The Problem of Depopulation in Melanesia as Applied to
Ontong Java," p. 53.
41. Hogbin, Law and Order in Polynesia, p. 140.
42. For additional sources consulted, see H. Ian Hogbin,
"Polynesian Ceremonial Gift Exchanges," Oceania, III (1932),
13-39; H. Ian Hogbin, "Coconuts and Coral Islands, "National Geographic Magazine, LXV (1934), 265-98; H. Ian Hogbin,
"Polynesian Colonies in Melanesia, " Journal of the Polynesian Society, XLIX (1940), pp. 199-220.

each of the three atolls formed the upper level, the remainder of the population formed the lower. The chieftainship was bestowed on the oldest man of the four kin groups eligible to hold the title. Newell believed that offices of the high chief and high priest were once combined. MacGregor, however, states that dual division may have existed throughout Tokelauan history. [43]

The village council of elders was the major means of regulation, integration, and control on each atoll. The chief usually did not sit on the council. The oldest member of the council represented him and acted as a liaison between him and the elders.

The high chief was not the supreme steward of land and sea. Most of the strategic resources were controlled by kinship groups. If a section of a kin group died out, the kin group and the village council discussed the reallotment of the group's land and the council heard all claimants from the village. The council could not arbitrarily alienate family lands. Certain lands set aside as communal reserves were under the "absolute" control of the village council, and it decided when these lands could be used. The council could place tabus on all lands. (On Fakaofu atoll the high priest participated). Breach of the tabu was supernaturally punished by the curse of the high chief. [44]

Most production was carried out by kin groups and was supervised exclusively by the head of the group. [45] Enterprises that involved village cooperation were determined and initiated by the village council. [46] Craft production was supported by family groups, not necessarily by the high chief.[47] There is evidence that the high chief did not engage in subsistence production. Although he owned land, "the families of the village consecutively supplied him with food. "[48] MacGregor reports that "The high chief might demand anything he saw from the food supply or property of others. "[49] It is

43. Gordon MacGregor, Ethnology of the Tokelau Islands (Bernice Pahau Bishop Museum Bulletin, No. 146 [1937]), p. 51.
44. Ibid., p. 58.
45. Ibid., p. 46.
46. Ibid., p. 53.
47. Ibid., p. 113.
48. Ibid., p. 51.   49. Ibid., p. 52.

difficult to understand how this right was enforced, given the nature of the power structure and the prevailing sanctions in the society.

In a few activities, the paramount chief was the focal point of a large-scale collection and redistribution of goods. For example, at the great annual ceremony, the paramount chief of Fakaofu received mats, pearl-shell pendants, food, and other offerings from the other atolls. The food was redistributed; the other goods were offered to the gods. When the high chief died, special rites were observed. Mats, pendants, and other goods were brought as gifts or offerings. Most were buried with the corpse. Most accumulations of goods and food occurred at the household or kin group level and were used for distributions in the kin group, for reciprocal exchanges between kin groups, or for feeding and rewarding canoe- and house-building experts. The group usually acted under its leader. [50] Food was gathered for village purposes, such as ceremonial observances, under the direction of the village council and was redistributed through feasts and allocations throughout the populace by an officer appointed by the council.

There was little differential consumption of strategic or even luxury goods between the two status levels. Choice parts of certain foods were reserved for the chief. Apparently the only insignia of rank of the paramount chief was a coconut leaflet chaplet.

The chief and the village council were the significant elements in the power structure. The chief and council members ". . . were elders of their community for advanced age was a requirement, if not the primary qualification, to hold office. . . . Even the heads of the kindreds were selected on this basis in preference to following the eldest line of patrilineal descent [i. e. , the theoretical succession pattern in kin groups] if this would bring a younger man into office."[51] Even among the elders there was a gradation of prestige according to age. MacGregor notes, "the importance of age is perhaps nowhere else in Polynesia so highly developed. Certainly the existence of only one or two hered-

---

50. Ibid., pp. 37, 39, 41, 58, 113-14.
51. Ibid., p. 49.

itary offices is unusual."[52] The emphasis on age also impressed Williamson who suggested that Tokelauan government was once a pure gerontocracy.[53] MacGregor's observations of Tokelauan government indicate limited political development. He speaks of the high chief as "the patriarch of the community"; and it is one of MacGregor's conclusions that "the Tokelau and Ellice atolls have the simplest and most democratic governments in western Polynesia, due to small populations, limited by the food supply."[54]

There is not much clear information about judicial practices. According to MacGregor, the high chief established the "laws."[55] His power of enforcing them was primarily, if not only, supernatural--the power of cursing.[56] The village council settled land disputes and "law" infractions with the "advice of or by consent of the high chief."[57] There is meagre evidence of a kind of judicial official who settled the disputes that were not taken to council.[58] Certain sea foods, notably whales, swordfish, and turtles were supposed to be brought to the temple (marae) as soon as they were taken, and distributed to the village after a suitable ceremony. Reputedly, anyone who kept one of these animals for himself--incredible in the case of whales--had his house, property, and canoe destroyed.[59] Lister indicates that punishments were generally mild, although it is possible that thieves were killed during famine.[60] Adultery was punishable by the destruction of property and goods of the wife and her kin group by the party of the outraged husband. No attempt was made to resist.[61]

52. Ibid., p. 49; see also p. 162.
53. Robert W. Williamson, Social and Political Systems of Central Polynesia (Cambridge, Eng., 1924), I, 373-76.
54. MacGregor, Ethnology of the Tokelau Islands, p. 162.
55. Ibid., p. 50.
56. Ibid., pp. 50-51.
57. Ibid., p. 53.
58. Ibid.
59. Ibid., pp. 151-52.
60. J. J. Lister, "Notes on the Natives of Fakaofu (Bowditch Island)," Journal of the (Royal) Anthropological Institute, XXI (1891), 54.
61. MacGregor, Ethnology of the Tokelau Islands, p. 42.

There was some tendency toward intrastatus or prestige marriages. "Frequently a match was initiated by the boy's father in order to unite two prominent families or to secure a girl of wealth and prestige."[62]

The greatest differential in the functional aspects of stratification occurs in the ceremonial sanctification of status, although by no means do the differences compare with the elaborate developments in some of the other Polynesian islands. The paramount chief was the direct descendant of the gods; his body was sacred and inviolable; he "lived apart from the daily activities of the community attended by his family and household."[63] The high chief occupied the position of honor at feasts, and his death rites were more formal than those of others. There is no record of a chief's language or special forms of obeisance.

Summary

Group III societies, Pukapuka, Ontong Java, and Tokelau were relatively unstratified. There were two status levels, the upper one containing very few members. Elders and the heads of kinship groups exercised the greatest prerogatives and played the dominant roles in socioeconomic and political affairs.

Access to resources mainly depended upon the heads of kinship groups. Wide powers of stewardship were not held by chiefs. In each Group III society, there were reserve communal lands. These were managed by elders in Tokelau and in Pukapuka, and by the priest-chiefs in Ontong Java. The most general tabuing powers were also held by elders in Tokelau and Pukapuka; in Ontong Java, the methods of placing tabus are not known. Violation of tabus on the use of lands was usually supernaturally punished, although in times of scarcity death was inflicted. In Pukapuka and Ontong Java, capital punishment was administered by a group that was chosen from the community. The identity of those who exercised such authority in Tokelau is not known. Communal production was stimulated primarily by the elders in Pukapuka and Tokelau, and by the priests in Ontong Java. Craft pro-

---

62. Ibid., p. 40.
63. Ibid., p. 51.

duction was indiscriminately supported by both chiefs and nonchiefs. Production by individual families was supervised by no higher authority than the family head. The Tokelauan chief did not produce an appreciable amount of the goods he consumed, while the priest-chiefs of Ontong Java evidently did. Information about this aspect of Pukapukan consumption is not specific.

The paucity of chiefly control over communal and craft production is correlated with a relatively small role in the regulation of distribution, especially redistribution. Most large-scale collections and redistributions of goods were directed by elders or males of the group as a whole. The relatively large proportion of reciprocal, nonintermediated exchanges between kin groups, as opposed to redistributions, can also be correlated with the slight degree of chiefly regulation of distribution.

Some foods were reserved for chiefs. The consumption of nonsubsistence goods that served as insignia of rank was limited to the ceremonial regalia worn by the Ontong Java leaders and the Tokelauan chief's coconut wreath.

None of the three societies' chiefs exercised arbitrary authority, and on Pukapuka and Tokelau, at least, the egalitarian council of elders was the most powerful political group. Collective kinship retaliations and responsibilities were the bases of punishments. In a few cases from Ontong Java, status differences were manifest in the ability of "strong" parties to inflict severe punishments; but generally chiefs did not administer more rigorous punishments than others in defense of their rights. In the three societies, there was almost complete dependence on supernatural sanctions.

A tendency toward marriage between individuals having prestige, if not between chiefly families, is indicated.

Ceremonial tabus surrounding chiefs were fairly well developed on Tokelau and Pukapuka where the chief's body was inviolable. The sacredness of the leaders of Ontong Java was effective only when they were officiating at tribal ceremonies. Elaborate forms of paying respect among Group III societies were most marked in Pukapuka. Methods of honoring the chief in Pukapuka compared favorably with those in Group IIb societies. Such customs were less pronounced on Ontong Java and Tokelau.

Elaboration in chiefly life-crisis rites was not highly developed. Special ceremonial forms occurred only in connection with death of the chief.

It does not appear possible to rate the relative stratification of the societies within Group III. The three may be considered equally stratified, or egalitarian.

6. Stratification and Productivity

THE GRADIENT OF stratification in Polynesia is illustrated in the preceding descriptions. It has been postulated that the degree of stratification in these societies is an adaptive feature related to increasing productivity. Polynesian cultures will now be classified on the basis of productivity and this classification related to the gradient in the degree of stratification.

Not all cultures are equally well adapted to the environments in which they are situated. Some exploit the external world more efficiently than others. The ability to derive need-serving goods from the external world may be called the productivity of the culture. It is necessary for all cultures to exploit nature for energy in the form of food. Therefore, productivity is best understood, if cross-cultural comparisons are to be made, in terms of ability to produce food. In any cultural situation two types of phenomena interact to sustain the population: the natural environment, and the tools and techniques used in exploiting it. To derive indices of productivity for Polynesian cultures, it is necessary to estimate the efficiency of technoenvironmental interaction in food production.

There are two methods by which efficiency of exploitation may be estimated. The first is to develop some measure which does not necessarily deal with formal qualities of environment and technology--such as irrigation, altitude, horticulture--but rather which measures their operation, e.g., in the form of input-output ratios. Thus one might use White's "amount of energy harnessed per capita per year . . . [and the] efficiency of the instrumental means of putting energy to work."[1] Another such measure, suggested by White, would be the number of man hours spent in food getting per capita per year.[2] This last would be an input-output ratio based upon the major exploitative activity, food getting. Neither of these measures can be applied to the available data on Polynesia, as observers were not particularly interested in measuring productivity. But the concept of productivity, and White's measures as well, have one implication that may be of considerable value in developing a further measure that is applicable. It is that, other factors being constant, the greater the productivity, measured in energy or man hours, the greater the surplus of subsistence goods produced by those engaged in food production.

It may be argued that this proposition is not necessarily valid, since an increase in productivity might be accompanied by a rise in the level of the producer's wants, and hence the surplus would remain constant, even diminish. For the problem at hand, the objection is not pertinent for two reasons: first, as the cultures compared here are historically closely related and have more or less the same foods and types of distributional systems, it is unlikely that a serious discrepancy in producers' wants would arise from society to society; second, and more significant, the surpluses which are being considered are food surpluses, and any discrepancy in wants that might arise would a priori be small. Human beings can consume just so much or so little food; in contrast to many other goods, the potential range is relatively small. The statement that surplus increases as productivity increases may be accepted for our purposes.

"Surplus" may be considered in two different senses, each of which has value in arriving at a measure of productivity applicable to Polynesia. One type may be designated "immediate surplus" (symbolized as "S_I") and refers to the ability of food producers to acquire, in a single exploitative activity, an amount of food beyond their immediate consumption needs, or an amount greater than would be needed be-

---

1. Leslie A. White, The Science of Culture (New York, 1949), pp. 368-69.

2. Ibid., p. 378. See also Leslie A. White, "Energy and the Evolution of Culture," American Anthropologist, XLV (1943), 335-56.

fore production is resumed again. Thus, in harvesting a domesticated crop, a large S_1 may be produced--much larger, for example, than in killing a small mammal. S_1 does not necessarily imply that the producer, in time, may not be able to consume all that he produces. A second type of surplus (symbolized as "S_c") is that food which the producer has left over after a full cycle, e. g., a year, of production. He has produced more than he can consume, and thus food is available to support other people. S_1 and S_c are not mutually exclusive; a rise in S_1 may produce S_c or a rise in S_c.

In treating Polynesian cultures it is particularly appropriate to use, as a measure of productivity, the ability to produce immediate surpluses. For it is precisely those foods produced beyond the immediate needs of the producers which were collected by chiefs and then redistributed by the system operating in conjunction with religious feasts and other occasions, as described earlier. With the exception of those foods siphoned off by the chiefs to support themselves and craftsmen, the food was redistributed among the commonalty. Therefore, other things being constant, a fairly accurate indication of the ability to produce S_1 may be gained by considering the greatest number of people encompassed in a single redistributive food network, and the frequency per annum of over-all redistribution in such a network. It should be noted immediately that the size of the unit will not necessarily be that of an entire island or group, but rather the number of people in the average distinct economic system. Polynesian cultures are compared below on this basis.

The ability of a producer to produce more food than he needs during a complete production cycle, is also a concept which lends itself to measures of productivity. Other things being constant, the greater the S_c, the greater the proportion of people in the society divorced from food production, that is, the greater the proportion of specialists. Polynesian societies can be compared on the basis of the degree to which they contain a division of labor between food producers and specialists who do not produce food, but the comparisons cannot be precise because the data contained in the ethnographic sources are often ambiguous and nonquantitative. Consequently, less reliance should be placed on this factor than on the size of the largest redistributive unit. Nevertheless, such estimates as can be made will be used as a check on the productivity measure derived from the size of the redistributive unit.

The second major method for estimating productivity--as opposed to these more or less "operational" measures--is one in which the environmental and technological conditions on each island are considered in light of their formal characteristics. For example, in most environments horticultural activities are usually more productive than collecting activities since the reproduction of the engery source is directly controlled. Hence, the number of man hours spent per capita in food getting--to relate this to an operational measure--would be less in horticultural groups than in nonhorticultural groups. A number of similar features of Polynesian ecologies can be analyzed in terms of their productivity implications; and thus by considering the specific technologies and environments, a further check can be made on the productivity classifications obtained through the use of operational measures.

In the proposition that a valid measure of productivity in Polynesian societies is the number of people encompassed in the largest single redistributive food network, and the frequency per annum of redistribution throughout this network, it is required that other things be constant. This requirement must be met if the measure is to be used cross-culturally. Specifically, within each society, every consumer must receive a proportionate amount or "bit." And we must be assured that redistribution is not used by chiefs for political expansionist purposes--that nowhere were bits made smaller than was customary in order that a chief might distribute less food per capita to more people and thus enlarge the number of his followers--otherwise the range of distribution might expand or contract irrespective of S_1 productivity. However, the data indicate that these conditions were met in Polynesia.

In many of the societies considered, some of the food collected by chiefs was used to support themselves and their subsidized specialists, the remainder of the food being given out in equal amounts to the remainder of the group, i.e., to the food producers. The amount taken out by chiefs, however, did not disproportionately affect the size of the redistributive network. If it did, one would expect the size of the network to decrease as the number of chiefs divorced from production and the number of specialists increased. The

converse actually obtained in Polynesia. The size of the redistributive network, the number of specialists, and the
number of chiefs divorced from production, all increase
correspondingly.[3]

Disregarding then any amount taken out by chiefs, is the
remainder of the food equivalently distributed in the large-
scale redistribution activities? Where data are available,
the answer is unequivocally affirmative. In Hawaii, for example, Malo describes the method of redistribution at the
annual Makahiki ceremony, wherein, after a proportion of
the large amount of collected food and goods had fallen to
the paramount, "portions were assigned to the remaining
chiefs and to the different military companies. To the more
important chiefs with many followers was given a large proportion; to the lesser chiefs, with fewer followers, a smaller portion."[4] Melville's description of a large fish distribution in the Marquesas is even more specific on this point.
After some fish had gone to the chief, "the remainder was
divided into numerous small packages, which were immediately dispatched in every direction to the remotest part of
the valley. Arrived at their destination, they were in turn
portioned out, and equally distributed among the various
houses of each particular district."[5] In the Cook Islands:
"The head fisherman took the large fish of a similar kind
and laid out one for each family. He then added fish in turn
to each heap until the pile was exhausted. Chiefly families
were given priority in distribution of the better or larger
fish, and a family of greater numerical numbers [sic]
might be given a few extra."[6] Mariner describes a great
Tongan feast in Vavau in which yams, hogs, and other foods
and goods were distributed: "The hogs were disposed of in
a like manner [i.e., similar to the disposal of yams]; the

---

3. The data verifying this point may be found as follows:
in chapters 2-5 (amount of chiefly separation from production), Table 1 (size of the redistributive network), and in
the next section of this chapter (number of specialists).

4. David Malo, Hawaiian Antiquities (Bernice Pahau Bishop
Museum Special Publication, No. 2 [2nd ed., 1951]), p. 143.

5. Herman Melville, Typee (New York, 1931), p. 234.

6. Peter H. Buck, Arts and Crafts of the Cook Islands (Bernice Pahau Bishop Museum Bulletin, No. 179 [1944]), p. 209.

greatest quantity to the greatest chiefs, who share them out to the chiefs immediately below them in rank, and these again to their dependents, till every man in the island gets at least a mouthful of pork."[7] In Pukapuka, every man, woman, and child was entitled to a share of given proportion in village food divisions.[8] Equal bit per capita distribution appears to be a general Polynesian phenomenon.

Chiefs apparently did not make bits smaller than customary in order to distribute to larger numbers of people. The scope was always defined by the kin relations of the chief and those of his descent group, for one was chief by virtue of one's status in a line of descent, which line stood in a defined relation to all comparable lines. It was this relationship between kin units that determined the range of distribution.

In at least two respects, therefore, the provision that other things be constant is met. But since this is no guarantee that all other factors are constant, attempts to measure productivity by the scope of the redistributive network must and shall be checked against other measures of productivity.

Table 1 (at end of this chapter) indicates in synoptic form the productivity of the Polynesian cultures considered according to the size and frequency of use of the largest single redistributive network for food. Unfortunately, accurate census materials are not available for the period at the commencement of European contact. The figures listed for size of the network vary considerably in accuracy. Where the redistributive unit was a smaller segment than an island or a group of islands, the number of people in such a unit may not have been recorded ethnographically. In that case, the population of the unit is computed by dividing the total population of the island or group by the number of autonomous redistributive segments, to arrive at an average. In such instances, when possible, some estimate of the range of deviation from the mean is made, based on the available evidence. The frequency of redistribution is also relevant, for if in two societies the size of the network be the same, that society in which the net-

---

7. William Mariner, An Account of the Tongan Islands in the South Pacific Ocean (3rd ed.; Edinburgh, 1827), I, 120.

8. Ernest and Pearl Beaglehole, Ethnology of Pukapuka (Bernice Pahau Bishop Museum Bulletin, No. 150 [1938]), p. 36.

work is used most frequently is most productive. The data do not provide quantification of frequency of over-all redistribution; sometimes they do not allow any conclusive statement regarding frequency. Three categories of frequency are defined. To each an arbitrary factor is assigned, multiplication of the size of the redistributive unit by which will yield an estimate of productivity. The frequency of over-all redistributions is considered "regular" and assigned a factor value of three if, in addition to annual collections and redistributions, surplus food also passes up and down the redistributive hierarchy at various times during the year. If only a few or less annual redistributions take place, the frequency may be considered "sporadic" and a factor of two assigned. If the interval between over-all redistributions of surplus food is greater than a year, the frequency is "rare" and a factor of one is given. In two cases, Tahiti and Samoa, the evidence does not permit exact specification of the size of the network of redistribution. It is difficult to say whether over-all redistributions in Tahiti were confined to units of the order of the twenty-odd districts, of which Papara would be an example, or of the three, higher-order units, of which the Teva division is representative. In Samoa, sometimes a "division" such as Aana of Upolu was a redistributive unit, but occasionally all Samoa, except for Manua, participated in a single network. In these situations, both units are listed in the table. In all cases where the size of the economic unit is smaller than the population of the island, the economic unit is designated by the name which usually appears for it in the literature. Where the estimate of population size was made, or refers to a period considerably after contact, the data are given in footnotes.

A comparison of the data given at the end of chapter 1 and Table 1 shows that a marked degree of correspondence obtains between the amount of stratification and the productivity of the society, as the latter is measured by the size of the largest distributive network and the frequency of distribution therein. Productivity on those islands containing the most stratified societies, Group I, does not overlap at all with the productivity of Group IIa societies. Group IIa seems to grade into Group IIb, but lack of specific information on the frequency of over-all redistribution on Uvea and Mangaia prohibits conclusive verification of this point. With the exception of Ontong Java, where the size of the redistributive unit is in doubt, there is a productivity break between Group IIb and Group III.

Within Group I, Hawaii was rated as most stratified, a rating duplicated in productivity. Samoa's somewhat lower stratification ranking than other Group I societies cannot be shown to correspond to productivity differences as the figures are not complete. Mangareva's rating as most stratified within Group IIa cannot definitely be correlated with the highest productivity rating within IIa societies because of poor data on the size of the redistributive unit in Easter Island, Mangaia, and Uvea. Uvea was considered to be less stratified than other Group IIa societies, but whether Uvean productivity is lowest of this Group cannot be ascertained. Within Group IIb, Marquesan society was rated as most stratified, Futunan least. By the measure used here, the Marquesan productivity is highest in Group IIb, but Futuna is not much lower, and does not rank below Tikopia of this group. As the Ontong Java data are incomplete, it is difficult to ascertain whether the productivity on this island was actually highest among Group III. The other Group III societies, Pukapuka and Tokelau, are very close together productivitywise, as they seem to be also in amount of stratification.

The amount of stratification, in terms of the major groupings outlined in chapters 2-5, is decidedly correlated with productivity measured in terms of the size and frequency of use of the redistributive network. The data are not exact enough to determine whether finer discriminations in stratification made within the major groupings are paralleled by productivity variations. It may be wise to refrain from building any conclusions on these results until productivity be checked by the other methods that have been proposed.

It has been postulated that the degree of specialization of labor in the social system should serve as an index of productivity, since the greater the surplus, the more people who would be divorced from subsistence production and hence be able to specialize in other types of production or services--other things being equal. Therefore, in order to measure productivity by specialization of labor, it would be necessary to know the number of kinds of specialists in the society, the percentage of the population so involved, and the part- or full-time character of the activities. However, the data on specialization in Polynesia are quite inadequate. Only fragments of such information can be found. The usual

114

Polynesian word for "expert" or "specialist" is some variant of <u>tohunga</u>. However, the meaning of the term ranges
down to "one who does a particular task well." In some instances ethnographers have gathered lists of the occupations
at which a person may be adept and published them as lists
of specializations. For example, Handy so lists twenty-sev-
en different specializations in the Marquesas. [9] Linton, a
bit more selectively one presumes, lists but two major specializations for the same culture! [10] Therefore, great emphasis cannot be placed on the degree of specialization as a
measure of productivity. The available materials are presented here for the light they sometimes throw on local productivity situations, but little reliance will be placed on degree of specialization as a measure of productivity in view
of the quality of the data. Where pertinent information is
lacking in the following summaries, it should be understood
that the data are unavailable. [11]

Hawaii. --Canoe builders were outstanding among the economic specialists. There were two types, those attached to
households of men of high status, and others. The former
were further specialized according to occupations such as
adz hafters or sennit braiders. [12] There were also housebuilders, men called upon to supervise house construction--
especially the chiefs' houses--adz makers, [13] bird snarers,

---

9. E. S. Craighill Handy, <u>The Native Culture in the Mar-
quesas</u> (Bernice Pahau Bishop Museum Bulletin, No. 9
[1923]), p. 144.

10. Ralph Linton, "Marquesan Culture," in Ralph Linton
and A. Kardiner, <u>The Individual and His Society</u> (New York,
1939), p. 145.

11. Specialization of chiefs as economic distributors has
already been used to indicate the amount of stratification
and thus cannot be used here to measure productivity. The
significance for productivity, however, is very slight because so small a proportion of the population is involved--a
proportion that is, in fact, fairly constant in the societies
considered.

12. M. K. Pukui (trans.), "The Canoe Making Profession
of Ancient Times," <u>Hawaiian Historical Society Papers</u>, XX
(1939), 27-37.

13. Malo, <u>Hawaiian Antiquities</u>, p. 51. (Were they dif-

diviners, healers, sorcerers, and various types of priests. The bird snarers, who collected feathers for chiefly costumes, worked seasonally.

Tonga. --Mariner lists eleven different types of experts (tufunga):canoe builders, undertakers, stone masons, net makers, fishermen (probably communal fishing directors), builders of large houses, tattooers, club carvers, barbers, cooks (?), and peasants. [14] A man may be a specialist in more than one thing, and the activities were not full time.[15] Besides, there were bards and several types of priests.

In the modern village of Pangai, the Beagleholes find that fifteen of 256 villagers (6 per cent) were experts. [16] In all cases, both modern and ancient, nonexperts were capable of performing specialist tasks, but they had less skill and training and hence might call in experts. [17]

Societies. --Henry lists eight different kinds of experts, three of which were types of priests. The others included doctors, directors of marae building, housebuilders, canoe makers, and fishing directors. [18] Canoe makers were divided into the same two types as in Hawaii, although Handy believes these were the same people differently designated when doing different work. [19] Henry also mentions tattooers

---

ferent from canoe builders?) See also N. B. Emerson, "The Bird-Hunters of Ancient Hawaii," Hawaiian Annual, XXI (1895), 75.

14. Mariner, An Account of the Tongan Islands in the South Pacific Ocean, II, 94. One presumes that most people were "peasants," that is, cultivators.

15. Edward Winslow Gifford, Tongan Society (Bernice Pahau Bishop Museum Bulletin, No. 61 [1929]), p. 144.

16. Ernest and Pearl Beaglehole, "Pangai, Village in Tonga," Memoirs of the Polynesian Society, XVII (1941), 42.

17. Specialization here and usually elsewhere in Polynesia was passed down to relatives through training. The training a skilled wood carver gave his son is apparently what is meant when it is written that the craft is inherited.

18. Teuira Henry, Ancient Tahiti (Bernice Pahau Bishop Museum Bulletin, No. 48 [1928]), p. 154.

19. E. S. Craighill Handy, Houses, Boats, and Fishing in the Society Islands (Bernice Pahau Bishop Museum Bulletin, No. 90 [1932]), p. 59.

and embalmers.[20] An expert's household or relatives acted as his assistants in performing a task.

Mention should be made here of the famous ariori entertainment societies of young adults, who traveled around the islands performing in various places. Many of them evidently did no other work. The bearers of the paramount chiefs were also exempt from subsistence production.[21]

Samoa.--Housebuilders were the same people as canoe makers. They formed a so-called "guild"; all traced relationship in a single line of descent.[22] There were master fishermen who directed communal fishing. Mead also reports carvers, masseurs, circumcisers, medicine makers, and sennit braiders. There were priests, especially a high priest in each village. Specialization was not full time.[23] Turner estimated that one of every 300 males was a master carpenter and had ten to twelve "apprentices."[24]

Mangareva.--Master fishers, carpenters, singers, tattooers, undertakers, spirit catchers, tooth treaters, goiter treaters, sorcerers, scholars, dancers, greater and lesser priests are mentioned by Buck.[25]

Uvea.--House and canoe building were done by carpenters called tufunga. At the time of Burrows' study, there were seventy of them on Uvea, or less than 2 per cent of the total population.[26] There were also healers and priests, and supervisors of turmeric preparation.

Easter Island.--Experts (maori) included: genealogy chanters, image carvers, and wood cutters.[27] There were

20. Henry, Ancient Tahiti, pp. 287, 295.

21. Ibid., p. 151.

22. Peter H. Buck, Samoan Material Culture (Bernice Pahau Bishop Museum Bulletin, No. 75 [1930]), pp. 22-23, 84 f.

23 Margaret Mead, The Social Organization of Manua (Bernice Pahau Bishop Museum Bulletin, No. 76 [1930]), pp. 38, 68, 69, and passim.

24. George Turner, Samoa (London, 1884), p. 157.

25. Peter H. Buck, Ethnology of Mangareva (Bernice Pahau Bishop Museum Bulletin, No. 157 [1938]), passim.

26. Edwin G. Burrows, Ethnology of Uvea (Bernice Pahau Bishop Museum Bulletin, No. 145 [1937]), p. 112.

27. Alfred Métraux, Ethnology of Easter Island (Bernice Pahau Bishop Museum Bulletin, No. 160 [1940]), passim.

also fishing directors, tattooers, and priests. Métraux
claims that there were professional warriors; there is also
some evidence to the contrary. [28]

Mangaia. --There were some fishing directors. Although
anyone could make a house, canoe, or net, experts made the
house-rafter designs and small nets and gave canoe-making
advice. [29] Skill in stone working, carving, and sennit braid-
ing usually went together. There were also priests and sorcerers. Specialization does not appear to have been full time.

Futuna. --House and canoe building were part of the carpentry expert's repertoire. There were two types of carpenters; one carried a hereditary title, the other did not. [30]
There were also healers, a turmeric preparation director,
and fishing directors.

Marquesas. --Handy's list of twenty-seven specialties has
been mentioned. However, professionals were not separately engaged in each of these activities. Furthermore, craftsmen also took part in subsistence production. [31] Linton
writes that the principal specialists were the house and canoe maker and the carver. [32] The former apparently supervised, rather than participated in, house and canoe construction. There was also a fishing director. There was at least
one priest per tribe.

Tikopia. --"Such specialization as exists is the development of extra capacity in a craft and not the practice of the
craft to the exclusion of others."[33] There were fish experts
of various kinds and skilled dancers, both called by specific
terms. Firth's description of the tufunga is quoted in full
since it seems to clarify the source of confusion in the Marquesan and other data: "The term tufunga is a generic title
for a skilled craftsman and has attached to it a number of ex-
planatory expressions indicating proficiency in tattooing,

---

28. Ibid., p. 138.
29. Peter H. Buck, Mangaian Society (Bernice Pahau
Bishop Museum Bulletin, No. 122 [1934]), passim.
30. Edwin G. Burrows, Ethnology of Futuna (Bernice
Pahau Bishop Museum Bulletin, No. 138 [1936]), p. 86.
31. Handy, The Native Culture in the Marquesas, p. 143.
32. Linton, "Marquesan Culture," p. 145.
33. Raymond Firth, Primitive Polynesian Economy (New
York, 1950), p. 113.

plaiting of sinnet, net-making, working of bowls or building of canoes. Here again there is no specific quantitative point of achievement at which the title may be attained and it is a matter of degree of activity and quality of the product rather than of specialization in the craft. But there is a difference to be observed. Whereas every man engages to some extent in agriculture, fishing, sinnet-plaiting, dancing, and minor woodwork, only a few are tattooers and canoe architects, though not exclusively. Women are also admitted to have special proficiency in crafts, particularly in the plaiting of mats. But the term tufunga is never applied to a woman."[34] The proportion of specialists is obviously a difficult matter to determine, and further information is lacking.

Ontong Java.--Specialization was rudimentarily developed. Every canoe crew, composed of the males of a joint family, had a member who constructed the canoe, often an elder of the family retired from the actual fishing.[35] This can hardly be called specialization. Hogbin also mentions a tattooer, and shark and bonito fishing experts.[36]

Tokelau.--There was a director of communal fishing. There were experts in charge of house and canoe building. Once there was a priest in each village. Apparently specialization was quite limited.[37]

Pukapuka.--The amount of specialization was small. All males could perform all men's tasks. Specialists were limited to canoe builders, medicine men, and priests. All, except perhaps the priests, participated in the daily routines.[38] There were no housebuilding specialists.

As for providing a check on productivity as derived from the size and frequency of redistribution, the data on the amount of

_____

34. Ibid.
35. H. Ian Hogbin, Law and Order in Polynesia (New York, 1934), p. 96.
36. Ibid., p. 131. See also H. Ian Hogbin, "Coconuts and Coral Islands," National Geographic Magazine, LXV (1934), 280.
37. Compare Gordon MacGregor, Ethnology of the Tokelau Islands (Bernice Pahau Bishop Museum Bulletin, No. 146 [1937]).
38. E. and P. Beaglehole, Ethnology of Pukapuka, p. 47.

specialization are far from satisfactory. However inadequate, the data above do seem to corroborate the main outlines of the productivity gradient. Group III societies, all of which rank lowest in productivity, as shown in the data at the end of chapter 1, were all undifferentiated as regards specialization of labor. Even partial specialization in Group IIb societies was usually limited to two to four major types of specialists. The societies of Group IIa rank higher in productivity than IIb societies and seem also to have had more different types of specialists--perhaps five or more. Mangareva, in fact, compares favorably with Group I. Uvea lists only three specialists, although the data are not complete. Finally, types of specialization were generally more numerous in Group I societies than in IIa, which corresponds to the difference in Table 1.

A final check on the productivity indices heretofore derived may be made by a consideration of exploitative techniques and environmental conditions. Here, formal characteristics of the ecological situation are considered. As a basis for evaluating the productivity implications of the qualitative aspects of technoenvironmental situations, certain principles can be adduced. First, two major deductions can be made: (1) Other factors, primarily environment, being held constant, productivity will vary as the techniques of exploitation vary. (2) The opposite, technology being held constant, productivity varies as the environmental situation varies. These two statements may be simply expressed as:

$$P = f(T), \text{ E being constant,}$$
$$\text{and}$$
$$P = f(E), \text{ T being constant,}$$

where P is productivity, T is technique of environmental exploitation, and E is environment.

From these abstract statements, a number of more specific propositions can be derived which will be useful in evaluating relative productivity. First, consider $P = f(T)$, E being constant. As already mentioned, one of the principles that may be deduced from this statement is that, other factors being constant, horticultural techniques of exploitation are usually more productive than hunting and gathering. Although the source of energy exploited in both cases is living organisms, in horticultural activities, because of the tools and techniques employed, the distribution and reproduction of the organisms are controlled; in collecting it is not so. The number of man hours spent per capita in horticulture, therefore, is less than, and the surplus greater than, in collecting. The presence of domesticated animals is also important in that respect. Polynesian cultures varied in the degree to which they depended on domesticated resources, thus this variation could be significant productivitywise.

Other derivations of P = f (T) which may be used are concerned with the productivity implications of particular horticultural techniques. For example, environments being similar, it is reasonable that the group possessing the greatest variety of crops will often have the greatest productivity. The reasoning is that the group with the greatest crop range will be able to cope with a greater variety of environmental conditions. Because Polynesian cultures varied in crop range, this feature must also be considered. [39]

Crops differ in the environments they require for fertility. If two cultures find themselves in the same type of environment, that culture will be more productive whose crops are best adapted to that environment. Crops, of course, are somewhat adaptable, especially if there is a selection of varieties. But if the outstanding Polynesian crops are considered, it is found that they did not all have the same "ideal" environments. The coconut, for example, seems to thrive in almost any kind of soil, even in coral sand and brackish water, but it grows best at altitudes between sea level and 2000 feet. [40] Once coconut has reached bearing age, it flowers and fruits continuously, and produces up to 100 nuts per year. It is a hardy, long-lived plant and requires little care. Bananas, on the other hand, require fairly humid climate, moist, deep, and rich soil, protection from the wind, good drainage, and sun, and heat. [41] Yams must have a deep, fri-

---

39. Unfortunately, the subspecies variation in crops is difficult to estimate in the literature, often because of a complete lack of data, and frequently because of the difference between botanical and native classification of variation. Consequently, such data will not be relied upon.

40. Earley V. Wilcox, Tropical Agriculture (New York, 1924), p. 58.

41. Otis Warren Barrett, The Tropical Crops (New York, 1928), p. 177. See also Henry A. Nicholls and John H. Holland, A Text-Book of Tropical Agriculture (London, 1929), p. 229. Bananas are, in many ways, a highly productive

able soil, fairly warm and dry. They are a seasonal crop.
They endure drought better than any root crop.[42] Yams can
grow very well at fairly high altitudes and are preservable
when out of the ground. Taro has a high yield. It may be
planted wet or dry but needs a fair amount of water in either
case. Taro bears continuously, and with an adequate drainage situation it can be left in the soil and harvested when
needed, which makes it a particularly useful crop. While
taro is quite adaptable to sun and moisture conditions, sweet
potato by contrast spoils with too little sun or too much moisture. Handy states that it is more valuable than taro because
it can be grown in less favorable localities, it matures in
one-third the time, and it requires less labor in planting and
care.[43] It does not, however, mature continuously as taro
does, only seasonally.[44] Sweet potato is best in light, friable, well-drained soil. It can be grown at considerable ele-
vations but does best in lowland conditions. Breadfruit usually bears three or four major crops a year, although with
a number of varieties the harvests may be staggered throughout a good part of the year. Breadfruit seems to flourish
best at lower altitudes (up to 1500-2000 feet). It requires a
warm, humid climate, heavy rainfall, moist soil, and good
drainage. It is reported that absence of any one of the conditions may be seriously detrimental.[45]

Thus, crops vary not only in environmental requirements
but also in the number of harvests and other characteristics.

---

crop. Nicholls and Holland report studies showing 4,000
pounds of bananas can be grown in the same area as 33
pounds of wheat or 98 of potatoes.

42. Barrett, The Tropical Crops, p. 374; see also Nicholls
and Holland, A Text-Book of Tropical Agriculture, p. 446.

43. E. S. Craighill Handy, The Hawaiian Planter (Bernice Pahau Bishop Museum Bulletin, No. 161 [1940]), p. 143.

44. Of course, with a great number of varieties with different growth rates, the effect may be one of continuous production. However, if a group domesticated a number of varieties, these would usually be spread out over the domain,
and as far as any one producer is concerned, crops would
be seasonal.

45. Wilson Popenoe, Manual of Tropical and Subtropical
Fruits (New York, 1920), p. 413.

Another factor which increases horticultural productivity is the development of special techniques of exploitation of soil such as irrigation, frequently found in Polynesia. Irrigation permits almost continuous production on the same land because of the replenishment of minerals through silt deposits of the irrigation water. Irrigation is quite superior, as a productive technique, to shifting cultivation. [46]

Thus, under $P = f(T)$, E being constant, there are a number of variable features of technological systems that should be noted when the formal characteristics of technology and environment are considered with a view toward estimating relative productivity: dependence on horticulture, range of crop variation, types of crops, adaptability of crops to environment, and special techniques of domestication. Under $P = f(E)$, T being constant, a number of similarly significant variable features can be determined. For example, technologies being similar, the greater the variety of environmental zones, the greater the possibility of wider and richer exploitation. High islands offer a marked contrast to low islands in this respect. Almost all the former are characterized by a greater variety of conditions as well as richer opportunities for plant growth than the latter. Different altitudes, soils, and conditions of water supply, in particular, contribute to the rich ecological diversity on high islands. On the low coral atolls, environmental differentiation is practically nonexistent. [47] Furthermore, environmental opportunities for horticulture on atolls are extremely limited. Water is a particular problem. The loose coral rubble that goes under the term "soil" is of no help, as it is so porous that whenever rains do occur organic materials quickly leach through.

Another feature of environment which varies from island to island, yet which is relevant to considerations of productivity, is the richness of natural exploitable biota. Availability of edible wild plants is, of course, important. But per-

---

46. Compare Karl J. Pelzer, Pioneer Settlement in the Asiatic Tropics (New York, 1945).

47. Compare J. Stanley Gardiner, Coral Reefs and Atolls (London, 1931); see also Otis W. Freeman, "Geographic Setting of the Pacific," in Otis W. Freeman (ed.), Geography of the Pacific (New York, 1951).

haps more crucial in Polynesia is the magnitude of fish resources. There is considerable variation in fishing opportunities. One variation is the general decrease in abundance and variety of fish from west to east in the Pacific.[48] A more important variation is the presence of reefs, especially of barrier reefs and lagoons, which offer unparalleled opportunities of adding to the food supply through fishing.[49] Some islands, e.g., the Marquesas, have no barrier reef or lagoon, and fishing resources are relatively poor.

All of these variable features of technology and environment are relevant to productivity differentials. So also are the presence and frequency of droughts, hurricanes, and the like which are apt to hamper exploitative activities considerably, if not to produce severe famine. Other things being equal, a culture subject to natural catastrophes, or to "lags" in the yearly cycle of harvests--with consequent food shortages or dependence on stored, previously harvested foods--is lower in productivity than the culture of an island not affected by such factors. The population-carrying capacity is reduced on islands which are apt to experience shortage and famine, and, consequently, the number of man hours per capita spent in food production rises. A deficiency in storage techniques would have the same result, other factors being constant.[50]

---

48. "The greatest abundance and variety of forms probably occur in the waters from the East Indies to Japan. The same types mainly, but in diminishing number, are found as one goes eastward through the islands to Hawaii. Yet between 400 and 500 species of shore fishes representing around seventy-five families are known from the Hawaiian Islands alone." John T. Nichols and Paul Bartsch, Fishes and Shells of the Pacific World (New York, 1945), pp. 61-62.

49. Ibid., pp. 55-56.

50. The significance of low productivity periods in exploitative activities has recently been pointed out by George A. Bartholomew and Joseph B. Birdsell, "Ecology and the Protohominids," American Anthropologist, LV (1953), 487-88: "Since biological factors vary with time, values for population equilibria are not to be measured at a given point in time. They fluctuate about a balance which is determined, not by the mean condition, but by extremes. Indeed, one of

The Polynesian islands that have been considered will now be examined from an ecological point of view to determine whether or not the relative productivities of the cultures check with the productivities as so far determined. The data are presented in the Appendix in a series of thirteen sections, one for each island.[51] These sections contain a number of headings which are designed to illustrate those variable features of technology and environment which are relevant in assessing productivity. Under "Environmental Opportunities" will be found the salient features of the environment, information on environmental diversity, abundance of natural biota, and suitability for horticulture. Under "Source of Food Supply," some indication of the relative dependence on domes-

---

the most firmly established ecological generalizations is Liebig's law of the minimum, which states that a biological reaction at any level is controlled not by factors which are present in excess, but by that essential factor which is present in minimal quantity."

Bartholomew and Birdsell are concerned here with the effect of food supply on population density; our concern is more with the range of size of economically autonomous units (which is essentially what Table 1 represents). The reason that population density has not been used here as a measure of productivity is that an increase in density does not imply an increase in productivity as we use that term. A coral atoll dependent on coconuts and fishing may have a relatively dense population. Yet hardly any surplus is derived; fishing and coconut gathering usually are daily activities. The number of man hours per capita spent in food production must be relatively high. This low productivity is reflected by the relatively low population (Table 1), but not by density, as the atolls can be extremely tiny in area.

51. Unfortunately, the material gathered for the Tongan group is not on a par with the information for other islands, and no chart has been made for these islands. For comparative purposes, the following range of food crops is known to have been cultivated in the Tongan group (the list may be incomplete): yams (the most important crop), plantains and bananas, breadfruit, coconut, taro (and kape, a taro variety), sweet potato, sugar cane, ivi (Tahitian chestnut), and turmeric.

ticated and nondomesticated foods is given. The other headings are self-explanatory. It is hoped that the Appendix contains enough material to enable the reader to draw conclusions about relative productivity in view of the general principles outlined above. In a brief summary, the data contained in the Appendix will be reviewed to see whether the hierarchy of productivity so derived correlates with the classification made of the amount of stratification in Polynesian islands.

Appendix sections I to XIII present the data on the technoenvironmental conditions of the islands (Tonga excepted). It was postulated that consideration of the formal characteristics of technology and environment would provide a qualitative check on the relative productivities as they have already been assigned. It seems indisputable that, in the main, the data do illustrate relative productivities (assessed according to the principles outlined above) that correspond to productivities measured by other means. As a short-cut method for the further comparison of productivity with the amount of stratification in different Polynesian islands, let us consider the productivities as they may be derived from the Appendix in terms of the categories (Groups I, IIa, IIb, and III) which we have outlined as representing the amount of stratification. In the process, the relation of the qualitative assessment of productivity to other methods of discerning productivity will become apparent, since the latter have already been found to correspond to the stratification groupings.

Group I societies were all characterized by a marked emphasis on domesticated food resources coupled with exploitation of a rich supply of noncultivated foods. Each had a wide range of crops (12 to 14), and the crops were used in a number of different ecological niches to which they were adaptively suited. Among the special techniques of domestication, irrigation was outstanding in Hawaii and to a lesser extent in Tahiti. In Samoa, swamp lands were drained. In all three areas, fish were abundant--especially in Samoa and the Society Islands where barrier reefs and lagoons are found--and were exploited by a wide variety of techniques. Edible wild plants were numerous, although they were not heavily relied upon. Hawaii and the Society Islands presented a great diversity of rich environmental zones to which crops could be adapted. Samoa also had environmental diversity, but it was somewhat more restricted--at least in area. In each locale, because of the height of the islands, water supply was not a problem. Droughts were infrequent; there was little seasonal variation in productivity level; and, because of the wide crop range, hurricanes could not do severe damage. Furthermore, the major crops could also be stored: taro in the ground, breadfruit in pits. The over-all picture of the Group I technologies and environments is one of extensive and intensive exploitation of a variety of conditions, sometimes by specialized techniques, at a continuously high level.

With respect to differences of productivity within Group I, Hawaii with its large-scale irrigation techniques and conscious and effective utilization of small ecological niches (such as the use of irrigation banks for subsidiary crops) stands above the field. In general the ecological situations of Group I societies afford a picture of productivity commensurable with that derived from the other measures used.

A striking feature of the environments of Group IIa societies is the relatively low height of the volcanic summits on each island. As a result of this, precipitation in high altitudes is definitely seasonal, and the drainage systems impermanent (or practically nonexistent in the case of Easter Island, where soil porosity is also a factor). This not only prohibited the development of irrigation on a large scale but, because of the seasonal character of the water supply, probably made for some seasonal declines in productivity. Even storage techniques did not make up for these declines when compared to Group I societies where production was high the year around, and where only a small part of the crops had to be stored, since most could be immediately consumed. The range of crops in Group IIa societies was generally less than in Group I, although Mangareva compares favorably with Group I. The crops were used in particular environmental situations, but environmental diversity does not compare with Group I islands--hence the scope of exploited environments was more restricted. Irrigation was practiced on Mangaia and Mangareva, but the extent was limited. On Uvea, swamps were drained for raising taro. On each island, the amount of very fertile soil was restricted to one particular area: the Mangarevan bays, the Uvean and Easter Island coastal areas, and the Mangaian puna lands. Natural biotic conditions varied significantly from the very rich fishing re-

127

sources of Mangareva and Uvea to the more restricted resources of Easter Island and Mangaia. There was a greater abundance of edible flora on Mangareva and Mangaia than on Easter and Uvea. In all islands, however, domesticated resources were more relied upon than nondomesticated. In summary, Group IIa societies rate definitely lower, according to the evaluating principles outlined, than Group I.

Within Group IIa, the evidence from the formal characteristics of the technology and environment supports a judgment of greater productivity for Mangareva. The greatest range of crops by far was found there, and fishing resources were very good. Definite, prolonged lean seasons, famines, and a restricted range of crops in Uvea, and the small range of crops combined with relatively poor fishing conditions on Easter Island indicate a lower productivity on these islands than others of Group IIa.

In Group IIb societies, ecological conditions show only a mediocre productivity level, although very close to some Group IIa societies. The Futunans used a considerable range of crops (10), but these were grown mostly in a small area, the shore strip. The interiors of the islands were not fully exploited, especially Futuna proper where the soil was acid and impervious. Not only was agriculture restricted on Futuna, but the fish supply was not abundant as it was in other islands. On the other hand, seasonal declines in productivity notwithstanding, severe famines were rare. Also, a special technique of domestication, irrigation, was found in Futuna. In the Marquesas, the lack of level land and the small distribution of fertile soil--both related to the deeply eroded nature of the islands--seriously limited technological developments, especially irrigation. There is, as in Futuna, no barrier reef or lagoon, hence fishing possibilities are restricted. Finally, although seasonal declines in productivity are not clearly indicated, severe famines occurred periodically. The crop range in the Marquesas is similar to the crop range in Futuna. On Tikopia, long seasonal drops in carrying capacity occurred. Again, a lagoon and barrier reef are absent, although the fringing reef was extensively utilized for fishing. The range of crops is comparable to those of Futuna and the Marquesas. Environmental diversity was extensively exploited on Tikopia, but land of every type was very restricted in area. In summary, Group IIb societies, although they had a fairly wide crop range, were limited in productivity by severe seasonal or cyclical declines which can be traced to environmental factors. Fishing resources were also poor as compared to islands with lagoons. Besides, in each case, exploitation was spatially limited. From these considerations the three islands seem about equal in productivity level.

The Group III societies may be clearly differentiated from those of Group II in productivity by the technoenvironmental situation. All three are found on coral atolls. The atolls are characterized by soil and water conditions not conducive to horticulture and by a lack of environmental diversity and edible wild flora. Furthermore, drought and famine were constant threats and reduced the productivity to almost preagricultural levels for long periods. Only the abundant fish supply made such islands at all inhabitable by nonindustrial peoples. In each case, the range of crops was far smaller than that of other societies considered. There is little difference among Ontong Java, Pukapuka, and Tokelau in the way of most or least productive. The technologies and environments are almost identical.

Summary

In the preceding discussions, the measure of productivity primarily used was: the greatest magnitude and the frequency of the collection and redistribution of the same goods-- since, in Polynesia, surplus production was distributed from a central agency. This measure was checked by a subsidiary measure based upon the degree of specialization, and by consideration of the formal aspects of the particular ecologies in terms of their productivity implications.

All measures of productivity correlated with the classification of the amount of stratification on the basis of four major groupings. The smaller difference in stratification between IIa and IIb than between I, II and III showed up to an extent in the measure based upon the size of the distributive unit and more so from consideration of the properties of the ecological conditions.

The four major stratification groupings were also, to an extent, subdivided, albeit the measure of stratification was not too refined. Hawaii was distinguished among Group I societies as being the most stratified. In terms of the network of food redistribution and in formal characteristics of the technoenvironmental interaction, Hawaiian productivity was the greatest of the Group I productivities. Samoa was classified as least stratified of Group I. That Samoan productivity was lowest in Group I is implied by consideration of Samoan environment but not by other measures. In Group IIa, Mangareva was estimated as most stratified, Uvea as the least--with the other two, Easter Island and Mangaia, about equal. Evidence from the amount of specialization and the formal aspects of Mangarevan technoenvironment indicates that Mangareva had the highest productivity in Group IIa. That Uvea had the lowest productivity in this Group cannot be documented as the evidence is incomplete, but the paucity of specialization and the technoenvironmental conditions are suggestive.

In Group IIb societies, Futuna was classified as least stratified, the Marquesas as most. In productivity as measured by redistribution, the Marquesas rank highest, but Futuna appears to have had a higher productivity than Tikopia, also of this group. No further clarification was forthcoming from other productivity measures.

Group III societies appear to have been equally stratified. Productivitywise, Ontong Java ranks highest by scope of redistribution, but the figures on Ontong Java may be seriously inaccurate because of the influences of acculturation.[52] In other measures of productivity, no significant differences within Group III were detected.

The deductions that have been made are supported by the evidence, at least as the evidence may be grossly measured. The amount of stratification is correlated with productivity.[53]

---

52. See pp. 226-30.

53. Compare Irving Goldman, "Status Rivalry and Cultural Evolution in Polynesia," American Anthropologist, LVII (1955), 680-97. In this article, Goldman attempts to demonstrate that political and social evolution in Polynesia has been promoted by "the dominant values of Polynesian cultures, those involving concern with social status [which have had effect] in one way or another . . . in the history of every Polynesian society " (p. 680). It is of interest that in many respects Goldman's classification of the degree of political development in the various islands corresponds with

the one developed here. In methodology, as well as in details of interpretation, there are vast differences. I cannot agree that variations of political development in Polynesia can be explained by an admittedly constant feature such as status rivalry. It is significant that Goldman writes that the directions of variation in Polynesian cultures are at least partially determined by "differing ecologies . . . variations in population density, varieties of subsistence techniques, levels of economic productivity . . . " (p. 680). However, aside from a table (p. 682) wherein these different ecological factors are charted, they play no role in Goldman's explanation of cultural differentiations in Polynesia. The table, in fact, shows only negative correlations between "ecology" and variations in Polynesian cultures. One can only conclude that Goldman is explaining differences in terms of the constant feature of status rivalry.

Furthermore, I am disturbed by Goldman's technique of assessing productivity in the various cultures. The basis for his productivity judgments (Table 1, p. 680) is nowhere stated except that they are estimated from monographs. It can be shown, as it is in the present work, that objective assessments of productivity in Polynesia do not correspond to Goldman's opinions. It is unfortunate that an important feature of cultural adaptation which has been extensively used to demonstrate significant relationships between different aspects of culture is so casually and confusingly treated. It must be inferred that Goldman dismisses it from consideration.

There does not appear to be a necessary logical or empirical relationship between status rivalry and Polynesian political developments such as increasing exploitation. The author's recent field work in Fiji, a closely related culture, indicates that the opposite relationship exists. Many times Fijian chiefs are unable to act coercively for fear of stirring criticism from members of the group that have aspirations to the chieftainship.

Finally, what is "status rivalry" but the operation of a particular kind of political system, the functioning of a specific structure? Status rivalry is not some disembodied value or an attribute of the Polynesian psyche, it is a social relation characteristic of a given political system. It is the political system that produces rivalry, not vice versa. Goldman is only dealing in tautology.

131

TABLE 1

PRODUCTIVITY AS MEASURED BY DISTRIBUTION

Island	Largest Redistributive Network	Size of Largest Redistributive Network	Frequency Factor	Productivity	Degree of Stratification[a]
Hawaiian Islands[b]	Island (Motu)	30,000	3	90,000	I
Tongan Islands[c]	Tongan Islands	20,000-25,000	3	60,000-75,000	I
Society Islands[d]	Tahitian "district" as Papara	8,250	3	24,000-[(68,000)x]?	I
	Tahitian "division" as Teva	68,000	?		
Samoan Islands[e]	"Division" as Aana of Upolu	$5,000 \left(\begin{array}{l}+10,000 \\ -3,000\end{array}\right)$	3	15,000-[(48,000)x]?	I
	All Samoa except Manua	48,000	?		
Mangareva[f]	Mangareva	4,000	2-3	8,000-12,000	IIa
Easter[g]	Easter	3,000-4,000	?	(3,000-4,000)x	IIa
Uvea[h]	Uvea	3,000-4,000	?	(3,000-4,000)x	IIa
Mangaia[i]	Mangaia	2,000-3,000	?	(2,000-3,000)x	IIa
Marquesas[j]	"Tribe"	1,500	3	4,500	IIb
Futuna[k]	Futuna	2,000	2	4,000	IIb
Tikopia[l]	Tikopia	1,250	2-3	2,500-3,750	IIb
Ontong Java[m]	"Tribe"	? -2,000?	2	? -4,000?	III
Pukapuka[n]	Pukapuka	435- 632+	3	1,305-1,896+	III
Tokelau[o]	? Tokelau	500- ?	3 or 2	1,500- (?)	III

a. See end of chapter 1, pp. 11 and 12, for system of classification.

b. A single island--there were eight inhabited islands in the Hawaiian Group--was, in most cases, the largest unit of over-all redistribution. See E. S. Craighill Handy, "Government and Society," and "Feasts and Holidays," in E. S. Craighill Handy (ed.), Ancient Hawaiian Civilization (Honolulu, 1933); William E. Ellis, A Journal of a Tour around Hawaii (Boston, 1825). At times the six large districts of the island of Hawaii (total population 75,000-100,000) were economically autonomous; at other times they were joined in one distributive system. See William E. Ellis, Narrative of a Tour through Hawaii (2nd ed.; London, 1826), p. 116. At the time of contact there were only four economically independent chiefdoms in the entire group. See Ralph S. Kuykendall, The Hawaiian Kingdom 1778-1854. (Honolulu, 1938), p. 30. Estimates of the total population of the group vary up to 400,000, but Bligh's estimate of 242,000 seems nearest the mark. See Edwin G. Burrows, "Breed and Border in Polynesia," American Anthropologist, XLI (1939), 16. Thirty thousand is thus the average number per island, which is usually given as the unit of redistribution. However, sixty thousand would be the average unit at time of contact. On Hawaii proper, the range would vary between 17,000 and 100,000 at different periods. The figure of 30,000 is somewhat arbitrarily taken as a mean size of the most encompassing redistributive network. It is probably conservative. Regular redistribution in such a unit is indicated. See David Malo, Hawaiian Antiquities (Bernice Pahau Bishop Museum Special Publication, No. 2 [2nd ed., 1951]), passim. See also Handy, "Feasts and Holidays," passim.

    c. Over-all redistribution was a fairly regular event throughout the Tongan group. See William Mariner, An Account of the Tongan Islands in the South Pacific Ocean (3rd ed.; 2 vols.; Edinburgh, 1827); see also Edward Winslow Gifford, Tongan Society (Bernice Pahau Bishop Museum Bulletin, No. 61 [1929]). The population was between 20,000 and 25,000 at the time of the first European contact. See Burrows, "Breed and Border in Polynesia," p. 12; Sylvester M. Lambert, The Depopulation of Pacific Races (Bernice Pahau Bishop Museum Special Publication, No. 23 [1934]), p. 15; Gifford, Tongan Society, pp. 4 f.

    d. Over-all redistributions in Tahiti were evidently regular in districts of the size of Papara. See E. S. Craighill Handy, History and Culture in the Society Islands (Bernice Pahau Bishop Museum Bulletin, No. 79 [1930]), passim; Arii Taimai E, Tahiti, ed. Henry Adams (New York, 1947); Teuira Henry, Ancient Tahiti (Bernice Pahau Bishop Museum Bulletin, No. 48 [1928]). The number of such districts on Tahiti is uncertain. Handy shows twenty-eight in a map, but five are in brackets and may be alternative names for other districts. See Handy, History and Culture in the Society Islands, p. 45. Twenty-six is taken as a compromise figure. Whether redistributions encompassed the three larger districts of Tahiti, of which Teva is an example, is not certain, nor would be their frequency. Cook's estimate of 204,000 population for Tahiti is taken as near the aboriginal mark. See Lambert, The Depopulation of Pacific Races, p. 5.

    e. The unit of redistribution is not clear. On Upolu, districts the size of Aana and Atua were "regular" redistributive entities. See Augustin Krämer, Die Samoa-Inseln (Stuttgart, 1902); and George Turner, Samoa (London, 1884). How many such districts there were throughout Samoa is disputed. Turner states ten, Krämer nineteen, and Keesing amends Krämer's figure to six. See Felix M. Keesing, Modern Samoa (London, 1934). Turner's figure is accepted as a compromise. Estimates for over-all population vary; Burrows' 50,000 at contact is accepted. See Burrows, "Breed and Border in Polynesia," p. 13.

Manua would be much less than the average of 5,000 for an economic unit, while Upoluan districts would be considerably greater, as population concentrated in Upolu. Occasionally, all Samoa, except Manua, was united. The paramount chief may have served as a focal point of pan-Samoan distribution at such times, but occasions such as these probably were very rare, if they existed at all.

f. Population estimates vary from 1,275 people in 1824 to an estimated 6,000 to 8,000 at contact. Buck holds the opinion that "the population [was at no time] greater than a few thousand." See Peter H. Buck, Ethnology of Mangareva (Bernice Pahau Bishop Museum Bulletin, No.157 [1938]), p. 11. Four thousand is a compromise figure. It is very difficult to estimate the frequency of over-all redistributions. It was at least sporadic and may have been regular. See Buck, Ethnology of Mangareva, pp. 164, 167, 433 f.; Honoré Laval, Mangareva: L'Histoire Ancienne d'un Peuple Polynésien (Braine-le-Comte, 1938), pp. 138-39.

g. Alfred Métraux, Ethnology of Easter Island (Bernice Pahau Bishop Museum Bulletin, No. 160 [1940]), pp. 14, 22. Métraux's estimate for the early nineteenth century is 3,000 to 4,000. The frequency of redistribution is difficult to estimate. The birdman was the focus of some collecting activities, but it is not clear whether or not what was accumulated was for his own support or was widely redistributed.

h. Edwin G. Burrows, Ethnology of Uvea (Bernice Pahau Bishop Museum Bulletin, No. 145 [1937]), p. 15. See Burrows, "Breed and Border in Polynesia," p. 11. The earliest population estimates do not go higher than 3,000, but Burrows estimates the aboriginal population at about 4,000. Over-all distributions occurred, but their frequency is not calculable from the data.

i. Peter H. Buck, Mangaian Society (Bernice Pahau Bishop Museum Bulletin, No. 122 [1934]), p. 6. Estimate of population size is for 1823. There were supratribal distributions, but the frequency of over-all distribution is not clearly indicated in the materials, although it was probably not high.

j. Linton writes that the tribe, the unit of collection and redistribution, was rarely more than 1,000. See Ralph Linton, "Marquesan Culture," in Ralph Linton and A. Kardiner, The Individual and His Society (New York, 1939), p. 150. Shilbeer, according to Williamson, estimated tribal size as between 1,500 and 2,000. See Robert W. Williamson, The Social and Political Systems of Central Polynesia (Cambridge, Eng., 1924), I, 317. Melville estimates the redistribution unit at 2,000 in one valley. See Herman Melville, Typee (New York, 1931), pp. 260-61. Fifteen hundred would be a compromise. The frequency was regular. See E. S. Craighill Handy, The Native Culture in the Marquesas (Bernice Pahau Bishop Museum Bulletin, No. 9 [1923]), passim.

k. According to Burrows, "The population has averaged about 2,000 during the period for which figures are available." See Burrows, "Breed and Border in Polynesia," p. 10. However, figures published by Burrows for dates between 1842 and 1931 indicate no year in which there were over 1,762 people, the figure for 1931. See Edwin G. Burrows, Ethnology of Futuna (Bernice Pahau Bishop Museum Bulletin, No.

138 [1936]), p. 10. Early missionaries were told by natives that the population was once much higher, so a figure of 2,000 is accepted. Overall distributions were apparently sporadic. See also ibid., pp. 97 ff., especially p. 111.

1. The highest recorded population for Tikopia was 1,281 in 1929. But population was on the increase then, and may not reflect pre-European conditions. See Raymond Firth, Primitive Polynesian Economy (New York, 1950). A figure of 1,250 is thus chosen. Firth's data give the impression that the large, over-all distributions were not too regular, yet something more than sporadic. (See ibid., pp. 222 f.)

m. According to the records of H. M. S. "Torch," the population of the group in 1900 was between 2,000 and 3,000. Hogbin believes this is too low, and he estimates the population for that time as between 5,000 and 6,000. See H. Ian Hogbin, "The Problem of Depopulation in Melanesia as Applied to Ontong Java," Journal of the Polynesian Society, XXXIX (1930), 45; see also H. Ian Hogbin, "The Social Organization of Ontong Java," Oceania, Vol. I (1930-31); and also H. Ian Hogbin, "'Polynesian' Colonies in Melanesia," Journal of the Polynesian Society, Vol. XLIX (1940). At Hogbin's time (1928, 1929), there were two tribes, each an economic unit, which would make the size of the unit somewhere between 1,000 and 3,000 based on 1900 figures. But evidence is adduced elsewhere (below) that there were more tribes than two in aboriginal days, which would make the size of the unit considerably smaller. No conclusion, then, can be drawn for the lower limit of the distributive unit although 2,000 may be accepted as a maximum. Major distributive activities only occurred when a tribe gathered for the annual sanga rites.

n. The range of recorded population between 1906 and 1925 was 435 to 632. See Ernest and Pearl Beaglehole, Ethnology of Pukapuka (Bernice Pahau Bishop Museum Bulletin, No. 150 [1938]), p. 13. A tidal wave of 350 years ago reduced the population considerably. Before that, according to the Beagleholes, the population was between 1,000 and 2,000. Ibid., p. 21. It is not reported how this figure was arrived at. However, the population most probably did not reach this figure at contact. Island-wide distributions were fairly frequent, that is "regular."

o. The available figures gathered in the 1930's for the three atolls, which once a year participated in a distributive network, are: 500 people on Fakaofu; 229 on Nukunono; 380 on Atafu. See Gordon MacGregor, Ethnology of the Tokelau Islands (Bernice Pahau Bishop Museum Bulletin, No. 146 [1937]), pp. 5-7. But Nukunono and Atafu probably were not connected in an economic system with Fakaofu before the nineteenth century (see below). In contrast, Olosenga, now uninhabited, once contained several hundred people and may have been in a joint distributive network with Fakaofu. The smallest possible economic entity is then Fakaofu (with 500 people), within which there was regular coterminous distribution. In any larger unit, if it existed, the frequency of large-scale distribution was probably sporadic as it was in MacGregor's time.

135

7. Stratification and History

POLYNESIAN CULTURES HAVE a common origin and together may be considered as a single genus undergoing adaptive radiation in particular habitats. Social stratification can be seen to be related to various features of the technological articulation of the cultures to these habitats. However, two diverse historical currents in Polynesia have been recognized for some time, and the possibility exists, therefore, that greater stratification is more a part of one history than the other, irrespective of adaptive aspects. I refer to the differentiation of western Polynesia from central-marginal, or eastern Polynesia.[1] This divergence apparently occurred fairly far back in Polynesian history and may represent the diffusion of cultural elements from two centers of radiating influence, Fiji in the west, the Society Islands in the east.[2]

If stratification were more closely allied to one or another of these historical entities, then a higher development should be found in either eastern or western Polynesia. However, the data do not support this proposition. Of the islands considered, Samoa, Tonga, Tikopia, Uvea, Futuna, Tokelau,

---

1. See Peter H. Buck, Vikings of the Sunrise (Philadelphia, 1938); Edwin G. Burrows, "Western Polynesia," Ethnologiska Studier, Vol. VII (1938); and Samuel H. Elbert, "Internal Relationships of Polynesian Languages and Dialects," Southwestern Journal of Anthropology, IX (1953), 147-73.

2. Burrows, "Western Polynesia," p. 91; compare Edwin G. Burrows, "Culture Areas in Polynesia," Journal of the Polynesian Society, XLIX (1940), 349-63.

Pukapuka, and Ontong Java are western; the Societies, Hawaii, Marquesas, Mangaia, and Mangareva are eastern. All four categories of stratification are represented in western Polynesia: Group I by Tonga and Samoa; Group IIa by Uvea; Group IIb by Tikopia and Futuna; and Group III by Tokelau, Pukapuka, and Ontong Java. Groups I, IIa, and IIb are represented in eastern Polynesia by Hawaii and the Societies, Mangareva and Mangaia, and the Marquesas, respectively. The fact that no eastern Polynesian atoll was considered may account for the lack of Group III stratification there. The historical difference between western and eastern Polynesia, therefore, does not account for the degree of stratification in the various cultures. On the contrary, the degree of stratification is seen to be entirely an adaptive variation when the cultures are classified on this historical basis.

Possible ways by which historical influences may operate nonadaptively on the amount of stratification in a particular culture have not been exhausted. If the historical factor is not constant, either the entire stratification system in a particular culture or some aspect of it may be elaborated beyond what is expectable with the prevailing degree of productivity. Unfortunately, the criteria of neither stratification nor productivity are fine enough to show exact proportional relationship between these variables and thus to clearly indicate where such "unexpected" results turn up. But occasionally, certain aspects of the degree of stratification in a particular island seem incongruously elaborated relative to other features of the system. These may be nonadaptive "survivals"--vestigial forms. A good example is the relatively elaborate sanctification of the high chief of Pukapuka. Despite the fact that the community elders were the most potent sociopolitical force, the high chief was surrounded by a fairly complex mana-tabu system and was paid respect through forms of obeisance comparable to those existing in more stratified societies. Similarly, the ceremonial sanctification of Tokelauan and Uvean chiefs was greater than one might expect relative to the roles of these chiefs in social and economic processes.

We interpret these cases as nonadaptive survivals in the stratification system. Both Tokelau and Pukapuka were settled from high islands where the degree of stratification was much greater than Pukapukan or Tokelauan life warranted, and both were settled within the last six hundred years. Uvea was settled around A.D. 1450--again relatively late--from more highly stratified Tonga, according to linguistic and genealogical evidence. [3] Nonadaptive survivals can affect aspects of the degree of stratification in particular cases. In the examples given, these survivals were persistences in the ideological sphere of culture. Such survivals could occur in social and economic spheres also and may be revealed in Polynesia if finer measures of stratification are developed and applied. But the most striking incongruities in this sense are very probably most frequent in ceremonial life. It has long been recognized that ideologies, in particular religious beliefs and practices, survive long after the particular forces which have brought them into being. It is not surprising then that ceremonial aspects of the degree of stratification are "overelaborated" in some cultures of Polynesia, especially those which have diverged but a short time ago from more highly stratified cultures. In short, ceremonial sanctification of status in Tokelau, Uvea, and Pukapuka is elaborated beyond other differential aspects of the status system, a fact related to the relatively nonadaptive character of ideology and thus understandable in terms of previous situations of the cultures, rather than their present adaptations.

---

3. Elbert, "Internal Relationships of Polynesian Languages and Dialects," pp. 163, 168.

8. Ramage Systems of Social Organization and Stratification

IN THIS AND the following chapters, the forms of social organization and social stratification in Polynesia will be outlined. An attempt will be made to relate these forms to aspects of the various technologies and environments. Three forms may be delineated; ramage, descent-line, and coral-atoll organization.

Ramage Organization

Despite the general similarity of form in the basic descent units in the high Polynesian islands of Hawaii, Tonga, the Societies, Mangareva, Mangaia, Easter Island, Tikopia, the Marquesas, and New Zealand, the literature bears no agreement on what this form might be called. Apparently what is one and the same thing, structurally, has been designated "clan," "tribe," "lineage," "descent group," or by a native term, e.g., hapu (Maori). The publication of Firth's We, the Tikopia in 1936, however, marked the beginning of a terminological revolution in Polynesian studies.

Although Firth used the word "clan" to describe certain Tikopian groupings, he recognized that he was dealing with something basically different from what was usually called by that term.[1] The Tikopian clan was a unilateral descent group but it was not exogamous, a feature which heretofore had been a hallmark of clanship. Furthermore, there was

---

1. Raymond Firth, We, the Tikopia (London, 1936), pp. 344-72.

not merely belief in common descent but an actual genealogical reckoning of patrilineal descent which served to differentiate people and groups within the clan according to their nearness of relation to the common ancestor. The entire system can be pictured as a genealogical tree with groups branching and rebranching from a major line of descent. [2] Great importance is attached to seniority in this system. Firth proposed that the term "ramage" be used to designate kinship groups of such nature since, "This term has the advantage of suggesting immediately by its etymology the branching process by which these groups attain individuality and yet keep their connection with the parent stem. It is also consistent in a metaphor with the expression 'genealogical tree.' The process can be correctly described as one of ramification."[3]

A ramage then is a nonexogamous, internally stratified, unilineal--in Polynesia, patrilineal--descent group. Distance from the senior line of descent from the common ancestor is the criterion of stratification. By this definition, segments of a ramage are also ramages. This implication is entirely consistent with the concept of ramification, although Firth does not exploit the concept in this way.

The best point of departure for an understanding of ramage systems is the customary mode of succession to the headship or leadership of a ramage. Barring defects in personality, the mode of succession is primogeniture; the eldest son succeeds to the position of his father. Given primogenitural succession to positions of leadership in the society, certain consequences follow that are essential to an understanding

---

2. Ibid., p. 371. As Firth points out, the tree metaphor is often used by the natives themselves.

3. Ibid. At approximately the same time that Firth applied the term "ramage" to this distinct type of organization, Paul Kirchhoff, in a brilliant paper, had isolated ramage organizations and called them "conical clans" in contrast to the "equalitarian clans" as one finds, for example, among the Iroquois. Paul Kirchhoff, "The Principles of Clanship in Human Society," Davidson Anthropological Journal, I (1955) 1-11. (This paper was written in 1934.) Firth's terminology is adopted here as it is more descriptive than Kirchhoff's and is already widely known.

of ramified social systems and the ranking systems which they produce. The major consequence is that an eldest brother in a family is differentiated from his younger brothers on the basis of his prior right of succession. Not only is this a differentiation in prestige, but it also permeates the childhood and entire life cycle of these individuals. The crisis rites of birth, puberty, marriage, and death of the eldest son are of an entirely different order of elaboration from those of his brothers. Training for leadership, both formal and informal, also mark off the eldest son. Not only is he differentiated from his younger brothers, but so also is every brother differentiated from every other in accordance with the respective order of birth and the consequent prospect of succeeding to the position of the father. Every brother is ranked by the principle of seniority. Sisters may also be integrated in this hierarchy. But with few exceptions, effective leadership is vested in the male, even though he may have an elder sister. Therefore, the position of women is not treated in this general discussion.

The seniority principle in the family is the microcosm of the ramified social system. The extension of ranking within a family to ranking within the entire society is clearly described by Gifford. [4] As a consequence of seniority, the descendants of an older brother rank higher than the descendants of a younger brother. In any given group which is descendent from a common ancestor, we can distinguish a senior line from a number of junior lines. Every individual within this group of descendants from a common ancestor holds a different status, one precisely in proportion to his distance from the senior line of descent in the group.

The Polynesian societies considered here are often single large-size ramages. The entire society can usually be analyzed as composed of sections of a single genealogical system at the apex of which stands the paramount chief. The paramount is the direct descendant on the senior line of the reputed founder of the society. Other members of the group are ranked in proportion to the closeness of their relationship to the main line of descent. Accordingly, people descendent from remote collaterals of the common ancestor

---

4. Edward Winslow Gifford, Tongan Society (Bernice Pahau Bishop Museum Bulletin, No. 61 [1929]), pp. 19-20.

are lower in rank than those descendent from a more immediate relative of the chiefly line (see Figure 1). People with the lowest status are those who have descended from younger brothers through younger brothers ad infinitum. The process of primogenitural succession and its consequent implications of seniority result in a ranking structure which encompasses the entire society. This does not imply that every individual keeps a full genealogical record back to the common ancestor of the group. On the contrary, usually only the paramount chief keeps such a record. However, the remembered ancestor of lower-ranking individuals or groups of individuals was usually a junior relative of the ancestor of a higher-ranking person or group. In this way the whole community forms a single ramified structure.

The position of the paramount chief is reinforced through deification of his ancestors, themselves former paramount chiefs, and through connecting this main line of descent to the important god or gods of the group. In consequence of divine descent, a certain sacredness and power (mana) is believed to be inherently a part of chieftainship. Often the sacredness of the chief is associated with supernatural power over the fertility of the land and people. The chief is surrounded with a number of tabus which vary in elaborateness from island to island. These tabus reinforce the position of the chief at the apex of the ramified system. The usual exogamic line in these societies is the second cousin. Chiefs, however, often marry closer in, thus strengthening socioeconomic prerogatives among the higher social ranks.

There is a certain inconsistency in the application of the rules of stratification to ramages of higher order in most of the societies. Whereas within large-size ramages--such as the Tikopian "clan," the Tongan "lineage," and Maori hapu--households are ranked relative to each other according to the descent of their founders, these larger units themselves do not appear to be totally superstratified, one above the other. One whole Tikopian clan does not occupy a higher level than other Tikopian clans. Whereas one large ramage may be said to "outrank" all others and supply the paramount chief of the entire society, it does not follow that all members of the highest-standing large ramage outrank all members of all other ramages of equivalent order of size. Instead, in most of the societies considered, the chiefs of the group are

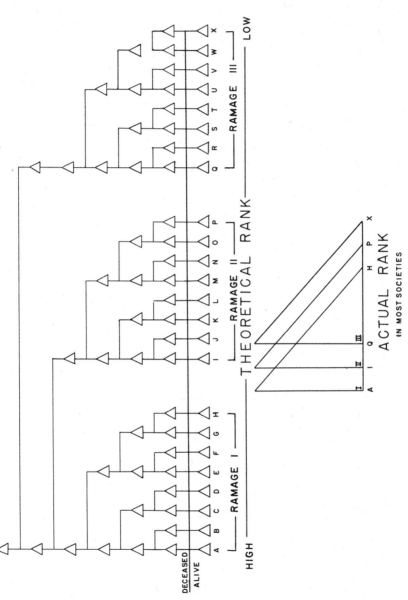

Fig. 1. The ramage organization in Polynesia

drawn from those senior in descent in the various large-size ramages and the lower-ranking members of all ramages are roughly equivalent to each other in status. Even in the ramage supplying the paramount chief there are people of low standing in the society. The heads of all large ramages comprise the chiefs of the society--these being ranked according to their distance from the senior line of the society--while the members of the different "clans" or "tribes" hold equivalent status if they are proportionately distant from the main line of descent within their respective ramages. Thus in Figure 1, in theory, all individuals from A to X should be ranked in that order, but in fact A, I and Q are all high chiefs, i.e., heads of large-order ramages; consequently E of Ramage I is roughly equal in status to M of Ramage II and U of Ramage III. While the extension of the principle of seniority of descent to its logical extreme would lead to superstratification of ramages, in practice this is not realized in most cases. In Hawaii and Tahiti alone a situation of at least partial superstratification of ramages occurred. How this was effected will be described shortly.

The discrepancy between rank by seniority and actual sociopolitical status, such as described, resulted in a certain flexibility in the ramage structure in most of the societies. There will always be more people descendent from collateral relatives of remote paramount chiefs than from collaterals of more recent paramounts. This implies that chiefs of lesser rank might have more followers than those of higher rank and than the close relatives of the paramount. Accordingly, high-order ramages whose leaders claim status by descent from a remote collateral of a remote paramount are frequently eliminated from the system of ramages, and the members are regrouped around people claiming descent from more recent offshoots of the senior line of the society. This must have occurred, for example, in Tonga. On Figure 2, a genealogical record of the ancestors of high-order Tongan ramages (haa), it can be noted that many groups descend from collaterals of relatively recent high chiefs. Gifford's discussion of the haa is instructive: "The whole system of lineages may be likened to a tree with trunk, limbs, branches and twigs. . . . Everything points to the necessity of a line of powerful chiefs for a nucleus about which the lineage groups itself. Without such chiefs it appears to wilt and die and its mem-

144

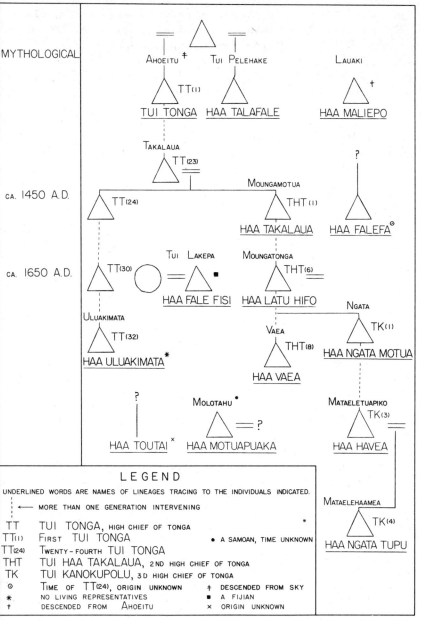

Fig. 2. Ancestors of the high-order Tongan ramages (lineages), haa (adapted from Edward Winslow Gifford, Tongan Society [Bernice Pahau Bishop Museum Bulletin, No. 61 (1929)], pp. 33-38)

bership gradually aligns itself with other rising lineages."[5] Genealogies evidently have been rearranged to accommodate such changes. In Hawaii, the shedding process became institutionalized. Each paramount chief, upon his accession, allotted leadership over the various large ramages among his close patrilineal relatives. As a result, the chiefly ramage became stratified above all others.

Other forms of mobility also produce flexibility in the system. Some families grow disproportionately large and put pressure on familial land resources. Pressures such as these are here and there relieved by adoption, by internal disputes and struggles between families, or by alignment with a mother's father's ramage rather than with that of the father. This last is produced through residence in the wife's household after marriage rather than the customary patrilocality, the children of the marriage taking membership in their mother's ramage. Such residence deviations are common in Polynesia; they are often called "matrilocal" and the consequent switch in the normal descent pattern is called "matrilineal." Both of these terms are unfortunate. To call such residence "matrilocal" obscures the fact that the wife's father is head and owner of the house; hence, no true matrilocal extended family exists. More often there is a bilocal extended family. "Matrilineal" likewise obscures the fact that descent is traced through a woman to her father, not her mother--the line of descent reached still being patrilineal. Hereafter, the tracing of descent through a woman into a patrilineal descent group will be designated as ambipatrilineal.[6]

Flexibility in the ramage structure may be produced on a large scale by interramage warfare, where the ramages are large groups within the same political structure. A paramount chief may be deposed in warfare of this kind and another ramage may usurp leadership. Often, in these cases, the divine descent of the paramount is retained and he becomes the sacred chief of the society while the victorious ramage takes over the secular chieftainship. A special situation obtains where victorious groups take over the positions

5. Ibid., p. 30.

6. This term was suggested to the author by Professor Elman Service.

of rank in the defeated unit while permitting its members to remain on the land. On a large scale this again can produce superstratification of high-order ramages.

As Firth points out, one of the most important features of ramages "is the principle of fission and dispersion in the creation of them."[7] The genealogical-tree metaphor gives the clue for ramage growth. As the branches diverge from the stem and the twigs from the branches, so does one household, as it grows in numbers, split from a parent household. The point of split is usually between two brothers, the younger often moving off with his offspring. If this continues for a sufficient length of time a new, large-order ramage may be created. The fission process results in a characteristic of ramage territoriality. Ramages, even of large order, are more or less localized groups. In Polynesia, the relationship to a certain territory is not always exact; there is usually only a fairly good correlation between ramages and certain districts of an island.[8] A perfect correlation is often prohibited by the tendency for the group which has budded off to move into any available uninhabited area. In consequence, a certain intermingling occurs between groups budded from different ramages in such areas.

The ramified system is a framework of social stratification. Differential status is inherent in the very process of ramification. In every ramified society, one can recognize two or three groups of statuses or status levels, which are functionally significant in terms of differential socioeconomic prerogatives. The position of the upper status level may be intensified by a degree of status endogamy. But since there is gradation of status, it is often difficult for either a native or an ethnographer to determine where one status level ends and another begins. In all ramified societies discussed here, the priestly hierarchy follows the genealogical

---

7. Firth, We, the Tikopia, p. 370.

8. This relationship has confused many ethnographers who have emphasized the district-territorial aspect of ramified groups rather than the genealogical aspect. See Peter H. Buck, Mangaian Society (Bernice Pahau Bishop Museum Bulletin, No. 122 [1934]); and also Edwin G. Burrows, "Breed and Border in Polynesia," American Anthropologist, XLI (1939), 1-21.

147

hierarchy. High priests come from high-ranking families; low priests come from families of lesser status.

The economic structure of ramified societies is identical to the ramage organization itself. In land tenure, for example, "overlapping stewardship" is found. Every individual has an enduring usufructuary right to a section of the resources of the society. But the head of every ramage is the manager or steward of all lands used by individuals of his ramage. Ramage heads, for example, have a primary voice in determining what is to be planted or worked on, or, by the power of tabu, what is not to be planted or harvested. In this system, lands of small-order ramages are incorporated in the lands of large-order ramages; and there are differing orders of stewardship, vaguely analogous to a feudal system of vassalages and fiefs, with which Polynesian land tenure is often identified. The system extends up to and includes the paramount chief in whom is vested the stewardship of the entire domain. What Firth writes of the Maori is true of ramified Polynesian societies in general: "The greater social group incorporates the rights of the lesser."[9] Thus a paramount chief can, for example, tabu any part of his domain--that is, prohibit the harvesting of certain crops, planting in certain land, fishing in the sea, and the like. The actual power to make and enforce such decisions varies with the amount of stratification in the society.

The ramified system is also the framework of the organization of production. Management of lands and the power, exercised by the ramage head (or steward), of prohibiting access to certain of the resources implies a certain control over production. As households produce most food and goods, most of the regulation is by household heads. Besides, there usually are certain communal activities involving suprahousehold labor. Such activities are initiated by the chief of the ramage involved or by the society's paramount chief if the manpower of the entire group is to be mobilized. The demand for labor is passed down the hierarchy of group heads until it reaches the household level. As these are kinship societies, such demands for labor are not regularized and specified by law, and the obligation to render service is an

---

9. Raymond Firth, Primitive Economics of the New Zealand Maori (New York, 1929), p. 343.

obligation to a relative superior in rank, not to a government. In islands with high productivity, such traditional obligations are often implemented by latent or actual physical force brought to bear by high-ranking chiefs. The food used to support suprahousehold labor is provided by the ramage head who initiated the undertaking. The role of ramage heads in the distribution system allows them to accumulate the necessary food.

Even specialized production seems to be organized along ramage lines. Where there are many specialists--usually part-time professionals--the specialty is ordinarily maintained within households or related households.

The system of distribution is again carried out in a ramage framework. This is the redistributive system by and large. In the islands mentioned, surpluses of food and other resources are constantly or periodically, depending on the crop or time of production, passed up the social hierarchy from household heads to heads of larger ramages and often to the paramount chief himself. Heads of ramages thus form the apex of an organization of accumulation. The paramount chief is the apex of an accumulation system of the entire society. The collected goods are then periodically redistributed among producers. The periods of redistribution, and often of accumulation, are occasioned by the many large religious ceremonies and feasts, life-crisis rites, intertribal visits, and the like. The scale of collection and redistribution correlates with the status of the presiding chief. For example, the entire society usually attends and contributes and receives food and goods if the life crises are in the high chief's family. A smaller gathering will mark a similar occasion in a family of lesser rank. It is for purposes of accumulating the wherewithal to celebrate such events that stewards exercise their tabu powers with respect to the resources of their areas.

Accumulated foods and goods are also used by ramage heads and the paramount chief to support extrahousehold labor. Because of their social status and role in the redistributive system, it is usually heads of larger-size ramages who contract for specialists and support them during the periods in which they engage in specialized production. [10]

_____

10. This does not imply that all distribution is of a redis-

149

As a rule, the function of ramage heads as regulators of production and distribution implies a certain liberation from actual food production. Variations of this have already been discussed.

Several points may be made to differentiate this economic system from systems that occur in state-organized societies with feudal or market-dominated money economies to which these Polynesian examples are, unfortunately, often likened. [11] The ramified system is first and foremost kinship organized, which is not true of the organization of feudal or money economies. All obligations, such as those of rendering surplus in the accumulation-redistribution system are phrased on a kinship basis. For this reason there is no specified amount of goods or services demanded by the ramage heads from their lesser-ranked kinsmen. Producers are expected to give only the kind and amount of goods they can spare. "Tax," "tribute," and "corvee," if they are to be applied to ramified Polynesian societies and economics, must be used only with reservations.

Nor are there specified punishments for refusing to render surplus production. The general underlying scheme regulating the application of sanctions to "wrongdoers" is not law, in the Austinian sense, but collective retaliation. Punishments, by necessity, vary with the kinship backing and support musterable by the respective parties involved. Naurally a high chief, by virtue of his position at the head of a large ramage, can muster a larger fighting force than a man low in rank, and therefore inequalities are apt to arise. But the paramount chiefs had no monopoly of coercive power and were not always able to punish recalcitrants with impunity, especially if the recalcitrant was himself head of a large ramage. There were many mechanisms, as we have seen, for preventing abuse of power by men of high rank.

---

tributive nature. There are many exchanges such as those between affinal relatives at life-crisis ceremonies of commoners that are simply reciprocal.

11. As already noted the Polynesian type of socioeconomic system has often been called, misleadingly, "feudalism." The terms "tax," "rent," "tribute," "king," "lord," "proprietor" have often been indiscriminately applied in the ethnographic accounts and in general discussions of Polynesian economics.

The "political" organization follows closely the genealogical framework of the society. Although the actual amount of authority exerted in the regulation of interpersonal affairs varies from island to island, it is usually true that ramage heads, in informal consultation with ramage members, determine the course of action of the ramage such as in punishing a wrong inflicted upon them. In matters concerning the entire society the paramount chief meets in informal council with the men of high rank, the heads of large ramages. If a course of action is decided, such as a plan of warfare, the ramage heads instigate the mobilization of the society by informing heads of smaller ramages in their domain. The process continues until the household and individual levels are reached.

The religious aspects of ramage organization have already been indicated. The position of ramage heads and especially of the paramount chief in the social hierarchy is reflected in beliefs in their divine descent, in their <u>mana</u> and tabu elaborations, in the ornateness of their life-crisis rites, and the like. The priesthood itself is a ranked structure that duplicates secular statuses.

This is the outline of the ramified social system and its economic, political and religious correlates as it may be generalized from its occurrence in the islands or groups of Hawaii, Tonga, the Societies, Marquesas, Tikopia, New Zealand, Easter Island, Mangareva, and Mangaia. In each of these islands there are variations of this pattern--some quite marked. These variations are now considered.

Tikopia.--Tikopia is the type site of ramified social structure. [12] Raymond Firth, in his brilliant study of Tikopian sociology, was the first field worker to isolate ramage organization as a distinct form of kinship grouping and to give it the terminology adopted here. [13]

There were three basic ramages, the household, the multi-

---

12. For principal sources, see the following by Raymond Firth: "Report on Research in Tikopia," <u>Oceania</u>, I (1930-31), 105-17; "Totemism in Polynesia," <u>Oceania</u>, I (1930-31), 291-321, 377-98; <u>We, the Tikopia</u>; <u>The Work of the Gods in Tikopia</u> (London, 1940); <u>Primitive Polynesian Economy</u> (New York, 1950).

13. Firth, <u>We, the Tikopia</u>.

household paito, and the multi-paito kainanga.* The paito
was composed of a number of households tracing descent
from a common ancestor, and was headed--with exceptions
due to occasional inadequate oldest sons--by a male senior
in descent. There was always a tendency after the death of
heads not on the senior line to revert to that line at the next
headship, if possible. The paito was not a residential unit;
it was scattered in various villages, although any given village had a preponderance of its members in one such ramage. But the household site of the common ancestor was the
ritual center of the group. Paito were created through a process of fission in response to increase in numbers. It is impossible to specify the exact moment when paito splitting off
occurred. "Related paito frequently speak of themselves as
one."[14] There were three types of paito all of which could
be found in the same kainanga: offshoots of chiefly houses,
descendants of immigrants who married local people, and
descendants of local individuals. Those from chiefly stock
were known as chiefly paito. However, only recent branch-
ings from chiefly lines were considered chiefly. "After some
time representatives of junior branches of the chiefly families cease to be considered as chiefly families (paito ariki)."[15]

Paito were composed of households often bearing ancestral names and living on similarly named plots. Although the
nuclear family was central to the household, it often absorbed more relatives, such as aged parents, and may be

---

*Editor's note: English language terms, rather than words
from native languages, have been used whenever practicable
in the preceding chapters, the object being to clarify the text
and to make the presentation more meaningful for purposes
of cultural comparisons and generalizations. The editor,
with the cooperation of the author, accomplished this by using consistently those English language translations--and only those--which were provided by the author at one or another place in the text. However, in the present and following
chapters, at the request of the author, the native words have
been retained as they appeared in the original manuscript.
See page 285 for glossary.

14. Firth, We the Tikopia, p. 355.
15. Ibid., p. 357.

best described as a patrilocal stem family.[16] New households were formed by fission. In most families, younger
brothers remained in the paternal household while older
brothers set up their own. In chiefly families, the opposite
situation occurred.

Kainanga were composed of a number of paito. There were
four kainanga on Tikopia. They were headed by chiefs (ariki),
who were, with a few genealogical exceptions, the descendants of eldest sons through eldest sons of the senior line of
the kainanga.[17] "The majority of members of each kainanga
are of common descent, their paito being offshoots in various generations from the original stock. . . . Other paito
have been incorporated into the clan by assimilation, usually
through the marriage of an orphan or an immigrant from another island with a daughter of the reigning chief. There are
many examples of this in the traditional literature."[18] Kainanga had a common deity, a temple, and totemic tabus.
Each was associated with a definite crop, and the chief of the
kainanga was ritually responsible for the fertility of that
crop. Marriage within the kainanga was permissible. The
second cousin on the maternal and paternal side was the usual exogamic line. Chiefs sometimes married nearer relatives.

The four kainanga chiefs were related, and their relationship may be traced genealogically. But Tikopian society was
limited in over-all political centralization, and this fact is
reflected in the genealogical reckoning as well as in the land
tenure and religious systems. One of the four ariki was considered senior in rank to the others. This seniority extended
to stewardship control over the interior lake and all canoes
on Tikopia. Contrary to our generalized description, however, the overlapping stewardship of this chief did not extend to land. The highest order of stewardship in land extended only to the four ariki. In ceremonial matters, the senior chief was believed to control the fertility of the land and
sea, and his ancestral god was the highest in the pantheon;
yet each chief, as has been indicated, had ceremonial control over the fertility of one crop--a ceremonial division of
labor not harmonious with centralized political control. This
merely partial emergence of centralized political control is

16. Ibid., p. 126.   17. Ibid., pp. 347-52.
18. Ibid., p. 362.

manifest in genealogies by the fact that although the chiefs were related, the relationship, as far back as it was traced, was an affinal one. They were not considered descendants of brothers, the eldest of whom was the ancestor of the chief senior in rank.

In the actual regulation of interpersonal affairs, the senior ariki did not exert greater influence than any other ariki. Firth believes that the seniority in rank of one ariki resulted from a centralization of ritual functions in one of a number of immigrant groups which populated Tikopia.

Another departure from the ideal ramified pattern occurred in Tikopia. There was a relative inflexibility in the ranking structure. Differential increase of ramages was allowed; the four kainanga numbered respectively (in 1926): 443, 365, 384 and 89. Neither ambipatrilineal descent nor military force was used to rectify the differential increase of ramages or to equalize the number of followers under men of equivalent status. Women usually do not appear on genealogies used to justify group affiliation, and there was a relatively low frequency of adoptions which resulted in severing connections with an original ramage. The custom of allowing free use of available garden lands to any member of the island community is a mechanism by which population pressure resulting from growth in familial size could be remedied without necessitating change in the ramage structure.

The genealogical system was the framework of social stratification. The two status levels, ariki and commoners, were brought about through the operation of the seniority principle. Some commoner families seem to have enjoyed greater ritual prestige than others. These are families said to be autochthonous in origin yet integrated into the kainanga structure.

New Zealand. --The Maori of New Zealand had a well-defined ramified social structure. The clarity of the system is enhanced by the close correspondence of ramages with localities. Villages were the rule and were usually inhabited by large-order ramages (hapu). This correlation of kinship and territory perhaps caused Burrows to advance the opinion that, of all Polynesian areas, ramification was most developed in New Zealand.[19]

---

19. Burrows, "Breed and Border in Polynesia," p. 5.

Three ramage orders can be distinguished: the whanau, the hapu, and the iwi. The whanau was a patrilocal extended family, sometimes a fraternal joint family headed by the eldest brother and sometimes a stem family headed by a patriarch. It was the household group; it ranged up to ninety-two members at the maximum. Ramages of this order branched off from one another. A number of whanau comprised a hapu, a group led by a chief (aho ariki) who was the direct descendant through eldest sons of the common ancestor of the various whanau. Hapu usually contained several hundred individuals. The largest ramage was the iwi, or "tribe," composed of a number of hapu. The iwi was led by the aho ariki who was the direct descendant of the founder of the tribe, a member of an immigrant canoe party. Tribes descendent from members of the same canoe party were called waka and occasionally formed military alliances, but the bond between them was often more sentimental than political or economic. Tribes occasionally acted as single political units and also, as the group in which accumulation and redistribution were sometimes coterminous, were the largest possible economic units. They numbered, very roughly, 3,500 on the average.[20] Both the hapu and the iwi were called by the name of the common ancestor prefixed by Ngati, Ngai, or Ati, meaning "descendants of." The ranking hapu in an iwi therefore had the same name as the iwi. Both hapu and iwi tended to be endogamous, which prevented dispersal of land interests to strangers. Marriage was generally prohibited between persons three generations or less removed from a common ancestor.

There was a general custom, in cases of interramage marriages, of permitting a man to affiliate with either his father's or his mother's ramage. Depending on the availability of land, an individual would be aligned primarily in one or the other, and eventually connection with the ramage whose lands were not used or resided in would be dropped. Firth calls this "ambilateral descent"; the term evidently refers

---

20. The native population of New Zealand was near 100,000. Best estimates that there were 18 major tribes and numerous tribelets. See Eldson Best, The Maori (Memoirs of the Polynesian Society, Vol. V) (2 vols.; Wellington, N.Z., 1924), I, 354.

to the phenomenon we have designated ambipatrilineal descent. The frequency and institutionalization of tracing descent to the mother's father's ramage may have been greater than in most other ramified systems. The mechanisms of change in ramage composition evidently usually solved the problems of differential growth of families, and maintained the existing status of the ranking system. Sporadically, however, a higher-order ramage expanded in power at the expense of other groups. Buck cites a case wherein one hapu rose in power within a tribe and assumed leadership in it. In the process the tribe was renamed by the name of the rising hapu.[21]

The ramified system was the basis of rank differentiation, and status levels emerged from it. The top level was the chiefly one composed of hapu and iwi leaders and their immediate relatives (rangatira). A second level was composed of more distant relatives of the chiefly line who had diverged from it in the normal process of primogeniture and ramification. This level (tutua or ware) contained the great majority of persons. Prisoners of war were used as menials. However, they were quickly absorbed into the tribal structure, as the females were taken by tutua as wives and by chiefs as secondary wives, and offspring of such unions were assimilated as tutua. Since all free members of the iwi were delicately graded on a genealogical hierarchy, it is difficult for both the ethnologist and the native to discriminate the point of difference between rangatira and tutua status. Best reported, "Inasmuch as all members of a tribe are connected with well born families, then it becomes a difficult matter to define the ware or tutua class. . . . Never have I met a native who would admit that he was a member of that class."[22]

---

21. Peter H. Buck, The Coming of the Maori (Wellington, N.Z., 1949), pp. 335-36.

22. Best, The Maori, I, 346.

For other principal sources of information consulted on New Zealand, see also H. B. Hawthorn, "The Maori: A Study in Acculturation," American Anthropological Association Memoir, Vol. LXIV (1944); Bernard Mishkin, "The Maori of New Zealand," in Margaret Mead (ed.), Cooperation and Competition among Primitive Peoples (New York, 1937); Edward Tregear, The Maori Race (Wanganui, N.Z., 1926).

Tonga.--The major ramage segment was the haa ("lineage" in the sources). There were thirteen in late times, averaging about 1800 members each. Such a major ramage was headed by the man on the direct line of descent from the common ancestor. Furthermore, the various haa traced descent to ancestors who were genealogically related (see Figure 2). Thus the entire society could be placed in a genealogical framework.

Major ramages were split into smaller branches, heads of which usually traced relationship to brothers. These smaller branches were further subdivided into yet smaller, but still probably suprahousehold, ramages.[23] The sub-haa ramages were called haa, faahinga, or matakali. The referents of these terms today are not ramages of particular orders of size, although Gifford's opinion is that such might have been the case in aboriginal times.[24] The smallest ramage was the natal members of the patrilocal extended family which was headed by the senior male. No suprahousehold ramage was exogamous or endogamous as such. Chiefs could marry as close in as cross-cousins; others married somewhat further out.

A great deal of ramage realignment is indicated by the fact that most haa do not date back further than A.D. 1600 (see Figure 2). Gifford also feels that the large number of place names--some the names of ancient chiefs--prefixed by the word haa is evidence that formerly there were more such ramages with fewer people per unit.[25] Ambipatrilineal descent, with residence in the wife's father's house after marriage and ambipatrilineal inheritance of land rights, and adoption, especially by the father's sister, were the major

---

23. "The splitting of major lineages into minor ones is well illustrated by the Haa Ngata Motua, by its branch the Haa Vakatola, and by the several subbranches of the Haa Vakatola. In time it is possible that these branches may grow into major lineages. On the other hand, they may die out." See Gifford, Tongan Society, p. 30. It is noteworthy that of the four subbranches of the Haa Vakatola, three are headed by brothers, "true" or classificatory, and one by a direct descendant of the senior line. Ibid., p. 39.

24. Ibid.

25. Ibid., p. 44.

mechanisms by which ramage realignment was effected. Status mobility within the ramified ranking scheme seems also to have occurred. In an example cited from one major ramage, the senior head by descent is lower in rank than heads of two of the ramage's subdivisions.[26] Gifford also finds evidence that, although theoretically chiefs were seated according to rank at councils, this ideal scheme frequently broke down which led him to speculate that the relative status of chiefs has varied outside of genealogical priority.[27] Internal struggles within ramages seem to have been the means by which such changes of precedence were produced.[28]

The ranking system and its crystallization into status levels was in the main determined by seniority of descent. The paramount chiefs, the heads of the various haa and perhaps of the major haa divisions, formed the chiefly status level (eike). There were at the time of contact three paramount chiefs. The highest, the Tui Tonga, was the direct descendant of the gods. Gifford and Williamson both find evidence that the Tui Tonga once exercised secular authority, at least over his home ramage on Tongatabu. At about A.D. 1470 he lost his temporal functions and became, instead, a highly sacred priest-chief.[29] The temporal powers were delegated, according to belief and the genealogical record, to a younger brother of the Tui Tonga who was given the title of Tui Haa Takalaua, and from whom a major ramage sprung. This office and line later gave rise to yet another office delegated to a younger brother, the Tui Kanokupolu, from which sprung another of the modern haa. The Tui Kanokupolu title gradually usurped the temporal prerogatives of the Tui Haa Takalaua, a process which continued under European influence. The situation has many analogies with the dual stratification system of Easter Island and Mangaia where a militarily dom-

---

26. Ibid., p. 40.

27. Ibid.

28. For example, Gifford talks of internal feuds on Eua (population, several hundred to 1,000), "some of which seemed to arise from offended dignity and questions of precedence." Ibid., p. 225.

29. Ibid., pp. 56 f. See also Robert W. Williamson, The Social and Political Systems of Central Polynesia (Cambridge, Eng., 1924), I, 167-68.

inant chieftain held supreme temporal power quite outside of the genealogical ranking structure. Here, however, the division of sacred and secular power was maintained, purportedly, within the genealogical system. The situation in Tonga is made even more intriguing by the fact that the office of Tui Haa Takalaua was created precisely at the time that Tongatabu was attempting to expand into Samoa, Futuna, and other islands and unifying the entire Tongan group politically. [30]

Aside from the chiefly status level there were "commoners" (tua) and chief's attendants (matapule). [31] The commoners' status was created through the normal process of primogeniture and the progressive lowering in status of descendants of younger brothers. The majority of the population were commoners. The chiefs' attendants ranked above the commoners and below the chiefs. Chiefs' attendants were ranked among themselves according to the chief they served. It seems that their ranking only partly derived from seniority, as Gifford finds evidence that they almost always were descendants of immigrants from other islands who attached themselves to chiefs. [32] Mariner reports, however, "[Matapule] rank is from inheritance; and they are supposed to have been, originally, distant relatives of the nobles, or to have descended from persons eminent for experience and wisdom. . . ."[33]

The Marquesas. --The household and the "tribe" were the significant ramages; there evidently was no unit of an intermediate order. The household was composed of a patrilocal extended family headed by the male senior in descent. Households of senior lines in the tribe were larger than other households. The so-called tribe consisted of a number of households tracing descent from a common ancestor of whom the chief (hakaiki) was the direct descendant. The tribe,

---

30. Gifford, Tongan Society, pp. 55 and passim.
31. See above, p. 22.
32. Gifford, Tongan Society, pp. 140-41.
33. William Mariner, An Account of the Tongan Islands in the South Pacific Ocean, ed. John Martin (3rd ed.; Edinburgh, 1827), II, 89. For additional information on Tonga see also Ernest and Pearl Beaglehole, Pangai: Village in Tonga (Memoirs of the Polynesian Society, Vol. XVIII) (Wellington, N.Z., 1941).

about 1,500 people, thus was a genealogically organized entity internally stratified by seniority of descent. In some cases, as on Ua Pou, there were evidently supratribal groups. But on the southern islands, from which most data come, the tribe was usually the largest sociopolitical unit. All Marquesan tribes traced their descent to the same ancestor; however, this elaboration of the genealogical reckoning was not a reflection of political unification or of over-all economic interdependence. There was no rule of exogamy or of endogamy pertaining to ramages as such, although the tribe was usually endogamous. Marriage with parallel cousins was prohibited; with cross-cousins it was preferred.

The ramage structure showed great flexibility. Individuals switched ramage allegiance by adoption as well as by ambipatrilineal descent. The frequency of permanent alignment with the mother's father's ramage was evidently comparable to its frequency among the Maori, for here also connection with the mother's group was regularly remembered and recognized.

Increase in the size of households led to increased productivity and distributions and, by these means, increase in prestige, but unlike most other islands considered in this chapter, it did not result in physical struggles for ascendancy. Rather, the increased prestige gained by larger size seemed to manifest itself in rearrangements of genealogical reckoning. As a result of the regular practice of tracing descent and maintaining connections with the mother's father's ramage, ". . . there was always some point in the line of descent at which one of the ancestors was higher than a contemporary ancestor of some other individual. Genealogies could thus be used to justify actual social relations. The various households went up and down in social prestige and position, and household heads selected which of the possible relationship terms they would use on the basis of which was superior or inferior. Because of the inbreeding [i.e., intermarriage within the relatively small "tribes"], it was always possible for a person actually on top to find a line of descent that was higher at some point than any other line."[34]

---

34. Ralph Linton, "Marquesan Culture," in Ralph Linton and A. Kardiner, The Individual and His Society (New York, 1939), p. 150.

There was a mechanism for dealing with households which grew large, distributed goods widely, and threatened the supremacy of the chiefs. Either the heir of the rising household was adopted by the chief or the eldest daughter was married to the chief's eldest son. This usually dissolved the upstart group, and the existing status system was maintained. All these rearrangements that resulted from increased size took place peacefully and within the genealogical system; a junior line did not seize the power of a senior line but became senior through manipulation of familial connections-- if the situation required it.

The status positions arose out of the ramified structure. Two levels can be demarcated. High chiefs (hakaiki) and their near relatives formed the chiefly level; the rest of the populace (mata-ei-nana), more remotely related to the main line, comprised the lower level. Refugees were absorbed, not enslaved, and captives were eaten. Thus, a third level was absent. [35]

Hawaii.--The smallest unit was the household, usually a patrilocal extended family, apparently somewhat larger in size in the case of chiefs. The household was probably headed by the male senior in descent. Beyond the household, the number of high-order ramages is uncertain. The largest ramage was an entire island led by the paramount chief who was reputedly a direct descendant of the common ancestor of the island populace. [36] An island was usually the political and economic unit. Island populations averaged about 30,000. An idea of the complexity of the ramage organization may be gained from Malo's breakdown of nine steward areas of diminishing order of size between the island community and the household. [37] These steward areas were sections of the is-

---

35. For additional information on Marquesas, see also R. H. Drioult-Gerard, La Civilisation des Iles Marquises (Paris, 1940); E. S. Craighill Handy, The Native Culture in the Marquesas (Bernice Pahau Bishop Museum Bulletin, No. 9 [1923]).

36. "Commoners and alii were all descended from the same ancestors, Wakea and Papa. . . . There was no difference between king and plebeian as to origin." David Malo, Hawaiian Antiquities (Bernice Pahau Bishop Museum Special Publication, No. 2 (2nd ed.; 1951]), pp. 52 and also 4.

37. Ibid., pp. 16-18. Handy and Wise only discriminate

land occupied by a number of households tracing common descent, i.e., ramages of different order.

One order of ramage, the ohana family group, has been well described by Handy and Pukui. [38] This ramage occupied a number of plots (ili) in a district (ahupuaa) running from sea to mountains. The ramage was composed of a number of households. "The pivot of the ohana was the haku (master director), the elder male of the senior branch of the whole ohana."[39] The ramage leader may have been an intermediate steward (konohiki) since chiefs of this level seem to have been stewards over sections of this type. [40] These chiefs were in some cases relatives of the paramount chief beyond two or three but within ten degrees of consanguinity. High chiefs (alii), closer relatives of the paramount chief, were leaders over districts occupied by a number of ohana tracing common descent. [41] Thus the ramified structure could in some cases encompass the entire sociopolitical unit. Handy records a poem or chant regarding the district of Ka'u, one of the six largest-sized districts (motu) of the island of Hawaii:

> Offshoots of one lineage are the people of Ka'u,
> From the uplands to the sea,
> From border to border. [42]

However, because of the large populations involved and the flexibility of the ramage structure, genealogical connections may have slipped into the background. Such indeed seems to be implied by Handy when he writes that the "tribalism" of Ka'u was unique in Hawaii. [43]

---

four orders of ramification. E. S. Craighill Handy, "Government and Society," and John H. Wise, "The History of Land Ownership in Hawaii," in E. S. Craighill Handy (ed.), "Ancient Hawaiian Civilization (Honolulu, 1933).

38. E. S. Craighill Handy and M. Pukui, "The Hawaiian Family System," Journal of the Polynesian Society, LIX-LXI (1950-52).

39. Ibid., LIX, 179.

40. Malo, Hawaiian Antiquities, p. 192.

41. Handy and Pukui, "The Hawaiian Family System," LIX, 177.

42. Ibid., p. 172.

43. Ibid.

No ramage seems to have been endogamous or exogamous as such. The usual restriction on first-cousin marriage may have generally prevailed, although high-ranking people married closer in. The paramount chief often married his sister or half sister.

Flexibility in ramage structure is indicated by the custom of adoption into ramages and by methods of tracing descent ambipatrilineally (revealed by the presence of women on status-validating genealogies). Structural flexibility was, in fact, an institutionalized aspect of the ranking system. At the accession of each paramount chief, theoretically at least, control over steward areas and over the ramages occupying them was redistributed. This distribution extended to relatives of the paramount chief within ten generations of a common ancestor. [44] Those who found themselves under a head eleven degrees of consanguinity from the paramount chief necessarily were realigned under a new alii or konohiki. In actuality, the distribution of stewardship did not always result in marked changes in the ranking structure as most konohiki evidently remained in their previous positions. [45] Warfare between high-order ramages, even within an island community, was a frequent occurrence and could cause drastic changes in the rank of the defeated group. Stewardship and positions of authority over vanquished peoples were distributed among the conquerors. Thus, a conquest hierarchy was superimposed over a genealogical hierarchy. This type of hierarchy affected succession to the paramount chieftainship (but it did not result in separation of temporal and sacred authorities or the abandonment of an inheritance-succession pattern to the position of the temporal paramount chief in peace time).

The Hawaiian custom of redistributing land rights upon the accession of the paramount chief has significant implications for the formation of the strongly centralized political structure present there. Here was a practice by which ramages descendent from remote collaterals of remote chiefs were eliminated, and the membership was regrouped under people closer to the chiefly line. The paramount chief could

44. Malo, Hawaiian Antiquities, p. 192.
45. Sanford B. Dole, "Evolution of Hawaiian Land Tenure," Hawaiian Historical Society Papers, III (1892), 6.

place near relatives in the positions of political importance, thus strengthening the integration of the polity. The logical consequence of full utilization of the land-redistributing prerogative would be a situation of superstratified ramages, one entire large chiefly ramage on top. Such also is the implication of conquest warfare and redistribution among the victors of the positions of power. These two features of Hawaiian ramage reorganization are connected, as Handy pointed out: "Everytime an Alii Nui [paramount chief] died or was overthrown, the new chief had the right to redivide all the land among his faithful followers, the alii who were younger members of his family, and others who were his dependents. A new king acted as a conqueror of the land, dividing the country among his followers."[46] Conquest warfare and institutionalized land redistribution combine to create a polity which approximates, if not actually realizes, a structure of a single ruling kin group and a number of only remotely related "commoner" groups. As such, the Hawaiian political structure contrasts sharply with that of most of the other islands. The social concomitants of the great degree of stratification in Hawaii are thus revealed.[47]

Society Islands. --The number and order of size of ramages are best known for Tahiti, but even here the documentation is poor.[48] Of the highest-order ramages (mataeinaa--

---

46. Handy, "Government and Society," pp. 21-22.

47. For additional principal sources of information on Hawaii, see also Edwin H. Bryan, Jr., Ancient Hawaiian Life (Honolulu, 1950); William E. Ellis, A Journal of a Tour around Hawaii (Boston, 1825); William E. Ellis, Polynesian Researches (2nd ed.; London, 1853).

48. Ramage organization, however, is evident even in relationship terms. The term "matahiapo" gives a clue to the entire ramified framework of the society: "First-born, male or female. Also applied to all representatives of a family stock descended in the line of first-borns. Thus, if I belong to a matahiapo family it means that at least one parent was a first-born right back to the god Taaroa. My first-born will carry on the matahiapo. All others are teina 'younger brother' or 'junior in rank.'" E. S. Craighill Handy, History and Culture in the Society Islands (Bernice Pahau Bishop Museum Bulletin, No. 79 [1930]), p. 23.

a term applied both to the ramage and the district in which
it was located), there were three on Tahiti, averaging about
60,000 people each. Each of the three was headed by the senior male of the area. Divided among the three major ramages were twenty-six lower-order ramages, each consisting
of 7,000 or more people on the average. These smaller
groups were the independent political units and for most purposes were the accumulation-redistribution units. The larger ramages, of which the Teva division of Tahiti is an example, functioned mainly as warfare confederations. Whether or not they represented coterminous accumulation-distri-
bution networks is uncertain. Within a smaller ramage, such
as Papara, were yet smaller units, amuiraa ("aggregation")
or pupu ("group"), headed by chiefs succeeding by primogeniture. There was also a ramage which Handy calls an "estate," which was evidently a section of an amuiraa; it was
called aia or aia tupuna. Handy believes that a unit called ati
was the extended family group among the lower status levels. [49] Ramages, as implied, were localized. Villages, however, did not exist; rather there were dispersed hamlet communities.

The ramage system was reflected in the system of ancestral temples (marae). Each family had a temple. The largest
temple in a district, that of the senior family, was considered the parent temple from which the others branched off.
There was an institutionalized method by which temples segmented which illustrates the growth of ramages by fission.
When a household divided and lands were partitioned, a
stone from the old temple was used as a cornerstone for the
new. The latter was consecrated to the same god as the old,
while the head of the segmenting group took an hereditary title associated with the older temple.

There is some evidence of flexibility of ramage affiliations
of individuals. Williamson cites reports which indicate flexibility of patrilineal descent, perhaps of ambipatrilineality. [50] Females, in the absence of male heirs, could carry
and pass on titles and land, which indicates that their children probably would align themselves with their mother's

---

49. Ibid., p. 11.
50. Williamson, The Social and Political Systems of Central Polynesia, II, 116.

father's ramage. Adoption into ramages was practiced. The stability of the genealogical hierarchy was also disrupted by military expansion of large ramages. Military ascendancy of one group over another could result in the subjugation of the defeated, a process calling for rearrangement of the ranking structure. It is Handy's contention, in fact, that the entire ruling status level was brought into power through conquest in Tahiti as well as in several other islands of the group. [51] This must have necessitated a change in the genealogical hierarchy of many localities, if it occurred. [52] The warfare between large-order neighboring ramages, at any rate, often produced a stratification of the leaders of the victorious group over the defeated, if the latter were allowed to survive, or if they acquiesced to the rule rather than fled. [53]

The status system was a function of principles of rank both by descent and by conquest warfare. Chiefs (arii), heads of major ramages, were senior descendants of the founder or conqueror of the population. Other members of the upper level, junior relatives of the chiefs (iatoai), held sway over sections of the high-order ramages and formed the principal warriors and body of retainers of the chiefs. Subchiefs (raatira) also headed large sections of the domains of the chiefs, while the commoners (manahune) formed the body of most ramages.

It is difficult to connect the subchiefs (raatira) with the genealogical tree of the chiefs (arii). [54] Handy believes no such connection obtained. [55] The chiefs appear to be a distinct ramage, ranked as a group above all others. The subchiefs, by contrast, seem to be senior members of ramages

---

51. Handy, History and Culture in the Society Islands.

52. Luomala's review of the evidence makes this large-scale conquest a dubious proposition. Katharine Luomala, The Menehune of Polynesia and Other Mythical Little People of Oceania (Bernice Pahau Bishop Museum Bulletin, No. 203 [1951]).

53. James Morrison, The Journal of James Morrison (Great Britain, 1935), p. 174.

54. Williamson, The Social and Political Systems of Central Polynesia, III, 148.

55. Handy, History and Culture in the Society Islands, p. 43.

embracing commoners. Ellis, in fact, includes the majority of the Tahitian population under the term raatira, thus overlapping Handy's manahune. This suggests the usual gradation of status within ramages. Ellis contrasts the land rights of chiefs and subchiefs in a way that would indicate that chiefly rights of stewardship derive from conquest, while subchiefs represent leaders of indigenous, conquered peoples who retained subordinate stewardship prerogatives: "[The raatira] were generally proprietors and cultivators of the soil, and held their land, not from gift of the king [i.e., the paramount chief], but from their ancestors."[56]

Thus, the status system of Tahiti apparently parallels that of Hawaii. A superstratified ruling ramage, set up through conquest, occupied the top positions of the society. Below this ramage were indigenous, conquered ramages headed by their own related chiefs. Hawaii differed in that the intermediate status there (the konohiki) were at least in part recruited from the chiefly ramage rather than from the conquered groups. This structural difference seems to have permitted Hawaiian paramounts to exercise greater authority than their Tahitian counterparts, who were forced to consult with the distantly related or unrelated subchiefs before they undertook important political actions. [57]

Easter Island. --There were several orders of ramages that developed through the usual process of segmentation. [58] The smallest was the household, a patrilocal extended family probably headed by the senior male and composed, at present,

---

56. Ellis, Polynesian Researches, III, 97; see also Morrison, The Journal of James Morrison, p. 174.

57. For additional principal sources of information on the Society Islands, see also Teuira Henry, Ancient Tahiti (Bernice Pahau Bishop Museum Bulletin, No. 48 [1928]); and Arii Taimai E, Tahiti (New York, 1947).

58. Routledge, in a private communication to Williamson, wrote of the process of generating ramages in terms of "smaller family units arising within the larger family unit, and again subdividing; and that process can be traced, not only in tradition, but in what appear to be comparatively recent times. 'The little clans were the children of the big ones.'" Williamson, The Social and Political Systems of Central Polynesia, II, 56.

of about nine people. Aboriginally, households of thirty or more were apparently not uncommon. A number of households tracing descent to a common ancestor formed a "subtribe" headed by the direct descendant of this ancestor. A number of similarly related subtribes formed the mata ("tribe"), of which there were about ten, averaging 300 to 400 people each. Most of the population traced descent to a common ancestor; many tribes were considered to be offspring of sons and grandsons of the first settler and chief. Both Métraux and Williamson believe that those mata which were not descendent from immediate relatives of the first settler were offshoots of mata that were, so that eventually the whole tribal system could be phrased on a genealogical basis. [59] No ramage was by rule endogamous or exogamous. Marriage was usually prohibited between relatives closer than second cousins. (An exception is noted below.)

This ramified structure was the basis of the genealogical ranking system. The mata descendent on the direct line from the first settler supplied the paramount priest-chief of the island (ariki mau) in the person of the eldest son of that line. Other members of the chiefly mata were, for the most part, similar in status to lesser members of comparable ramages, although they appeared to have enjoyed some greater prestige from their descent than members of other mata. Other chiefs, on the main line of their respective mata, shared the upper status level with the paramount priest-chief. Métraux is of the opinion that a professional class of warriors (matatoa) exercised the real power, but this view rests on tenuous evidence. [60] Native traditions stressing the importance of warriors and a missionary dictionary distinguishing matatoa from paoa ("ordinary soldiers") seem to be the major supports for the interpretation. [61] Although Métraux states that warriors ruled the mata, he does not indicate from what position on the genealogical ranking system this class might come and offers no evidence that they weren't actually the

---

59. Alfred Métraux, Ethnology of Easter Island (Bernice Pahau Bishop Museum Bulletin, No. 160 [1940]), p. 123; Williamson, The Social and Political Systems of Central Polynesia, I, 389.

60. Métraux, Ethnology of Easter Island, pp. 138-39.

61. Ibid., pp. 135 f.

168

tribal chiefs to begin with. Although it cannot definitely be established that these warriors were or were not the heads of tribes, it can be established that the hereditary chiefs of tribes were war leaders.[62] Thomson writes, in a statement endorsed and cited by Métraux, that "Clans [mata] were always led to battle by the chief."[63] It appears, then, that any statement that warriors, as persons distinct from mata chiefs, were "the actual rulers of the tribes" is misleading. Furthermore, Thomson writes, "There was no class of professional fighters or soldiers; every able bodied man was supposed to be a warrior and compelled to do duty in time of war."[64] Possibly the traditional emphasis on the matatoa results from occasional usurpation of the position of mata chief by a leader of a powerful junior line.

In actuality, a dual ranking system occasioned by differential military power of the mata combined with the system of rank based on seniority occurred in the uppermost levels of the Easter Island power structure.[65] The dual ranking system in paramount chieftainship was manifest in the institution of the birdman cult.[66] At yearly intervals there was an institutionalized scramble among the leaders of the militarily ascendent tribe for the egg of a certain bird. The finding of this egg by one of these men or his "servant" meant that the man became birdman for a year, the incarnation of the god Makemake, and the holder of many economic, social, and political privileges. The ariki mau, head of the genealogical hierarchy of the island, did not participate in the egg

---

62. This is, in fact, true all over Polynesia. Chiefs were the outstanding war leaders if not the actual outstanding warriors.

63. William J. Thomson, "Te Pito Te Henua, or Easter Island," United States National Museum, Annual Report (1889), p. 476.

64. Ibid., p. 475.

65. Rising in status through military power was not the only flexibility in the ramified system of Easter Island. Ambipatrilineality of descent reckoning indicates that the usual realignments of ramage memberships also occurred.

66. Métraux, Ethnology of Easter Island, pp. 333 f.; Williamson, The Social and Political Systems of Central Polynesia, I, 398.

hunt. The position of the birdman, therefore, was one of co-existent supremacy with the ariki mau.

It is the contention of Williamson and of many others cited by him that the birdman competition was the method by which the secular chieftainship of the island was determined.[67] Williamson makes the plausible suggestion that the competition was a pseudo one; certain evidence leads him to believe that the outcome was settled beforehand: "Prior to the competition an ivi-atua, a divinely gifted individual having the power of prophecy, would dream that a certain man was favoured by the gods, and would win; and in the actual hunt the gods intervened. . . . I gather from this that the result was governed by arrangements made beforehand, upon which the prophet's dream was perhaps based."[68] Early accounts agree that the ariki mau was a sacred ruler in the main. His divine powers were great, but he lacked temporal powers and he had almost no authority outside of his own tribe. There are hints that he once did have. But it is certain that the birdman had widespread secular powers as well as religious privileges. The birdman usurped some of the functions in the accumulation-redistribution system from the paramount chief by descent, and the relative weakness of supreme control by the island high chief in the overlapping tenure pattern is apparently related to this split in sacred and secular rule.[69]

Métraux, however, is reluctant to agree with Williamson in regarding the bird cult as competition for secular supremacy. He emphasizes instead the religious nature of the egg-hunting ceremony and derives the secular powers of the birdman from his sacredness as incarnation of Makemake. He criticizes Williamson's interpretation on the grounds that such an institutionalized temporary secular "kingship" has no analogue in all of Polynesia.[70] However, Métraux's arguments can be countered on many points, including that just mentioned. A temporary position of secular paramount

---

67. Williamson, The Social and Political Systems of Central Polynesia, I, 402 f.
68. Ibid.
69. Ibid., pp. 402-4; Métraux, Ethnology of Easter Island, pp. 129-30.
70. Métraux, Ethnology of Easter Island, pp. 340-41.

chieftainship going to the head of a militarily dominant group has occurred in Polynesia, in Mangaia to be specific.[71] Even so, it seems unjustifiable to reject the apparent character of an institution on the grounds that it did not elsewhere occur in Polynesia. The giant stone heads or the birdman cult itself did not occur elsewhere, yet certainly they existed in Easter Island.

To the status levels that crystallized out of genealogies, the chiefs and nonchiefs, can now be added those that emerged from warfare and the military dominance of certain tribes. The birdman and his immediate relatives must be added to the upper status level composed of members of the senior descent lines of the mata. Members of tribes defeated in war (kio) and used as menials or forced to yield surplus to members of the conquering tribe form a lowest level below the majority of the populace. It is difficult to say whether kio were absorbed into second status level of the tribes that defeated them, as happened among the Maori. My impression is that the status was not permanent, and besides, there was an opportunity for a defeated people to rise up and turn the tables on the conquerors.[72]

Mangaia.--The minimal ramage in Mangaia was the household, a patrilocal extended family (matakainanga). It was headed by the male senior in descent. A number of households with an ancestor in common formed the "tribe," (kopu, pare, or e). The tribe had a specific name, often that of its common ancestor with or without a prefix meaning "descendants of" (Ngati). Tribes grew by fission. Evidently there was a ramage between the tribe and household in order of size, as a number of descendants from a common ancestor less remote than the tribal ancestor might call themselves "Ngati so-and so." The tribe was headed by an ariki, usually the direct heir on the main line of tribal descent, although many exceptions to genealogical succession resulted from the differential growth and power of senior and junior lines, and from emphasis on ability in war as a succession

---

71. Buck, Mangaian Society.
72. For an additional principal source of information on Easter Island, see also Mrs. Scoresby Routledge, The Mystery of Easter Island (London, 1919).

criterion. The tribes probably averaged about 200 or 300 people each.

An unusual feature of the Mangaian ramage organization was exogamy of the tribal groups. Buck feels that this custom arose through a process of institutionalization of the custom by which the tribes of the first settlers, Ngariki, supplied wives to immigrant groups. Another feature in which Mangaia departs from the ideal ramified system is the lack of genealogical system embracing all the large-order ramages, or tribes. Certain tribes traced descent from the reported original settler, and they supplied the two paramount priest-chiefs of the island; but others maintained traditions of descent from immigrant groups. The lack of genealogical unity was reflected in the lack of overall overlapping stewardship.

The tribes were more or less localized in the districts of the island of which they were allegedly the original inhabitants. It is significant that the correlation is not exact. [73] Buck's ethnographic report is confused regarding the nature of district organization, some of which confusion stems from the fact that in the early nineteenth century, a district-territorial organization was formally created, apparently at the expense of the tribal organization. Evidence will be adduced shortly that this may have resulted from European contact.

There was perhaps more mobility of individual ramage alignment in Mangaia than in any other Polynesian island. Land pressure and the loss of land through warfare resulted in many changes of ramage membership, the mechanisms being adoption and the seeking of protection from a wife's or mother's father's tribe with resultant absorption. It was frequently the custom to share children alternately between the father's and mother's father's ramage, adoption by the mother's father being the mode by which the switch in alignment was effected. Residence in the wife's father's household after marriage was common. Ambipatrilineal descent was prevalent.

Warfare was a mechanism by which differentials in strength, power, and growth of families were realized, and these differentials upset the theoretical ranking system based on seniority. On every level of ramification, growth in the power

---

73. Buck, Mangaian Society, pp. 106-7.

of junior ramages could overturn the ranking structure. Buck speaks of the powers of the warriors (toa) as Métraux spoke of the matatoa of Easter Island: "In the course of history the prestige of the toa (successful warrior) began to overthrow that of the rangatira (chief)."[74] But to interpret this to mean that warriors, coming out of nowhere socially, could take over control of tribes or the island as a whole is, I believe, a mistake. War leaders here, as elsewhere, were heads of ramages. What is probably meant by such a statement is that the heads of powerful junior branches of a larger ramage could rise up and take away the power of the senior line, or that a good warrior would be chosen a ramage head in preference to a poor warrior, despite seniority differences. Thus Buck writes: "A hereditary chief could not rely on his seniority alone, but, to maintain his power in the tribe, he had to be a warrior as well. Te Uanuku of Ngati-Vara held the mangaia through his personal prowess as much as through his being the first born son of Mautara. None of his descendants displayed military leadership, and though his family is recognized as the kiko mua, the leadership in the tribe passed to junior branches of the family."[75] Tribes and families rose and fell, fought, and grabbed supremacy outside of the system of genealogical priority. In this sense is the prestige of toa best understood. Buck states: "The power of a chief was influenced by the number of people who gave him allegiance. This depended on the male increase in his particular family group, and in the number of outside people he could support in his establishment. Seniority of blood, though revered, was somewhat theoretical as compared with the practical advantages of number."[76]

The rise and fall of ramages reached a climax in the method of determination of the paramount chief of all Mangaia (mangaia), the "Temporal Lord of Mangaia"(TLM). On the upper levels of the ranking structure, as in Easter Island, there was coexistence of the system of genealogical priority with a system based on military might. At the top of the genea-

---

74. Ibid., p. 110.
75. Ibid., p. 110. Emphasis, M. D. S. Mangaia refers to the paramount chieftainship of Mangaia, discussed later. Kiko mua means "First-born son of a first-born son."
76. Ibid., p. 110.

logical system stood the two priest-chiefs, members of the Ngariki, descendants of the original settlers of Mangaia. At one time, according to Buck, the Ngariki held supreme secular authority as well, but this authority waned and the secular leadership was made one of the spoils of war.[77] Succession to the TLM went to the leader of the tribe which had come into military prominence through conquest of another tribe. Rule was only temporary; the rise of another tribe brought in a new TLM. The longest recorded reign was twenty-five years. The dominant tribe took possession of conquered lands and assumed supremacy over the remaining inhabitants. Lands held by other tribes and the supremacy of their chiefs were not affected, although all recognized the suzerainty of the TLM.

In the early nineteenth century, however, something radically different happened. The two dominant tribes divided the island into six districts and assumed positions of authority over all the districts. The division took place under the aegis of the TLM, Pangemiro, whose actions seem peculiar when viewed against previous Mangaian institutions. Not only was there a sudden centralization of the secular domain under him, but the same thing occurred in the sacred realm, for the two high priest-chief titles were combined. Pangemiro acceded to office in 1814 without battle; when an advantageous alliance was made by him, the chiefs deserted the previous TLM. After Pangemiro had quelled an internal revolt in 1823, his position as TLM was secured; the division of the realm was apparently not made before this date. The abrupt centralization of power suggests that European influence might have been involved. The suggestion is strengthened by the fact that Cook visited Mangaia in 1777. Furthermore, a whaler's captain landed at the beginning of the century, and another in 1814. Finally, in 1823 Pangemiro not only consolidated or reinforced his TLM position, but within two months

---

77. "The history of Mangaia illustrates the attempt of the Ngariki to keep the position of Temporal Lord of Mangaia within their own tribe, and their ultimate failure through the ambition of the warlike Tongaiti. Once precedent was broken down in this direction . . . temporal power was the reward of war and not of hereditary descent. . . . "Ibid., p. 34.

missionaries came to Mangaia. [78] It appears unlikely that centralized power administered on a territorial, nontribal basis was an autocthonous development. The stratification system was based both on genealogy and on war. On the upper level can be placed the two priest-chiefs, the TLM, and the heads of the various tribes with their near relatives. "Commoners" were the junior offshoots of senior lines and formed the majority of the population. Those defeated in war either were absorbed into other tribes through adoption, marriage, or the like, or lived in margin-al lands. This level was not a permanent one; the social system operated to assimilate or re-establish the defeated in a kinship framework. [79]

Mangareva. --The basic ramage in Mangareva was the household, as usual, a patrilocal extended family, some-times including collaterals and members of groups defeated in war. These members of other ramages are called by Buck "servants" (kio). He does not mention the possible lineal or affinal relationship to the household to which they were at-tached. Laval pointed out that kio could also mean descend-ants. [80] The households were headed by the male senior in descent. Another, higher-order ramage (vao, paa, ivi, or inao) is not clearly distinguished from the "tribe" (also inao). Inao were composed of groups of households descendent from a common ancestor. They were designated by the name of the common ancestor prefixed with "descendants of" (Ati). [81]

78. William Wyatt Gill, From Darkness to Light in Poly-nesia (London, 1894), pp. 323 f. ; Buck, Mangaian Society, p. 83.

79. For an additional principal source of information on Mangaia, see William Wyatt Gill, Life in the Southern Isles (London, 1876).

80. Honoré Laval, Mangareva: L'Histoire Ancienne d'un Peuple Polynésien (Braine-le-Comte, 1938), p. 286n.

81. "Owing to the lapse in native education following the advent of Christianity, the present people cannot connect genealogically with their tribal ancestors, but there is little doubt that most, if not all, the tribal names have been de-rived from eponymous ancestors." Peter H. Buck, Ethnol-ogy of Mangareva (Bernice Pahau Bishop Museum Bulletin, No. 157 [1938]), p. 140.

They were apparently led by chiefs who were descendent in the senior tribal line. The ancestors of all the tribes could be placed, with some exceptions, in a genealogical system.[82] The tribes were localized in various districts, usually on a bay. The localization was not precise; some tribes were found in two or more geographical regions. Unfortunately, Buck emphasizes the territorial aspect of tribal organization and speaks in terms such as "district chiefs," belying the ramage, kinship nature of the social organization.[83]

The ramage system was quite flexible both through the mechanism of ambipatrilineal descent and through the operation of physical force. Adoption and nonpatrilocal residence were mechanisms by which individuals were switched from one ramage to another. But the major changes in the ramified structure resulted from warfare and struggles over power. These occurred from the top to the bottom of the genealogical framework: "The history of Mangareva consists of struggles between different families and districts [i.e., "tribes"] in their attempts to gain power or avenge defeats."[84] The principle of seniority was never a certain determining factor of succession; usurpation of the position of the senior male was always an imminent threat. "The question of whether or not departures from the pattern [of seniority] became established depended on [the junior lines'] being able to hold by force the position they had usurped."[85] In struggles between major ramages, inao, the victorious group took possession of the lands of the defeated. Such lands were redistributed among the members of the victorious group. The defeated who remained after the slaughter took "protection" in other tribes.

Although hereditary succession to the title of the para-

---

82. "Unfortunately . . . the lack of family [genealogies, also a result of missionary influence] prevents our linking up the various chiefly families (togoiti) with particular tribes. We can only assume from the tribal organization in other parts of Polynesia that the tribes had their ruling chiefs who belonged to the senior family line descending from the eponymous ancestor." Ibid., p. 142.

83. Ibid., passim.

84. Ibid., p. 36.

85. Ibid., p. 157.

mount chieftainship of Mangareva was not a certainty, and the rule was often challenged by junior lines of the tribe holding this position as well as by others--called "commoners" although their familial connections are unknown--once the title was established, it did not slip out of the major line of descent for any length of time. A dual stratification system with a split between the temporal and secular powers did not occur. The paramount chieftainship of Mangareva was established at the time of a certain Anuamotua, twenty-two generations before 1900, according to genealogies. After his death the rule was divided, but eight generations later a direct descendant of his line reunited the entire group, and thereafter the rule remained more or less stable.

The basic status levels emerged out of the operation of seniority. These were the "nobles" and "commoners" according to Buck and Laval.[86] After this, there is confusion in the sources. The "nobles" were of three types, togoiti, akariki, and momomomo. Togoiti were descendants of Anuamotua, and they evidently were chiefs of most of the tribal districts. However, some tribal chiefs were called akariki, and there were some akariki who were not of Anuamotua's line. It is possible that they traced their descent to pre-Anuamotua chiefs and ruled over groups outside of the genealogical framework that encompassed most of Mangareva. On the other hand, according to native traditions, all previous sources of chiefly blood were abolished in Anuamotua's time.[87] Another possibility is that non-togoiti akariki were upstart chieftains of the junior lines of their tribes. Momomomo were relatives not living in togoiti households, but related to togoiti directly within four generations from a common ancestor. This then was the limit of the upper status level.

Much confusion is caused by the term, pakaora. Generally it refers to those victorious in battle, both chief and commoner, who shared in the redistribution of conquered lands. Pakaora were evidently stewards of these lands under the tribal chief, akariki. The term ragatira, according to Buck, originally referred to junior members of chiefly lines, but was

---

86. Ibid., pp. 142 f.; Laval, Mangareva: L'Histoire Ancienne d'un Peuple Polynésien, pp. 223 f.

87. Buck, Ethnology of Mangareva, p. 143.

extended to include pakaora of any kind holding a large steward area.[88] The term kio was given to menials in households of men of high rank. It has been translated as "servants" or "descendants." Most kio came from tribes defeated in war. Kiore is referred to as the lowest status, people without lands. It probably refers to people defeated in war who were fugitives or had not yet been assimilated into other groups. Finally, tau seems to have been another general term for "commoners," or for one who held land as a steward under someone else. Laval's discussion of these terms is quite revealing.[89] He wrote that by his time, (the first half of the eighteenth century) pakaora was practically synonymous with ragatira. Furthermore, tau, meaning "holder of lands under nobles," was equated with pakaora and ragatira. Finally, tau were also called "kio." Thus, in reality, all these terms signified a position of understewardship. The basic distinction was between togoiti or akariki and urumanu, while kio referred perhaps primarily to those who were defeated in war and took refuge elsewhere.[90]

Summary and Interpretation

Many departures from the ideal ramage system described in the beginning of this chapter have been noted in our survey of Polynesian ramified societies. There is great variation in the ability of individuals to change their affiliations in the ramage structure. For example, Tikopian ramages were inflexible, an individual apparently had no choice of ramage affiliation. Elsewhere, as in the Marquesas, close ties were maintained with one's mother's ramage, and membership in that group rather than in one's father's ramage was evidently frequently sought. Adoption frequencies similarly varied from island to island and contributed to the degree of permissible flexibility of the ramage structure. It is obvious that no

---

88. Ibid., p. 147.

89. Laval, Mangareva: L'Histoire Ancienne d'un Peuple Polynésien, pp. 223-24, 286.

90. Additional consulted source of information on Mangareva: S. Percy Smith, "Notes on the Mangareva or Gambier Group of Islands, Eastern Polynesia," Journal of the Polynesian Society, Vol. XXVII (1918).

facile explanation of these wide variations is to be made. I shall only suggest that factors such as population density, availability of free land, and differential land fertility may have some bearing on the question of flexibility of the ramage system.

Flexibility in ramage affiliation does not profoundly alter ramage structure. Major structural differences are produced through such developments as dual chieftainship and superordinate ruling ramages. Moreover, these aspects of ramage organization seem linked together and can be observed as part of a political maturation of ramification.

In New Zealand, the Marquesas, and Tikopia, chieftainship was a relatively stable institution. Rank and succession to office closely followed the principles of genealogical seniority. Political units in New Zealand and Tikopia were divided into a number of high-order ramages, the heads of which were the high chiefs of the polity. In all three societies, members of different ramages held roughly equivalent status if they were proportionately distant from the main line of descent within their respective ramages. There was no one superordinate chiefly ramage. Divine and temporal powers were united either in chiefly persons or in persons under chiefs' control.

In Easter Island and Mangaia, chieftainship was comparatively unstable. Large-size ramages ("tribes") struggled for political supremacy. Secular authority became a spoil of war, and hence was a temporary position. Dual chieftainship developed, the paramount chiefly descent being removed from the sphere of combat and given only sacred powers. It is significant that military ascendancy did not bestow high rank in the genealogical structure. Under such conditions, no superordinate chiefly ramage could develop. The seniority in descent of the priest-chief being unalterable, it is affirmed that the traditional ramage system cannot be overthrown. Victorious "tribes" were able to lay claim to high secular chieftainship and take over control of defeated groups, but the other "tribal" chiefs did not thereby lose status and their position in their own domain was not challenged. Mangareva presents a picture similar to Easter Island and Mangaia with the exception that no dual chieftainship developed. There was instability in the paramount chieftainship, but the traditional main line of descent was always able to recapture the leadership. Warfare between "tribes" was more decisive; conquer-

179

ors appropriated their victims' land and forced the defeated to find "protection" elsewhere. An entire high-order ramage might drop out of the power structure. What seems implied in Mangareva was a rather widespread regrouping of ramages around closely related chiefs. This tended to produce a chiefly ramage stratum at the top level of the society.

Such a trend is clear in Tonga. The ethnography and genealogies (see Figure 2) show the tendency to center chieftainships of all large ramages (haa) among close relatives of the paramount chief. At the same time, as in Mangaia and Easter Island, there was a split between sacred and temporal rule. However, the split did not remove the secular chieftainship from the genealogical hierarchy, thus it remained stable. Secular rule merely devolved upon a junior line of the senior ramage of Tonga. Consolidation of power and modification of the ramage ranking structure through the development of a chiefly ramage is emerging.

In Tahiti, and to a greater extent in Hawaii, a single ramage spread over all positions of authority and became a ramage of chiefs. Conquest warfare, with the defeated governed by the victors, was one mechanism by which this was effected. In Hawaii, especially, it was not possible for heads of ramages tracing descent to remote collaterals of remote chiefs to assume positions of authority. The chiefly ramage, by reserving the right to redistribute offices upon the accession of each new paramount, guaranteed that the single ramage character of the ruling group would not be altered.

These variations of ramage systems illustrate a developmental sequence from political structures based on distinct ramages headed by chiefs more closely related to their followers than to each other to monolithic polities headed by a ramage of chiefs who were at best only remotely related to the people they ruled. It is not accidental that this developmental sequence closely follows the gradient of stratification described earlier in this work. Variations of this type in ramage systems are the structural concomitants of differing degrees of stratification.

We have not in this chapter in any way explained the ramage system and its variations. We have merely outlined the social mechanisms by which status differentials are produced. It remains to do the same for other sorts of Polynesian social organizations, and to then determine if these types--ramage systems included--can be understood as adaptive varieties in the Polynesian cultural genus.

180

9. Descent-line Systems of Social Organization and Stratification

THE ABORIGINAL SOCIAL organizations of Samoa, Futuna, and Uvea offer a contrast to ramified systems just discussed. To my knowledge, the contrast has been overlooked in the ethnological literature of Polynesia. In Samoa, Uvea, and Futuna, the political system was one of localized, discrete, patrilineal descent lines. The descent lines held titles, and the titles bestowed office in local territorial entities, villages and districts. Status did not depend--at least not in the same way as in the ramified system--on distance from the main line of descent, but rather on the traditional position of one's title in the territorial hierarchy of titles. I propose to call this a "descent-line" system of social organization and stratification. Since only three variants of the descent-line system are considered here, each will be described in detail without first describing the general pattern.

Samoa. --Samoan political organization was concerned with a system of titles which, although accruing to patrilineal descent lines, took on hierarchical significance in the local context of the village and of larger territorial groups. With these titles went privileges of sitting on certain councils (fono), positions of precedence in ceremonial kava servings, and a place in the order of title calling which served as a customary preface to important social activities. As Mead[1] described this titular system:"Names and their rank, not individuals are units of construction. . . . The individual may

---

1. Margaret Mead, The Social Organization of Manua, (Bernice Pahau Bishop Museum Bulletin, No. 76 [1930]), p. 11.

move about at will, but the name, the post, the position in the kava ceremony, and the right to make speeches, are constants, sustaining a fixed relationship to all other names in the series." In ramified systems, on the contrary, it is precisely the individual which is "the unit of construction," and the relationship between titles is dependent upon the genealogical relationship between people.

In Samoa, titles were held in paternal descent lines. Each village contained a number of unrelated descent lines, although a particular line could be found in a number of villages. Unlike the ramified systems, succession to titles was not necessarily by primogeniture but could go to any son or brother of the former holder of the title. Suitability for leadership and propinquity of residence were the final criteria of selection.

Titles conferred positions in the village council (fono). Only title holders (matai) could sit on this council and each held a rank based on the traditional relationship of his title to others of the fono. Position of the title in councils was thus the ultimate determinant of status. Titles were of two types, chiefs (alii) and talking chiefs (tulafale). Talking chiefs were the ceremonial attendants of chiefs; each talking chief was attached to a specific chief and took his status according to the title of the chief. Therefore, among title holders, chiefs and talking chiefs held every grade of status; chiefs did not, as a group, outrank talking chiefs as a group. Talking chiefs were the speakers of the chiefs, kept their genealogies, and acted as distributors in feasts.

The descent-line system of Samoa and its hierarchy of titles will be considered, first, from the viewpoint of the structure of kinship groups and, second, from that of local groupings. The basic domestic unit was the extended family, usually patrilocal, sometimes bilocal. The members of one or a few families who traced common descent--in all, up to fifty or more people--formed a local descent line in a village called "ainga," a term also used to refer to an egocentric, bilateral kindred, or "sa," connoting "line of descent." A sa in a village was normally but a section of a multilocal group which had other branches scattered in several villages. Such multilocal descent lines were also called "sa." The village sa section was sometimes further subdivided, but the term of reference for these lesser branches is not clear. Each multilocal sa held titles in village councils which were

182

filled by the heads of the local sections. One sa section was considered the ranking branch in the entire larger sa and held the highest title the line could bestow.

A sa having sections in a number of villages gives the appearance of related ramages with heads of varying rank. In truth, the ranking of the titles of local sections within the larger descent line probably stems from the division of one local group from another in the course of village segmentation (see below). However, the rank relationship between sa branches and the titles thereof was not established by seniority of descent, and did not involve the development of senior and cadet lines through primogeniture. The connection between branches of a sa was variously phrased genealogically, even affinal connection was sufficient; descent of related sections was not necessarily traced from a brace of brothers.[2]

More significant in distinguishing descent lines from ramage organization is the fact that the relationship in rank between titles of a given village or district was not based upon differences in seniority in the descent of the different lines demonstrable on some genealogical tree. Rather, the various lines in a village or district were genealogically distinct.[3] Priority on the basis of age of the sa sections might have been the determining factor as to which section held which local title of what rank, but the local hierarchy of titles involved more than offshoots of a single sa.

Local hierarchies were established in traditional, pseudo-historical, mythological terms. A title was traced through a line of male title holders to a god or legendary incident. Again, unlike the ramified system, it was the title whose descent was reckoned, not individuals. The kinship structure was not an over-all system of interconnected ramages operating as a framework from which statuses emerged, but rather a number of unrelated descent lines holding status titles that were traced to certain gods or legendary incidents.

---

2. Robert W. Williamson, The Social and Political Systems of Central Polynesia (Cambridge, Eng., 1924), II, 3 f.

3. Through intermarriage, of course, interrelationships between different families could be established, but these relationships were not the basis of title holdings.

In ramified systems, each household is ranked according to the genealogical priority of its head; but in Samoa, a man of chiefly descent only ranked as high as his title, perhaps lower than a man whose father was not a chief but who inherited a high title from some other paternal relative. In consequence, untitled members of the household of a high matai did not rank much higher than members of a low matai's household.

The possibility that the descent-line system developed out of a system of genealogical priority cannot be overlooked. There was a myth to the effect that the god Pili, a descendant of other gods, divided Upolu among three of his sons. In two of the autonomous Upolu divisions, the high chiefs traced descent from Pili. Furthermore, some traces of primogeniture were found by Mead, and she believes that primogeniture, formerly present, had disappeared.[4] Among the evidences of former dependence on primogenitural succession, and perhaps ramification, was the elaboration of crisis rites regarding the birth of the first child. Mead writes: "The birth of the first child was regarded as much more important than any subsequent birth. . . . A greater emphasis upon a first birth is one of the few Samoan remnants of the prestige of the first born."[5]

The local descent lines were composed primarily of descendants of males through males (tama tane). Sisters of these men, however, and their immediate descendants formed a distinct organization (tama fafine) which had many ritual functions as well as economic prerogatives in affinal gift exchanges and the power to veto the disposal of land. This group was usually headed by the oldest sister of the male head. As females usually married out, the tama fafine lacked the cohesiveness, length, and breadth of membership of the tama tane.

A fuller understanding of the descent-line system is gained when it is viewed in its local setting, and the organization on a territorial basis is examined. The aboriginal settlement pattern was one of villages, usually located near the seacoast. A village usually contained more than five different, unrelated sa sections. The village did not exceed

---

4. Mead, The Social Organization of Manua, p. 144.
5. Ibid., p. 89.

400 people. Each sa in the village held one or more titles in the village fono. Not all of the possible titles in a village were necessarily operative at a given time. Usually one title was highest in rank; the holder of such a title was the village chief. The village with its fono was the sociopolitical unit.

The village fono contributed representatives to fonos of a district of several villages. High-ranking village titles conferred the prerogative of sitting on the district fono. In a similar manner, the multivillage fonos contributed representatives to larger, multidistrict fonos. These were the "division" fonos, which, for most purposes and at most times, were those of highest order. Division fonos governed what was usually the largest social, political, and economic unit in Samoa, such as the divisions of Aana, Atua, and Tuamasanga in Upolu, or the Manuan group as a whole. All fonos ratified titles of the members, installed the high chiefs, and made preparations for war. The district and division fonos functioned solely in these activities. The paramount chief, the man with the highest title in each division, had the title Tui followed by the name of the division, e.g., Tuiaana, or Tuimanua. Such a chief usually traced his title to an illustrious god through a line of males. These chiefs were the heads of certain sa which had representatives in many of the villages, and thus the division gave the appearance of being under the domination of one particular family. However, much power was held by a number, usually less than ten, of other high-ranking men in each division known as the orator chiefs (tulafale alii). Genealogical connection can sometimes be demonstrated between the paramount and the tulafale alii, but the connection is often affinal. The tulafale alii are not necessarily members of the paramount s sa. Furthermore, near relatives and heads of known branches of the high chief's sa may rank lower than these tulafale alii. [6]

Occasionally, one high chief gained control of the titles of the three great divisions of Upolu. [7] Such a person became

---

6. See Williamson, The Social and Political Systems of Central Polynesia, II, 3-39, passim.

7. Four titles were actually involved, two were from Tuamasanga. One of the titles referred also to dominion over Savaii.

the paramount chief (<u>tafaifa</u>) of all Samoa, except Manua. [8]
His reign was only temporary, and although the precedent
was established before contact with Europeans, the position
was not a permanent Samoan institution. The paramount
chief was the leader of the infrequent <u>fono</u> of all Samoa (save
Manua) and was the focus of an occasional redistributive network of that scope.

Flexibility was, in fact, an outstanding feature of the Samoan ranking system. Warfare does not seem to have operated frequently as a mechanism of flexibility except in the
superstructural spheres. On the other hand, a liberal number of adoptions and alliances with the mother's father's
descent line through ambipatrilineal descent did take place.
The social organization showed great adaptability in reflecting the differential growth of families and their consequent
differential ability to produce and distribute a large surplus.
Through lavish distribution the head of a <u>sa</u> section gained
prestige, and with this prestige his title moved upward in the
system of titles in the <u>fono</u>. With the aid of manipulations by
the talking chiefs, a title could be created or a title could be
raised in the hierarchy, which would reflect the increasing
economic importance of the title holder. Then again, the
opposite might occur, which would reflect the economic decline of a title holder. As Mead acutely notes: "The title
held by the poor or undistinguished sinks gradually into dis-
repute. The lesser title held by the rich and the ambitious
rises in the scale; myths of its origin are manufactured, the
genealogies are rearranged, the phrasing of the [order of
titles] altered slightly; and a different set of fixed and unalterable relationships is established."[9] Or, "A shift in power
from one house to another means a shift in the genealogy of-
tenest on the lips of pedantic talking chiefs."[10]

Mead also gives a graphic idea of the frequency of shifts
and the amount of flexibility. "So flexible is the social structure, so minutely adapted to manipulation, that it is possible
to change the appearance of the <u>fono</u> in twenty years."[11] It
is this flexibility and the creation of new titles around rising

8. Felix M. Keesing, <u>Modern Samoa</u> (London, 1934), p. 54.
9. Mead, <u>The Social Organization of Manua</u>, pp. 21-22.
10. <u>Ibid.</u>, p. 135.
11. Margaret Mead, "The Role of the Individual in Samoan

kin groups that gives a clue to the process of sa separation and thus points out a marked departure from the ramified system. The local sa has the tendency to break up into new and entirely distinct descent lines, to fragment along the line created by the establishment of a new title: "The Samoan tendency is continually to break up old lineages into smaller ones. Each generation adds a few new eponymous ancestors of small descent groups. An emphasis upon village organization, upon the creation of new titles, and upon the households surrounding each title accounts for this feature. . . . The existence of a large number of small titles of recent origin or low prestige amply provides for this multiplication of family groups. For example, the family of Asoao in Faleasao may control half a dozen small titles, but all of these title holders and their children may prefer to lay claim to being members of the Sa Asoao. But when the family becomes more numerous, the small title rises in prestige through the united labor of large descent groups, and some of the branches of the family will cease to comment upon their remote relationship to Asoao and use the new title with the prefix, 'family of.'"[12] This is a crucial difference between descent-line and ramified systems. When fission occurs in ramages, it occurs between descendants of brothers, but the common ancestor and unity of the group is maintained. In Samoa, fission results in fragmentation of a group and the loss of ties between two lines of descent.

The appearance of a given sa in a number of villages is intelligible in terms of village growth and fission. A given segment of a village--or a fishing settlement attached to the village--that contained households of several of the village sa grew in size. The neighborhood bond was emphasized and carried on in fono life until the village fono itself split into two fonos, hence the village into two villages. The split was rapidly codified by the creation of a ceremonial pattern for the new fono by its talking chiefs, undoubtedly based on the pattern in the old village. Thus, the local sa were duplicated; the sa became multilocal.

Status levels, of course, emerged out of the descent-line

Culture," Journal of the (Royal) Anthropological Institute, LVIII (1928), 495.
12. Mead, The Social Organization of Manua, p. 134.

system and its titular emphasis. The titled were markedly differentiated from the untitled in socioeconomic and religious functions, privileges, and obligations. The council of title holders was the dominant force in Samoan life. Thus, two distinct status levels emerged, those with titles and those without. Every title occupied a different position and rank, and high titles were further distinguished from low titles. This distinction had some functional significance with regard to differential cultural roles, but the significance was not as great, or perhaps not as well documented, as the distinction between "titled" and "untitled." The different roles of the status levels have already been outlined. In contrast to the ramified systems, power was vested in councils rather than in individuals; the emphasis was upon the representative bodies not on the chiefs themselves. Consequently, in Samoa, supreme stewardship, the application of sanctions, control over production, and leadership in warfare were activities assumed by fonos of which the high chief was a necessary feature, not by high chiefs in consultation with lower-ranking chiefs and relatives. A marked territorial emphasis was a feature of the descent-line system in contrast to the relationship emphasis of ramage organization, although both had elements of breed and border, and both were kinship, nonstate organizations. [13]

Futuna. --The social organization of Futuna was very similar to that of Samoa. The principal difference was that the

---

13. For additional principal sources, see also Peter H. Buck, Samoan Material Culture (Bernice Pahau Bishop Museum Bulletin, No. 75 [1930]); Wilhelm von Bülow, "Der Landbesitz der Eingeboren auf der Insel Savaii," Globus, Vol. LXXXI (1902); John Wesley Coulter, Land Utilization in American Samoa (Bernice Pahau Bishop Museum Bulletin, No. 170 [1941]); Augustin Krämer, Die Samoa-Inseln (Stuttgart, 1902); Margaret Mead, Coming of Age in Samoa (New York, 1950); E. Schultz, "The Most Important Principles of Samoan Family Law, and the Law of Inheritance," Journal of the Polynesian Society, XX (1911); Erich Schultz-Ewerth, "Samoa," in Erich Schultz-Ewerth and Leonhard Adam, Das Eingeborenenrecht (Stuttgart, 1929-30), Vol. II; Reverend John B. Stair, Old Samoa (London, 1897); George Turner, Samoa (London, 1884).

Futunan system of titles was much smaller in scope. The one chief in every village, the district paramount chiefs, and certain district functionaries were the only ones with titles. Most descent lines were very short and carried no titles whatsoever.

The smallest social unit was the household, a patrilocal extended family (kainga) composed of eight persons on the average, and twenty-five at the maximum. The kainga was practically coextensive with the kutunga, the counterpart of the localized sa in Samoa.[14] The kutunga was a group of persons, often confined primarily to one household, that recognized patrilineal relationship. It had a name which could be that of a distinguished ancestor, a place of residence, or an animal regarded as the incarnation of a god. Titles of village or district chiefs were held in certain kutunga. Kutunga split off from one another and formed new kutunga. The bonds between such separated kutunga eventually grew looser and the relationship was forgotten. Thus, as in Samoa, the local pattern of grouping was one of attenuated, discrete patrilineages. The fissioning of kutunga seems to have been a response to pressure of increasing numbers.[15]

Territorial units were villages of 100 to 200 people, combined in districts of 500 or 1,000 people. Each type of unit had a council, but there was no island-wide title or council. Unlike the Samoan council, the Futuna village council was theoretically composed of all adult males of the group, "but in practice, the older men are the most regular attendants."[16] Each village had a chief; the title was held by one of the kutunga in the village. Village chiefs (aliki fenua) and one or

---

14. "Kutunga" was usually synonymous with kainga. It is clear that kutunga could have members in other villages, but it is not clear that this means kutunga branches or merely women--more rarely, men--who had married out. See Edwin G. Burrows, Ethnology of Futuna (Bernice Pahau Bishop Museum Bulletin, No. 138 [1936]).

15. "Where there is more than one house on the property of a single kindred, the occupants of each have a certain claim. Permanent establishment of such claims may be the way, or one of the ways, in which the splitting of kindreds is brought about." Ibid., p. 84.

16. Ibid., p. 100.

two other functionaries formed the district fono, consisting
solely of titled men and headed by the district chief (aliki
sau). The district council titles were arranged in a definite
hierarchy that was symbolized in kava-ceremony seating and
title-calling procedures. The descent of the district chief
was traced far back to a god. The lines of village-chief titles were also elaborated, but other genealogies were much
shorter.

Succession to title was, as in Samoa, patrilineal but without a definite rule. The rank position of a title was apparently qualified by warfare or internal struggles. In one district,
for example, succession to the district chieftainship alter-
nated between two rival kutunga. Burrows states that the establishment of precedence between titles "has uniformly been
by prowess in war."[17] As the succession pattern indicates,
the hierarchy of titles did not depend on seniority of descent
as it did in ramified systems. There is no evidence of genealogical connection of any sort between the kutunga which
supplied the various titles in a district. Neither did the paramount chiefs of the districts trace descent to a common ancestor.

Yet there is evidence of ramage practices. The birth of
the first male child was elaborately celebrated. There was
a pattern of stewardship over land of the kutunga that ac-
crued to "the senior man of the [descent line] . . . called
taokete (elder son) or pule (master)."[18] However, primogeniture was not the rule in succession to title, and the hierarchy of titles was not based on seniority. The ramage traits
may have been survivals from times when primogeniture and
seniority were significant principles of the ranking which
pervaded the entire society, a situation that was certainly
not present at the time of European contact. Also, there was
no pattern of overlapping stewardship except insofar as the
fono might be considered the supreme steward of its territory.

The status levels emerged clearly from the system of titles. The titled were distinguished from the untitled, and
through activities of the district council this distinction was

---

17. Ibid., p. 89. This statement seems to be supported
by native traditions. Ibid., pp. 17-56.

18. Ibid., p. 82.

accompanied by differing roles in economic, social, and religious life. As in Samoa, and as was generally characteristic of descent-line systems, membership in a kutunga holding a title did not automatically bestow high rank. Other characteristics of descent-line systems, found in Futuna but not in ramified systems, were emphasis on territorial units and the regulation of affairs by chiefs in a council rather than by a chief with counselors.

Uvea.--Uvean social organization is difficult to classify. There were many aspects of ramification, including emphasis on the ceremonial celebration of first births, gradation based on seniority in households, and succession of the first-born son--with exceptions due to unfitness--to the headship of the household and stewardship over its lands. There is no precise information on the pattern of succession to important titles, but it appears that primogeniture played some role, except in the case of the highest titles on the island, which often changed hands in warfare. In a personal communication, Burrows states that primogeniture was, in fact, the major criterion determining succession.[19] But despite these practices of a ramage nature, Uvea must be classified as a descent-line system because it was characterized by attenuated kinship groups, descent lines, and lacked an overall ramified network from which status, reflecting genealogical position, would emerge. The order of precedence among titles was not based on seniority. In his personal communication, Burrows writes: "The order of precedence among Ministers [i.e., the high titles of the island, described below] governs seniority among lineages, rather than being governed by it. What determined this order is a matter of 'historical accident,' now for the most part irrecoverable."[20] This fragmented system of descent lines holding titles, arranged in a hierarchy not based on seniority of descent, links Uvea typologically to Samoa and Futuna.

The Uvea descent lines were, in fact, similar in composition to the Futuna descent lines. The basic domestic unit in Uvea was the patrilocal extended family, a household (api).

---

19. Burrows also informed the author that there is little evidence that Uvea once had an over-all ramification system. Edwin G. Burrows, personal communication.

20. Ibid.

The api had a name and from three to twelve members. Api grew from one another by fission and thus a number of adjoining ones might have shared the same name. Burrows distinguishes the api from the kainga, "lineage," another small, named group composed of people tracing common patrilineal descent.[21] Actually the memberships of the api and the kainga overlap. The core of the api consisted of members of one kainga. The difference between these groups was that the household, as a domestic group, included persons who married in, while the lineage, as a descent group, excluded these but included natal members who married out.[22] However, it is characteristic of all descent-line systems that the effective descent group practically corresponds to the household, at least the natal members of the household. Therefore, household fission becomes equivalent to lineage fission, and such was evidently the case in Uvea, where lineages were short in genealogical depth and usually unrelated. The only exceptions were certain lineages which were anciently segmented from lineages holding titles. Although the segmented lineages were distinct for all practical purposes, some memory of an old connection may have been maintained.[23]

The village, about 200 people, contained a number of unrelated kainga, one of which supplied the village chief. All adult males participated in a village council. However, in

---

21. Edwin G. Burrows, Ethnology of Uvea (Bernice Pahau Bishop Museum Bulletin, No. 145 [1937]), pp. 64-66.

22. "Including the living, the average numbers of a lineage would coincide with those of the household. The household usually constitutes . . . a patrilocal extended family. . . . Living members of the lineage would be the same, minus outsiders (usually women) who had married in, and plus members (usually women) who had married out . . . my figures for a household . . . apply as well for a lineage." Burrows, personal communication.

23. "When a lineage becomes unwieldy it splits up. The Tamahaa, which traces its ancestry to a king, has branched off and is regarded as a separate lineage. But the connection with royalty is commemorated in the name and still carries the fahu [i.e., a permissive affinal kin relationship] privilege." Burrows, Ethnology of Uvea, p. 64.

192

council proceedings, "the heads of lineages take precedence."[24] Each village also has a guard, an official responsible to the council; his duties are not clearly described and the office could be of European origin. In modern times, the village chiefs unite in district councils in which they are seated and served kava in a definite order of precedence. However, the district organization is a European invention, even though the fono form has an aboriginal basis.[25] The highest fono is the island fono composed of the paramount chief and six or seven other lesser chiefs ("ministers") ranked in a definite order. These lesser chiefs reside in the paramount chief's village, and with the exception of the chief of that village, they are not village chiefs. It is possible that formerly the chiefs of the villages sat on the island fono. They were called village elders (matua fenua) or village chiefs (aliki fenua). The paramount chief and the other island chiefs were called "kau aliki." Another title, chief's attendant (matapule), was hereditary in certain descent lines.

A great deal of flexibility in the order of precedence among titles is noted by Burrows.[26] The native traditions record many examples of succession to the paramount chieftainship effected through warfare and assassination. Other shifts in precedence occurred with respect to other titles; some "ministers" (island high chiefs) which outrank village and other ancient chiefs have new titles. One line, Hoko, now that of a village chief, formerly, according to tradition, supplied the high chief. Native traditions are full of stories of factional rivalry, and this was probably the major mechanism accounting for shifts in the titular hierarchy. Adoptions, some residence after marriage in the wife's household, and ambipatrilineal descent indicate that changes in descent line alignment occurred on all levels of the society, probably occasioned by differential family growth.[27]

---

24. Ibid., p. 78. Burrows does not elaborate; he must mean precedence in debate. These heads of lineages do not hold titles, and in personal communication, Burrows refers to them as "chairmen," not comparable to the Samoan matai.

25. Ibid., pp. 5 and passim.

26. Ibid., pp. 70-71.

27. For additional principal sources, see also Edwin G. Burrows, "Breed and Border in Polynesia," American An-

Status levels emerge from the descent-line and title systems. The two levels are those with titles and those without. Unlike Samoa and Futuna, and probably related to the marked number of ramified customs, membership in chiefly descent lines seems to have conferred extra prestige. The various prerogatives of the two status levels have already been described. The emphasis here again was on territorial units and council administration. [28]

Summary and Interpretations

Descent-line sociopolitical systems have been described as local groupings of relatively small, unrelated, patrilineal units which fill titles in territorial, administrative divisions such as villages and districts. The titles are arranged in a traditional order of precedence symbolized by seating position in administrative councils (fonos) and in the order of kava serving at the meetings of such bodies and other ceremonial occasions.

A number of variations are apparent. There is variation in the elaboration of the titular system. Futuna had the least complex hierarchy of titles; there were only village chiefs, one to each village, and the paramount chief of the district. Although the island occasionally participated in a single distributive activity, there was no island supreme chief. Uvea had a separate set of island chiefs as well as a chief in each village and some matapule titles. In Samoa, every descent line in a village held at least one title. The system was also extended to district and division levels, and occasionally to all Samoa, there being a supreme chief for each such regulatory segment. Furthermore, the Samoan titular system was divided into two categories, chief and talking chief. These variations can be correlated with variations in efficiency of technological exploitation, as Futuna, Uvea, and Samoa rank in that order of productivity (see Table 1). Elab-

thropologist, Vol. XLI (1939); S. Percy Smith, "Uea, or Wallis Island, and Its People," Journal of the Polynesian Society, Vol. I (2nd ed.; 1909).
28. However, again perhaps related to ramification, the high chief in the councils did most of the talking or ordering, the others, as in Tonga, merely concurred.

oration of the titular hierarchy is, in fact, an elaboration or increase in the amount of social stratification and is thus correlated to technoenvironmental efficiency.

There are variations in degree of mobility in the status system and in the manner of effecting changes in the rank of a title or a descent line. On all three islands, differential growth of descent lines results in changes in the order of precedence in the titular hierarchy. In Samoa, these changes were accomplished in a peaceful and institutional manner. The council patterns and genealogies were rearranged by the talking chief in accordance with changes in the ability of descent lines to make lavish distributions of food and goods. In Futuna and Uvea, however, internal struggles, assassinations, and warfare were the major mechanisms involved in rearrangements of the titular hierarchy. One factor which may account for this difference is the presence of greater amounts of available, arable land in Samoa than in Futuna or Uvea, land which was never fully utilized by the aboriginal population.[29] One possible reason for this ecological situation is the fact that land plots generally decrease in size and to some extent in agricultural value as one moves inward from the sea.[30] It would be difficult for an inland-dwelling population to exist, as it would have to produce a surplus to exchange for sea products to which it would have little or no direct access.[31] Only a large coastal family then could divorce part of its labor resources from the rich sea areas and take advantage of this freely available land. A greater surplus could be produced by such a family, hence a greater distribution and greater prestige.

The peaceful flexibility of the Samoan stratification system can be thus related to the relative abundance of unused land. In Futuna, and to a lesser extent Uvea, there does not

---

29. Mead, The Social Organization of Manua, p. 65; Coulter, Land Utilization in American Samoa, passim; Buck, Samoan Material Culture, p. 551.

30. Coulter, Land Utilization in American Samoa.

31. Coulter notes the plight of a village on Tutuila which had used up all the good taro lands in the vicinity and was pushing up the forested slopes so that "The nearest taro lands to the village, about 0.1 of an acre, are now about two miles away." Ibid., p. 27.

seem to have been such a proportionately large quantity of unused land. Most of the Futunan interior was unarable because of desert and heavily acidic soils (see Appendix, IX). On Uvea, the interior was arable only in spots, which seem to have been fairly well occupied by the various kainga, as is indicated by numerous plantation sites. [32]

Furthermore, interior land in Samoa is well watered and suitable for continuous, but limited, taro production, whereas that in Uvea and Futuna is not (Appendix, III, VI, IX). In summary, the greater restriction on unused land in Futuna and Uvea, with the differential growth of families and villages, may have produced internal struggles over land which would also result in changes in the hierarchy of titles. In Samoa, with a relative abundance of free land, the same results seem to have come about through peaceful expression of the ability of a larger family to produce and distribute a greater surplus than could a smaller family.

---

32. Burrows, Ethnology of Uvea, pp. 12-13.

10. Ramified and Descent-line Systems: Interpretation

RAMIFIED AND DESCENT-LINE SYSTEMS present a number of contrasts. The former, through the mechanism of primogeniture, is characterized by a seniority principle which pervades all unilineal groups and sometimes the entire society; the status of a given person is thus a function of his distance from the main line of descent in his kin group and community. The descent-line system also contains inherited statuses, but primogeniture is not necessarily the mechanism of inheritance. The ranking principle in descent-line systems is a traditional mythological order of precedence, an order having outward manifestations in kava ceremonies and other activities. [1] In descent lines, there is no over-all graded hierarchy of statuses as there is in ramages. In ramified societies, kinship units, ramages, are common-descent groups related to other similar groups in a larger ramage descendent from a common ancestor of further remove. Smaller groups are thus incorporated in larger groups headed by higher relatives, the whole structured as a genealogical tree. The paramount chief, the direct descendant of the gods, stands at the apex of the society. By contrast, in descent-line organizations, groups of relatives who trace common descent are often no larger than

---

1. Symbolization of status in kava ceremonials or other similar activities could have occurred, of course, in ramified systems, e. g. , the Tongan kava ceremonial and fono arrangements, or the seating arrangements on the ancestral marae of the Society Islands.

a moderate-sized, patrilocal extended family. These descent lines confer various titles, but the importance of the titles is not determined by the seniority of the line. The importance of the line is determined by the position of the title in the social hierarchy.

Both ramified and descent-line systems have territorial as well as kinship bases. Large-order ramages are usually localized in given territories. It is the ramage, however, that is the most important political administrative unit; the territorial bonds are subsidiary. In the descent-line systems, by contrast, political action is primarily along territorial lines--a correlate of the fragmentary nature of the kinship groupings. Along with emphasis on locality goes government by councils of representative heads of the descent lines. One of the titles in each council is always supreme, thus there are high chiefs. In ramified systems, the high chief controls regulatory functions; in certain instances he might consult informally with lesser chiefs, but this could be dispensed with.

These same differences between the ramified and descent-line systems are reflected in forms of economic and sociopolitical processes. In the land-tenure structure, for example, the ramified systems are associated with the pattern of overlapping stewardship, a pattern in which the supreme chief is the supreme manager of the society's resources, while the heads of ramage segments are subordinate stewards managing the lands of their ramages. In descent-line systems, the head of the descent line is steward of the descent line's holdings, but all such holdings are subordinated to the local council of titled chiefs. "Overlapping stewardship" can be extended to cover descent-line systems as well, but high-order stewardships are held by councils, not by individuals.

Similarly, in distributive activities, there are contrasts. In both cases, the distributive system is mainly of the redistributive form. But in ramified systems, the focal points of accumulation and redistribution are ramage heads. In descent-line systems, small-scale redistributive activities are undertaken by descent-line heads, but activities involving more than just a few descent lines are usually organized and undertaken by councils of titled men.

The organization of production, especially communal production, is also different in the two systems. In ramified

198

systems, communal production is organized along ramage lines and initiated by ramage chiefs or heads. Communal production in descent-line systems is organized on a territorial basis, usually the village, and is initiated and directed by the local council. Craft specialization, such as Samoan carpentry, is organized along lines of descent, just as in ramified systems. Crafts are associated with particular kinship groups in both cases. Such organizations have been called "guilds" by Polynesian ethnologists. [2] They differed from medieval European guilds in at least two significant ways. First, they were common descent groups. [3] Second, the "guild" was not a price-fixing organization since there were no prices and the economy was not of the market form. It is true that in certain cases, if it appeared that the workers would not be well fed or given ample reward for their services, no member of the "guild" would work further on the project. But this did not involve a failure to live up to a stipulated price for a stipulated service. [4]

In socioregulatory matters differences between ramified and descent-line organizations can also be seen. Political actions, such as the punishment of wrongdoers, are usually taken up by the fono in descent-line systems but by the individual chiefs in ramified systems. In decisions concerning peace and war, the chief usually initiates the project in ramified systems, albeit he consults with lesser chiefs in particular instances. In descent-line systems, however, war and peace are phrased as fono decisions.

In summary, the two systems, ramified and descent-line, differ significantly, not only in the nature of kinship structure and in the principles dictating the order of precedence

---

2. For a description of one so-called guild, see Peter H. Buck, Samoan Material Culture (Bernice Pahau Bishop Museum Bulletin, No. 75 [1930]), pp. 84 f.

3. Thus a proficient carpenter in Samoa who was not a member of the descent line of Tangaloa was adopted into it. Ibid., p. 84.

4. Turner wrote of the Samoan custom of pledging to work and to support, on the part of the craftsmen and "entrepreneurs" respectively, that "Nothing was stipulated as to the cost; that was left entirely to the honour of the employing party." George Turner, Samoa (London, 1884), pp. 157-58.

of status, but also in the processes of economic and social life. Two types of factors, broadly speaking, historical and adaptive, can be adduced to account for differences between ramified and descent-line organizations.

Historical Background

Ramified and descent-line systems may have historical bases. All societies having each type might have a distinct cultural source. The two forms, in other words, may have developed in separate centers and spread into particular, exclusive areas. Tracing the distinction in social organization to different sources, of course, does not fully explain this cultural variation. On the other hand, the possibility of distinct histories must be taken into account in order to assess the role of adaptive factors in an explanation of the differences.

For some time, ethnologists have differentiated two spheres of exclusive cultural influence in Polynesia, a western and a central-marginal, or eastern (see chapter 7). Regional variations in the distribution of aspects of material culture, kinship practices (not including ramified and descent-line systems), and mythology have led to the conclusion, primarily through the detailed comparisons of Edwin G. Burrows, that these two areas were, in fact, historically diverse--perhaps as a result of the dissemination of culture from two distinct centers.[5] This conclusion is corroborated by a recent linguistic analysis.[6] Among the island groups represented here, Samoa, Tonga, Futuna, Uvea, and Tikopia would be included in the western group, while Hawaii, the Societies, New Zealand, the Marquesas, Mangaia, Mangareva, and Easter Island would be eastern.

It does not seem unreasonable that the geographical dis-

5. Edwin G. Burrows, "Western Polynesia," Ethnologiska Studier, Vol. VII (1938); Edwin G. Burrows, "Culture Areas in Polynesia," Journal of the Polynesian Society, Vol. XLIX (1940); see also Peter H. Buck, Vikings of the Sunrise (Philadelphia, 1938).

6. Samuel H. Elbert, "Internal Relationships of Polynesian Languages and Dialects," Southwestern Journal of Anthropology, IX (1953), 147-73.

tribution of descent-line and ramified structures might correspond to the west-east historical dichotomy. There is some positive correlation. Futuna, Uvea, and Samoa are all western and all examples of descent-line systems, while all the eastern groups have ramified organizations. However, Tonga and Tikopia are both ramified and western. Furthermore, according to Elbert's classification of Polynesian languages, Tikopia, a ramified island, is linguistically closely related to Samoa, which has a descent-line system.[7] Also from linguistic evidence, Futuna and Uvea are more closely related to Tonga than to Samoa, all of which is not what it should be if the historical factor were the only factor.[8] Certainly, if a group came from an island with a particular type of social organization, it would tend to recreate that organization if it settled in an uninhabited area. But other elements beyond historical similarity or diversity are needed in any attempt to explain these variations in social system. Descent-line and ramified systems can also be understood as results of cultural adaptations to the natural environment--as adaptive variations. An explanation of organizational differences from this point of view may elucidate the problem.

Ramified and Descent-Line Systems as Adaptive Alternatives

Leaving aside, temporarily, the question of internal historical relationships, these Polynesian societies can be considered as members of a single culture type adapting to various local habitats. The two systems, the ramified and the descent-line, may represent differing adaptations related to variations in ecological conditions. In particular, the distribution of natural resources, i. e., of the zones of exploitation, may have been a factor prejudicing the development of ramified or descent-line systems.

Apparently, the crucial difference between ramified and

---

7. Ibid., p. 164. Firth, however, records traditions of Tongan contacts in Tikopia. See Raymond Firth, We, the Tikopia (London, 1936).

8. Elbert, "Internal Relationships of Polynesian Languages and Dialects," pp. 163-64.

descent-line systems is whether or not kinship relationship is maintained between households or patrilocal extended families which have segmented because of increase in size. In both organizations, large groups of this nature divide, which gives rise to two distinct alignments of patrilineal kin. In ramified organizations, the split usually takes place between the families of two brothers. The relationship between the households is maintained, and the two households are ranked according to the seniority of the brothers. In descent line systems, the connection between segmented families may be remembered for a time, but gradually the tie weakens and dissolves, and two discrete groups are formed. Practically all other differences in the two systems are related to this difference in the segmentation process. In economic matters in ramified systems, such as land tenure and redistributive activities, the divided households also remain interconnected; the senior household head exercises supreme stewardship and is the focal point in cooperative accumulations and distributions. Similarly, productive activities involving the labor of the two households would be led by the head of the senior household. By extension of the same principles, such productive and distributive activities might encompass any number of related households, an entire ramage of large size, no matter where its diverse branches were located. In descent-line systems with discrete groupings, the head of each group exercised such regulatory economic functions, but if distribution or production involved many groups or descent lines, the heads of all met in council.

The maintenance of kinship ties between two groups derived from a common group seems to be an adaptation to economic necessities of cooperation. In particular, it may be postulated that ties will be maintained between two branching households if there is a tendency for such households to become specialized or semispecialized in production of surplus goods. Thus, if one household produces a surplus of fish--or might be able on some specified occasion to produce such surplus--while another, because of its inland situation, could more easily produce a surplus of a cultivated food, some advantage would certainly be served if these households could maintain their kinship bonds. By means of redistributive activities in which one household acts as a focal point of accumulation and redistribution, or by means of direct exchange, such inequalities or potential inequalities in consumables might be remedied; the surplus production of different foods or goods might be equitably distributed.

It may be further postulated, therefore, that if a budded-off household tends to move into or gain access to a resource area which could be efficiently exploited to produce strategic surpluses different from those produced by the original group, there would be a tendency for ramified organization to develop. The ramified system is adapted to the exploitation of different, widely spread resource areas, which adaptation on an economic level is manifest in sporadic, seasonal, or total specialization of familial production. On the other hand, if in the process of fission, the household or family which buds off tends to move into an area identical to that of the parent group as regards the type of strategic goods producible, the kinship tie between the two groups might weaken and dissolve. Descent-line systems are thus adapted to exploitation of similar resources by the different lines. If families are inhabiting a common resource area, then any surplus which is produced by one would be more or less contemporaneously produced by all. Any variations in the amounts of familial surplus might be equalized by a community distribution involving all the families of a locale, and a territorial distributive network would be advantageous.

If these deductions be correct, empirical evidence, (other factors being constant) should show ramified systems in islands in which there is a variety of scattered resource zones differentially exploited by families or small groups of families. Or, inversely, ramified systems would be expectable on those islands where a single patrilocal extended family could not efficiently exploit the total range of available resources on a high level. However, where resource areas are clustered in time and space so that a single familial group could cope adequately with the total range of available exploitative techniques, descent-line systems would be most frequently found. As a further corollary, we should expect to find ramified systems most often in association with a scattered, hamlet type of settlement pattern, while descent-line systems might frequently be found with a nucleated, village type of settlement arrangement. The data on the ecology of the ramified and descent-line systems may now be reviewed in test of these expectations. (Much information on the distribution of resource areas is contained in the productivity data in the appendix, hence the following descriptions are relatively brief and of a summary nature.)

Tonga (ramified). --The greatest part of the information regarding Tongan settlement pattern and resource conditions concerns the principal island, Tongatabu, a raised coral island. The grouping together of houses into villages in Tonga is a modern phenomenon; in aboriginal times, the settlement pattern was of a scattered, hamlet type.[9] The soil of raised coral islands, such as Tongatabu, was fertile on any part of the island and was fully exploited. As the range of crops was great, it does not seem likely that a single family produced, or could produce, all.[10] Furthermore, since all of the large island of Tongatabu, for example, was inhabited, families living inland had little or no access to sea resources.[11] A familial group of this type exchanged inland products for sea food with certain trading partners called tofia brothers, who were members of their own large-order ramage living near the sea.[12] The ramified system in Tonga was associated with familial specialization of production and scattered settlement.

Marquesas (ramified). --There was a widely scattered distribution of resources in the Marquesas (see Appendix, VIII). Breadfruit, the main crop, seems to have been grown at altitudes up to 1000 feet and was seasonally harvested. Taro, however, was grown and harvested continuously, primarily near streams, and as these were often intermittent in their lower reaches, it was probably often grown in upland regions. Other crops, such as sugar cane, were mostly grown in the lower vegetation zone, while fishing, of course, was carried out on the shore. There were no villages. The settlement pattern was one of small clusters of houses scattered about the valley floors.[13]

---

9. Edward Winslow Gifford, Tongan Society (Bernice Pahau Bishop Museum Bulletin, No. 61 [1929]), pp. 6 f.

10. James Cook, A Voyage to the Pacific Ocean . . . in the Years 1776, 1777, 1778, 1779, and 1780 (London, 1784), I, passim.

11. Tongatabu is 99.2 square miles.

12. Gifford, Tongan Society, pp. 146, 177.

13. E. S. Craighill Handy, The Native Culture in the

There is mention of a class of so-called professional fishermen in the Marquesan literature. Perhaps this refers to an organization of deep-sea fishermen which functioned periodically to provide for general distributions under the chief's direction. [14] Anyone could fish when he wanted to. [15] Undoubtedly, those living near the shore fished most frequently and exchanged their surplus for inland foods. Handy mentions that small fishing parties (of household strength?) might "barter" their surplus for inland products such as breadfruit. [16]

Mangaia (ramified). --Definite scattered zones of exploitation existed on Mangaia despite the relatively small size of the island (about twenty-eight square miles). The rich puna lands on the interior border of the raised reef (makatea) were used for cultivating wet taro. Each region was known for its particular type of taro. [17] The upland valleys grew sweet potato, some dry taro, ti, and uncultivated pandanus; Morinda citrifolia and Tahitian chestnut were also found there. Pockets of soil on the makatea were used for sweet potato, arrowroot, and wild-growing candlenut. The sea, with its fringing and barrier reef, formed still another frequently exploitable area (see Appendix VII). With the scattering of resource zones, it is likely that there was semi-specialization of production by small groups.

Gill reported that the people of his time lived in vil-

Marquesas (Bernice Pahau Bishop Museum Bulletin, No. 9 [1923]), pp. 9, 42. Melville writes of the Tapai Valley: "The valley is some nine miles in length, and may average one in breadth, the houses being distributed at wide intervals throughout its whole extent, principally, however, toward the head of the vale. There are no villages." See Herman Melville, Typee (New York, 1931), pp. 260-61.

14. Handy, The Native Culture in the Marquesas, passim; see also Ralph Linton, "Marquesan Culture," in Ralph Linton and A. Kardiner, The Individual and His Society (New York, 1939); and Melville, Typee, p. 233.

15. The Native Culture in the Marquesas, p. 173.

16. Ibid., p. 168.

17. William Wyatt Gill, From Darkness to Light in Polynesia (London, 1894), p. 113.

lages.[18] However, Buck points out that, although during peace there was some concentration of people along stream banks in the puna lands, "In no district were the dwellings grouped together to form villages."[19] Baessler reported that village settlements were a product of missionary influence, previous to which houses were scattered throughout the island.[20]

Society Islands (ramified).--Most of the information comes from Tahiti although on other islands environmental conditions and exploitative techniques were substantially the same. A wide range of crops was present; they were utilized in a variety of environments. The maritime flats, one to four miles wide, were cultivated extensively with lowland banana, breadfruit, taro, and subsidiary crops. Mountain banana grew in various upland-valley recesses. There were upland irrigation terraces for taro near mountain streams, and yams also were grown in high locales. The lagoon, the reef areas, fresh-water lakes, and rivers were all utilized for fish and other forms of water life, while various wild plants growing in a number of different zones were utilized. The range and spread of resource zones on these large islands were undoubtedly beyond the exploitative capabilities of a small ramage (see Appendix, II). A segment of the population, living near the sea, concentrated on fishing and exchanged surpluses for inland products.[21] Smith stated that the small islets of Tethuroa, twenty-four miles from Tahiti, were occupied by 3,000 people who were "principally employed in fishing for the chiefs of Otaheite, and bring back breadfruit and other things in exchange."[22]

18. William Wyatt Gill, Life in the Southern Isles (London, 1876), p. 8 and passim.

19. Peter H. Buck, Mangaian Society (Bernice Pahau Bishop Museum Bulletin, No. 122 [1934]), p. 135.

20. Cited by Robert W. Williamson, The Social and Political Systems of Central Polynesia (Cambridge, Eng., 1924), I, 263.

21. E. S. Craighill Handy, Houses, Boats, and Fishing in the Society Islands (Bernice Pahau Bishop Museum Bulletin, No. 90 [1932]), pp. 69-70; William E. Ellis, Polynesian Researches (2nd ed.; London, 1853), I, 138.

22. William Smith, Journal of a Voyage in the Missionary

Besides the spatial variation in resource zones, there was also a temporal factor. Breadfruit and fish were most abundant in the rainy season, while taro (fei), sweet potato, and other inland foods were abundant in the drier months. Some of the arii group moved from sea to interior in the latter period, but the majority of the population remained as situated despite the seasonal variation.[23] According to Smith, the fact that the trade winds blow from the south, ". . . occasions a great difference in the breadfruit season, between the north and south sides of the island . . . the breadfruit harvest commences on the north side about November, and continues till the end of January; whilst on the south side, in some parts it begins in January, and continues in different districts till November."[24]

The settlement pattern was not of the village type. Ellis reports about the former inhabitants:"In the bottom of every valley, even to the recesses in the mountains, on the sides of the inferior hills, and on the brows of almost every promontory, in each of the islands, monuments of former generations are still met with in great abundance."[25]

Hawaii (ramified). --A tremendous variety of widely scattered environmental zones on Hawaii were exploited for different foods. Soil, altitude, rainfall, and water variations made for a multitude of ecological niches, for the utilization of which the Hawaiian selected from an impressive crop list[26] (see Appendix, I). Valley bottoms and sides, streams, stream borders, the sea, various altitude levels, types of

Ship Duff to the Pacific Ocean in the Years 1796, 7, 8, 9, 1800, 1, 2, etc. (New York, 1813), p. 32.

23. Handy, Houses, Boats, and Fishing in the Society Islands, p. 79.

24. Smith, Journal of a Voyage in the Missionary Ship Duff to the Pacific Ocean in the Years 1796, 7, 8, 9, 1800, 1, 2, etc., p. 37. Some few kinds of breadfruit were present to a limited degree all year round in many areas.

25. Ellis, Polynesian Researches, I, 163.

26. Compare E. S. Craighill Handy, The Hawaiian Planter (Bernice Pahau Bishop Museum Bulletin, No. 161 [1940); see also E. S. Craighill Handy and M. Pukui, "The Hawaiian Family System," Journal of the Polynesian Society, LIX (1950), 173.

soil, and vegetation covers were utilized for different purposes. The range of exploitable areas and techniques in any
given season or throughout the year was well beyond the productive capabilities of any given household. Specialization in
certain types of food production existed on the household level.[27]

An excellent example of familial specialization of production is provided by a fairly large-size ramage, the ohana,
described by Handy and Pukui.[28] The ramage as a whole exploited a triangular section of land stretching from the sea-
shore far back into the mountains. The ohana was composed
of a number of households, some living inland and exploiting
areas suitable for certain crops, and some living close to
the sea, growing other crops and fishing. A constant sharing
and exchange of diverse foods and other goods and services
took place between these productively specialized households. The exchanges took two forms: (1) reciprocal gift giving, and (2) redistributions in the form of feasts supervised
by the senior member of the entire ohana.[29]

The Hawaiian settlement pattern was one of small clusters
of huts spread about the islands, both in the interior and
near the shore, "wherever a living could be secured."[30]
There was "no development of village or town communities."[31]

Mangareva (ramified). --The major resource areas in
Mangareva were the sea and the flat lands of the valley bottoms. Crops were grown in a number of scattered locations:
breadfruit in various parts of the lower levels; taro in lowland swamps and in irrigated terraces far up the valleys.
The shore, lagoon, and outer reef were particularly rich
areas of exploitation (see Appendix, IV). Specialization in pro-

27. Handy, The Hawaiian Planter, pp. 163-64 and passim, especially maps of resource areas.

28. Handy and Pukui, "The Hawaiian Family System."

29. Compare Peter H. Buck, Arts and Crafts of the Cook
Islands (Bernice Pahau Bishop Museum Bulletin, No. 179
[1944]), p. 517, who also provides a description of the economy
of an ohana.

30. Handy and Pukui, "The Hawaiian Family System,"
p. 180.

31. Ibid., p. 173.

duction occurred among those living on the shore and those living inland, and fish were exchanged for inland products, especially breadfruit, the production of which was limited in area because of soil conditions. Unfortunately, the literature does not specify whether or not this "trading" went on between members of the same ramage.

Most settlements were scattered clusters of huts near the shores and in the valleys, although there were house sites also on hill slopes, near upland water seepages, and even on the summit of Mount Duff. [32]

Tikopia (ramified). --Although present to some extent, the amount of resource diversity and the degree of familial specialization in subsistence production appear to have been smaller on Tikopia than on the islands just described. Firth notes that with few exceptions "the major food plants are found fairly well spread over the island."[33] The exceptions are coconuts, sago, and pulaka (allied to taro) which grow better on the lower reaches of the island than on the higher slopes. Taro, the staple, although widely distributed, seems to have been most grown in favored areas such as Rakisu on the plain in the southwest. [34] But slight differences in resource zones such as these are mitigated by the fact that Tikopia is a very small island, only about three square miles in area. It would seem unlikely, with all lands relatively accessible from the coastally located settlements, that here was a great deal of familial specialization of production.

Nonetheless, some production differences appear. There were wide individual variations in the degree to which the men participated in fishing, and industrious cultivators planted about twice as much taro as other men. [35] Perhaps this last is to be linked to the prevailing tendency for familial orchards to be correlated with residence. Although the land holdings of a household might have been quite scattered, "Those [plots] in a remote district are often left for relatives to work, so that in a generation or two they are apt to

---

32. Peter H. Buck, Ethnology of Mangareva (Bernice Pahau Bishop Museum Bulletin, No. 157 [1938]), pp. 11, 36, 166, 199.

33. Raymond Firth, Primitive Polynesian Economy (New York, 1950), p. 64.

34. Firth, We, the Tikopia, p. 375.

35. Firth, Primitive Polynesian Economy, pp. 63, 67.

pass from one branch of a house [i. e. , a paito, a multihouse-hold ramage] to another. "[36] With a degree of regional diversity (as has been just noted), one might infer a slight specialization of production from such localization of land use. Moreover, there was quite a bit of food exchange, on a reciprocal basis, between districts of the island: "Scarcely a day passes without baskets of food being carried from one village to another or across the island in payment of some obligation. "[37]

Careful consideration of the evidence leads to the conclusion that the selective factors postulated as determinants of the differentiation of ramage from descent-line systems--regional diversity of resources and familial specialization or semispecialization in production--were present but were not as pronounced on Tikopia as on the islands previously described.

With regard to the pattern of settlement, nearly all the population was concentrated on the coast, especially where canoe landings were easily made, and where the fringing reef offered the best fishing possibilities. Aboriginally, there were a few scattered houses inland. At the time of Firth's study, there were twenty-five groupings of houses dispersed along the coasts, among which the population of about 1300 was divided. Firth calls these groupings, "villages"; they might be better described as hamlets of about fifty people each. The hamlets contained people of a number of different ramages, but usually members of a single "clan" (maximal ramage) predominated in each. [38]

New Zealand (ramified). --Each "tribe" had one predominant and several subsidiary subsistence modes from among the following: agriculture, fishing, and forest hunting and collecting. Each mode embraced a variety of activities, thus predominantly agricultural tribes could grow taro, sweet potatoes, and ti. [39] Consequently, a fair range of exploitative activities was undertaken by any one tribe. The Tuhoe, for

---

36. Firth, We, the Tikopia, p. 389.
37. Raymond Firth, "Report on Research in Tikopia, " Oceania, I (1930-31), 109.
38. Firth, We, the Tikopia, pp. 65 f.
39. Eldson Best, Maori Agriculture (Dominion Museum Bulletin, Vol. IX [1925]).

example, a forest tribe, lived on rats, birds, ferns, berries, bulrush and other roots, fresh-water fish, and a number of collected fruits. [40] As many productive activities might go on concurrently, a given household group (whanau), which was the major production unit, probably did not exploit the complete range of foods. [41] Such tasks as bird snaring could be undertaken for long periods of time by small groups of the hapu, a surplus being taken and preserved. [42]

Despite this more or less rudimentary familial specialization, the Maori were concentrated in villages much of the year. The villages were composed of a single large ramage, the hapu. The individual household, however, might move out to the forest, sea, or garden land during the proper food-getting seasons. [43] The village pattern seems related to defensive needs. At the same time, the village pattern was also consistent with exploitation of a number of different resource areas found in every direction from a habitable area. New Zealand has more of a continental than an island topography. Unlike smaller Polynesian islands, exploitable zones, if scattered, would not be distributed in concentric zones running from the sea inland to a mountain, but might be scattered in all directions from a given habitation point.

Easter Island (ramified).--The distribution of resource areas in Easter Island evidently was less scattered than in most other islands with ramified systems (see Appendix V). The majority of the evidence indicates that agricultural pos-

40. Eldson Best, "Food Products of Tuhoeland," New Zealand Institute Transactions, XXXV (1902), 45-111.
41. A work calendar compiled by Firth shows that many activities could have gone on in the same month, undoubtedly within the same tribe since more than one mode of subsistence was relied upon. Raymond Firth, Primitive Economics of the New Zealand Maori (New York, 1929), pp. 57-60.
42. Ibid., pp. 149 f. Such a situation is also implied by Firth when he states: "A man who is skilled in the snaring of birds . . . may devote himself largely to this work [for that part of the year when birds can be snared]." Ibid., p. 207.
43. Ibid., pp. 78, 108-09; see also Eldson Best, Forest Lore of the Maori (Dominion Museum Bulletin, No. 14, and Polynesian Society Memoir, No. 19) (Wellington, N.Z., 1942), pp. 68 and passim.

sibilities, and settlements as well, were concentrated along the coast, and that the range of crops was not particularly great. Rain rapidly leaches through the soils in the interior, sharply limiting agricultural possibilities there. Lack of water in the interior also influenced the settlement pattern. Métraux gives the impression that the interior of the island was only very sparsely inhabited and cultivated. [44] Routledge reports: "The lower portions of the island [this would include a great deal of the interior which is a low rocky plain] were the most densely populated parts, especially those on the coast, and the settlements on the higher ground appear to have been few."[45] However, Routledge also writes: "The old man [i.e., an informant] . . . was brought out to Raraka [about a mile inland from the coast], roved around the mountain telling with excitement who occupied the different houses in the days of his youth."[46] A definite indication of familial specialization is given by Routledge: "Fish are not very plentiful, as there is no barrier reef, but they were an article of diet, and were bartered by those on the coast for the vegetable products obtained by those further inland."[47]

The actual settlement pattern is difficult to establish. Métraux continually mentions villages in his report.[48] From descriptions of travelers, cited by Métraux, the "villages" apparently were many and consisted of small clumps of houses--a situation perhaps parallel to Tikopia.

Futuna (descent-line).--Cultivation of Futuna proper was confined to the narrow shore strip and the tips of the adjoining ridges.[49] The red, dense acidic soil of the interior does

44. Alfred Métraux, Ethnology of Easter Island (Bernice Pahau Bishop Museum Bulletin, No. 160 [1940]), pp. 124, 151, and passim.
45. Mrs. Scoresby Routledge, The Mystery of Easter Island (London, 1919), p. 221.
46. Ibid., p. 216; see also William J. Thomson, "Te Pito Te Henua, or Easter Island," United States National Museum, Annual Report (1889), p. 457.
47. Routledge, The Mystery of Easter Island, p. 218.
48. Métraux, Ethnology of Easter Island.
49. Scattered holdings on interior Alofi were held by Futunan residents, an arrangement that only dates back to the early nineteenth century. See Edwin G. Burrows, "Topography

not hold moisture and is not suitable for cultivation with aboriginal techniques. Thus, all the resource zones, (including the sea) were confined to the immediate vicinity of the
shore (see Appendix IX). These zones were arranged in narrow concentric bands so that familial lands, running in parallel strips from the shore inward, encompassed the entire
range of exploitative possibilities. [50] Familial specialization
of strategic production was apparently nil. Fission of households was in the form of lateral expansion, and no new resource areas were likely to be encountered by newly created
segments.

All permanent dwellings on Futuna were on the narrow
shore strip, most within fifty yards of the shore, a concentration understandable in terms of the areas of exploitation.
Each valley mouth furnished some land for irrigated taro
flats, consequently settlements were in the nature of villages
at the valley mouths. On Alofi, there is some evidence of
more scattered habitation in earlier times. [51]

Samoa (descent-line). --The area around the coast af-
forded the best horticultural as well as fishing activities.
The hillsides slope more moderately there, and swamps
suitable for taro cultivation are formed between the back of
the beach and the interior hills. Furthermore, larger
streams, flowing to the sea, form wide arable valleys at
their mouths. In most places within one to two miles inland
the mountains become too steep and high, and the soil too
thin, for large-scale production. Without the possibility of
producing surpluses for exchange with coastal groups, inland areas were usually not feasible for habitation (see Appendix, III). [52] The plight of a village on Tutuila which has

---

and Culture on Two Polynesian Islands," Geographical Review, XXVIII (1938), 220.

50. Four zones of exploitation, aside from the sea, can be
demarcated in each family plot: a shore zone in which coconut predominated; a zone of breadfruit, banana, and arrowroot; a zone of taro patches, and the slopes of the adjoining
bluffs on which yams, dry-land taro, and bananas were
raised. Edwin G. Burrows, Ethnology of Futuna (Bernice
Pahau Bishop Museum Bulletin, No. 138 [1936]), p. 81.

51. Ibid., pp. 9-10.

52. John Wesley Coulter, Land Utilization in American

used up all good taro land in the vicinity of the coast has already been noted. The taro plots are now about two miles inland, but because of the difficulty of cultivation due to the steep slope (and possibly the long walk), these plots are only 0.1 acre in area.[53]

Familial specialization was rudimentary. Mead reports that each household was a self-sufficient economic unit.[54] Coulter writes that the members of a family in a village owned and worked five to ten plantations from one-twentieth acre to three or four acres in area situated in scattered locales, usually in the near vicinity of the village.[55] Specialization of production occurred, but by villages, not families. Sometimes, although rarely, there were inland villages that exchanged local produce with shore villages.[56] It may be precisely because villages dispersed into new resource areas that the connection between a sa in two different villages was maintained, while within the village, and within the same resource area, it was forgotten.

The settlement pattern was one of nucleated villages, almost always on the coast.[57] Keesing notes that the village pattern was prevalent from the beginning of Samoan history.[58] In Manua, according to tradition, villages were once further inland, about as far from sea as present villages are from taro plantations. Now they are on the shore.[59] Such a difference would, of course, not be significant from the point of view of familial self-sufficiency, as access to all productive zones is maintained in either case.

Uvea (descent-line). --The coastal area, with its abun-

Samoa (Bernice Pahau Bishop Museum Bulletin, No. 170 [1941]).

53. Ibid., p. 27.

54. Margaret Mead, The Social Organization of Manua (Bernice Pahau Bishop Museum Bulletin, No. 76 [1930]), p. 70.

55. Coulter, Land Utilization in American Samoa, pp. 17-18.

56. Turner, Samoa, p. 16.

57. Felix M. Keesing, Modern Samoa (London, 1934), pp. 15, 20, and passim; see also Augustin Krämer, Die Samoa-Inseln (Stuttgart, 1902), passim.

58. Keesing, Modern Samoa, p. 15.

59. Mead, The Social Organization of Manua, p. 45; see

dant fish supply and its streamlets (at the base of the bluff on the inland side of the shore strip), was a rather rich area. But unlike Samoa and Futuna, Uvea was arable in much of the interior. Yam, a staple cultivated food, for example, only grew in the interior. Plantations now and in aboriginal times penetrated a few miles inland (see Appendix, VI). Each family held a number of "patches widely scattered about the island."[60] It is difficult to establish the presence or absence of familial specialization. The diversity of resource areas seems to argue for specialization. On the other hand, the relatively limited crop range and the widely scattered nature of a household's gardens argue against specialization.

Information on settlements is again noncommittal. The present pattern of settlement is seaside villages, and Burrows feels "confident that seaside villages, mainly in the present locations, antedate European contact."[61] On the other hand, there is evidence of pre-European "habitations and forts in many parts of the interior. House platforms are common in the central bush, and Henquel's history relates events in many places far from the sea."[62]

Summary and Interpretations

There is evidence that shows that the differences between ramified and descent-line systems are related, to some extent, to diverse historical traditions. But because some islands with common histories manifest different forms of organization, it was suggested that the forms might also be considered from an adaptational point of view--that they are, perhaps, associated with particular types of exploitative techniques operating in different environmental situations. It was reasoned that connection between segmented households would tend to be maintained if, in the process of seg-

also Erich Schultz-Ewerth, "Samoa," Das Eingeborenenrecht, II (Stuttgart, 1929-30), 707.

60. Burrows, "Topography and Culture on Two Polynesian Islands," p. 217.

61. Edwin G. Burrows, personal communication.

62. Edwin G. Burrows, Ethnology of Uvea (Bernice Pahau Bishop Museum Bulletin, No. 145 [1937]), p. 12.

mentation, the new household was apt to move into a new resource area and thus specialize in a particular type of strategic production. Maintenance of ties would result in the
growth of interconnected ramages and a hierarchy for purposes of effecting equitable distribution of goods, by both reciprocal and redistributive methods. If, on the other hand,
a new household moved into an area identical in exploitable
opportunities to that in which the parent household was situated, connection between the two would weaken and dissolve
and descent-line systems result. As a corollary, descent-
line systems could be expected to be associated with concentrated or village settlement patterns and ramified systems
with scattered settlements.

In most of the societies examined, this postulated relationship was found to hold. It is apparent, however, that there
was a great deal of variability in the selective factors, i.e.,
regional diversity of resources, which were posited to effect
the differentiation of ramage and descent-line systems. The
ultimate test of the hypothesis, one for which data and techniques are unfortunately lacking, would be to analyze each
case in terms of its history and the particular intensity of
selective pressures present. Without this test, one cannot
assert that the hypothesis has been conclusively demonstrated. Tikopia, Easter Island, and Uvea, for example,
are crucial cases in that they are exceptions or near exceptions to the general hypothesis. In these instances, the technoenvironmental conditions seem uncommitted as far as prohibiting or promoting familial specialization is concerned.
Little selective pressure in favor of either ramage or descent-line systems is apparent. In the case of Easter Island,
it would seem that its historical alignment with eastern Polynesia, where ramage systems predominate, would favor the
formation of a ramified organization under conditions of selective indifference. The same explanation might be relevant for Tikopia, but the historical derivation of Tikopian
culture is not clear. In Uvea, this interpretation is evidently insufficient, as Uvea, a descent-line society, was apparently settled from Tonga, a ramified society.[63] Existing evidence seems to offer no explanation of the Uvean exception.

_____

63. Ibid., p. 18; see also Elbert, "Internal Relationships
of Polynesian Languages and Dialects," pp. 163-64.

Inexplicable exceptions to the hypothesis such as these indicate that its probability is lower than 100 per cent. It is hoped that further research in Polynesia will help to explain the exceptions, or will allow a modification of the hypothesis so that it will better account for the differentiation of ramage and descent-line systems.

A speculation that might arise from the presence of ramage elements in all descent-line systems is that they diverged and developed from ramage organizations. Proto-Polynesian culture may have been ramage-organized. Another interpretation, suggested by the recent studies of Professor Murdock and Professor Goodenough, is that both ramage and descent-line systems developed from a common ancestor, a nonunilinear descent group, under the selective conditions outlined in this chapter. [64]

_____

64. George P. Murdock, Social Structure (New York, 1949), pp. 228-31, 349-50; see also Ward H. Goodenough, "A Problem in Malayo-Polynesian Social Organization," American Anthropologist, LVII (1955), 71-83. Goodenough's article appeared after this manuscript had been completed; hence, a full discussion of his stimulating hypothesis could not be undertaken here.

11. Social Organization and Stratification on Polynesian Atolls

THE SOCIAL ORGANIZATIONS of the Polynesian atolls show a marked degree of variability, both among themselves and by comparison with the descent-line and ramified systems of the high islands. Completely different selective factors are to be encountered on low islands. In contrast to volcanic groups, adaptive differentiation in social structure on atolls cannot be attributed, for example, to problems engendered by surplus distribution. The low islands are distinct from the volcanic islands in having low productivity, small and sporadic surpluses, frequent famines, high population densities in small areas, and certain peculiarities of resource distribution. Social forms in the atolls should be considered in light of these factors. Also significant is the fact that most of the atolls have been settled in the relatively recent past from high Polynesian islands. Some elements of ramage and descent-line systems can, therefore, be expected in the atolls, and variations in place of origin, degree of isolation, and length of time of occupation probably contribute to social differences in the low islands.

Five atoll cultures are examined in detail in this section: Manihiki-Rakahanga, Tongareva, Tokelau, Ontong Java, and Pukapuka. They are first described roughly in the order in which they diverge in social type from high islands, and then an attempt is made to understand the adaptive characteristics of their social organizations.

Examples of Atoll Organization

Tongareva. --The social organization of Tongareva was of

the typical ramage type. The diagnostic characteristics of ramified societies, primogeniture, an over-all seniority system with a subtle gradation in status, an emphasis on ceremonial observances in the life of the first-born, and overlapping stewardship corresponding to a system of interconnected ramages, were all present in Tongareva. There were three major lines, from one of which (or all three through intermarriages) each individual traced his descent. The existence of three lines rather than a single one is related to the political fragmentation (see below) of the atoll.[1] The major ramages were the household and the "tribe." The household group consisted of a patrilocal extended family, including up to three or four generations of patrilineally related relatives. As with all other Polynesian groups, bilateral cousin exogamy was the rule. In this case, third cousins were permissible spouses, second and first cousins were not. The first sons often established new households if many children were born in a single family, so that headship of an original household might pass to a younger son. However, the social position of the father, and his rule, if any, over a number of households passed to the eldest son.

A number of households tracing descent from a common ancestor were united in a larger group, a "tribe." According to Buck, ancestral kinship connections within the three major lines of descent were "relegated to the background"; instead, the tribes, tracing descent to more recent ancestors, formed independent groups inhabiting particular islands or sections of one of the larger islands.[2] Each tribe had a name, in an early period that of the common ancestor, although, according to Buck, these were later changed to territorial names referring to the islets in which the tribes were localized.[3] Moss estimated eight tribes, which, with Buck's estimate of the precontact population at about 2,000, makes an average of 250 people per tribe.[4] The senior fam-

---

1. It may also be related to economic differentiation of groups, but unfortunately data on distributive activities, especially large-scale ones, have not been preserved.
2. Peter H. Buck, Ethnology of Tongareva (Bernice Pahau Bishop Museum Bulletin, No. 92 [1932]), pp. 26, 45.
3. Ibid., p. 31.
4. Ibid., p. 9; see also Robert W. Williamson, The Social

ily of each such group supplied, by primogenitural succession, the tribal high chief (ariki). As each tribal group represented a segment which had budded off from one of the major lines, the tribal chiefs were ranked on the basis of seniority. This ranking was of importance in determining the leadership among tribes allied for military purposes. [5] The organization of regulatory functions was based on the ramified framework of the tribe; the chief was the tribal leader, and the household heads comprised an informal discussion group consulted by him.

The two status levels crystallized out of the genealogical system. The tribal chiefs, ariki, and their households constituted an upper status level. The rest of the populace, related to the chiefs, formed a second level. [6]

Manihiki-Rakahanga. --Manihiki and Rakahangan culture can also be classified with the ramified systems. Succession to status was through primogeniture, and the differentiation between senior and junior lines pervaded the entire group. Any person's status was proportional to the closeness of his relationship to the main lines of descent in the society. [7] Knowledge of the over-all genealogical record was poorly preserved by most people, a feature which Buck attributes to the supposed original settlement of the atolls by members of a single biological family, headed by a defeated warrior, whose immigration was unaccompanied by priests.

---

and Political Systems of Central Polynesia (Cambridge, Eng. , 1924), III, 383.

5. Buck feels that the term ariki was properly applied only to the senior chiefs of two of the three main lines and that its appropriation by other chiefs was somehow illegitimate. Legitimate or not, it was certainly in use by the tribal chiefs. Buck, Ethnology of Tongareva, p. 50. See also E. H. Lamont, Wild Life among the Pacific Islanders (London, 1867).

6. Also consult S. Percy Smith, "Tongarewa, or Penrhyn Island, and Its People," New Zealand Institute Transactions, XXII (1889), 85-103.

7. "Seniority was all-important in the old social structure in deciding rank and title and relative degrees of influence in family and community gatherings." Peter H. Buck, Ethnology of Manihiki and Rakahanga (Bernice Pahau Bishop Museum Bulletin, No. 99 [1932]), p. 32

The result was that, although the people knew the story of settlement, "only a few could trace a connected line from Toa [that is, the original settler] to themselves. Most could trace pedigrees to ancestors through six to twelve generations but could not connect them with the main lines."[8] However, a skilled native genealogist could demonstrate the interrelatedness of all families.

The household group, a patrilocal extended family in many cases, was the fundamental ramage. It was headed by the male senior in descent. Younger sons often moved into their wives' households. The numerical strength of the household group is not available, although on comparative evidence, it probably did not exceed ten or twelve people on the average.

An understanding of higher-order ramages is gained from an exposition of the history of Manihiki-Rakahangan organization as reconstructed by Buck from the native traditions and modern organization.[9] Traditions trace the colonization of Manihiki and Rakahanga to a single biological family. Buck considers Manihiki-Rakahanga organization to have developed from this family into a number of ramage segments. The first division was between the families of two brothers, although the groups remained in a unified polity. In the eleventh generation after settlement, the two lines diverged because of a quarrel, and two ariki (high chief) titles were established. The two lines then each divided into two sublines, "tribes," the junior ones being led by the younger brothers of the arikis; thus, at the time of contact, there were two supratribal groupings of two tribes each.

The major segments of the ramage structure were then the supertribal groups, each led by an ariki with a title, and each composed of descendants of a common ancestor. Each supertribal group was divided into two tribes. The tribes were headed by chiefs, senior members of the senior line in each. Tribal chiefs of junior tribes were called whaka-manu. As the largest recorded population of the two atolls totals less than 900 persons, the tribes probably did not exceed 250 on the average.[10] The tribes were known as mata-

---

8. Ibid., p. 21.
9. Ibid., pp. 43 f.
10. Ibid., p. 11. A 1906 census showed a total of 873 per-

keinanga; they also had names which may have been the names of their respective common ancestors. The tribes were split into smaller ramages, tukuwhare, composed of a number of households tracing common descent. Such "subtribes" usually traced descent to brothers, often those of the first ariki of the supertribal groups. The tukuwhare contained between thirty and fifty persons.

Most of the duties of the two arikis were priestly; they hardly interfered in secular matters, which were carried out by the papa, executives attached to the ariki, and by the tribal chiefs and subchiefs. The papa, tribal, and subtribal chiefs formed the hui rangatira, the assembly of chiefs, which acted as a consulting group to the ariki. This group of chiefs and their households were a separate status level from the remainder of the population.

Tokelau. --Tokelau is difficult to classify with either descent-line or ramified systems. Unfortunately, many elements of the social organization are still obscure to us even after careful study of the ethnography. Contradictions appear in the literature, especially in MacGregor's ethnographic study. [11]

The smallest social unit was the household. Households were located in villages; there was one village on each of the three Tokelauan atolls, Fakaofu, Atafu, and Nukunono (and formerly also on Olosenga, now uninhabited). MacGregor writes of the household as composed basically of a nuclear family with the addition of maternal and paternal relatives. Its affairs were directed, "by the senior mother and her husband. "[12] The group apparently had no name.

A group tracing patrilineal descent to a common ancestor, the "kindred," was, according to MacGregor, the most significant kinship unit. It evidently included a number of households. Unfortunately, the exact composition of this group as well as that of the household is difficult to determine. [13] It

sons for the two atolls. At that time, each atoll was separately inhabited. Previously, one or the other atoll was inhabited at a time, the population shifting with the food supply.

11. Gordon MacGregor, Ethnology of the Tokelau Islands (Bernice Pahau Bishop Museum Bulletin, No. 146 [1937]).

12. Ibid. , p. 45.

13. Goodenough analyzed Tokelauan organization as com-

is also difficult to understand the determinants of succession to headship. Both of these problems are bound up with the customs of residence after marriage and with patterns of inheritance and control over kindred lands, but precisely in these matters contradictions appear in MacGregor's report. Residence after marriage, or after the birth of the first child, seems to have been patrilocal in the case of the eldest son and daughter, but with a bilocal option (depending on availability of land) for younger sons and daughters. The direction over the kindred lands, according to MacGregor, usually went to the eldest son, a ramified practice. This position of stewardship should correspond to the position of headship over the kindred. [14] But primogeniture does not seem to have been the succession rule either to headship of the kindred or to any title of office. MacGregor writes that the normal succession pattern was: first to younger brothers of the deceased, and then back to the eldest son of the eldest brother. He interprets this as a compromise between gerontocratic and primogenitural customs. [15] Yet, if the succession, besides being patrilineal, was based solely on age, how different would the pattern be? It seems that age was actually the determining factor in succession to headship of the kindred. MacGregor writes in a later passage, "Even the heads of the kindred were selected on this basis [i.e., on the basis of age] in preference to following the eldest line of patrilineal descent if that would bring a younger man into office." [16] Thus, the head of the kindred did not have to be the eldest son at all, i.e., the one who reputedly managed lands. But MacGregor also writes that the kindred head managed the lands. [17] Furthermore, he says that the eldest son re-

---

prised of an unrestricted nonunilinear descent group and in addition a restricted (by rules unrecoverable) nonunilinear descent group. Ward H. Goodenough, "A Problem in Malayo-Polynesian Social Organization," American Anthropologist, LVII (1955), 76-77.

14. Williamson made this deduction regarding Tokelau, as he had no data on familial life, although he had information on land matters. Williamson, The Social and Political Systems of Central Polynesia, III, 382.

15. MacGregor, Ethnology of the Tokelau Islands, p. 46.
16. Ibid., p. 49.   17. Ibid., p. 46.

sided patrilocally, but that the kindred head lived with his wife's family; hence his eldest sister managed the daily life of the household. [18] Finally, it is reported that, as the kindred head's eldest son was the heir to headship, the kindred head's eldest sister adopted him in order to rear him in the chief household of the kindred, where presumably he would have been living anyhow. [19]

Only a vague conclusion can be drawn from these data, namely that although age and sex are the predominant qualifications for leadership in the kindred, some cultural emphasis is placed on seniority. Ramified practices do appear to some extent in the kindred. A second element of ramification is the special, institutionalized attention paid to first births.

Another point on which the literature must be interpreted is whether or not the kindreds were organized into a larger kin organization of some kind. According to MacGregor, the kindred "is not a stable institution but increases with each generation. When it becomes too large to function as a unit, it gradually regroups itself into new kindreds." [20] This regrouping was accompanied by a division of lands. The crucial points are whether or not the kindreds maintained genealogical connection, and whether this connection, in terms of seniority of descent, determined the stratification structure. Genealogies were kept that reached further back than the common ancestor of the kindred, and kinship was reckoned with all who could demonstrate relationship to an individual's own ancestor. Furthermore, the formation of the Atafu kindred by branching and subdividing from the family of the original settler, as recorded in native traditions, does give the impression of an interlocking system of ramages. But Atafu was so recently settled (1833 or later, after European influence began), that the evidence from that atoll might at least be held in abeyance. [21] In Fakaofu, the paramount chief was chosen because he was the oldest member in one of the four lines descendent from the brothers who reputedly sired the population of that atoll, an indication of underlying rami-

18. Ibid.
19. Ibid., p. 47.
20. Ibid.
21. Ibid., pp. 25, 28-32.

fication. All of the evidence shows at least "underlying"ramification, coupled perhaps with an egalitarian emphasis on
age. But we found no clear statement to the effect that all
lines of descent were interconnected and that their heads
were graded on a genealogical basis. Gerontocratic succession would actually be incompatible with that type of structure. There is no assurance that a genealogical framework
was the basis of rank. Furthermore, MacGregor's interpretation of men's house organization suggests that it was not
(see below), and that the kindreds were more or less discrete.

Each atoll had a village, and each village had several
men's houses. On Fakaofu, two of these houses served as
garrisons for the village guard. Although one of MacGregor's
informants told him that men's house membership was based
on neighborhood in the village, MacGregor believes that membership was originally based on kinship. In support of this
argument, he points out that the term sa, meaning "family
of" in Samoa, appears in many of the names of the men's
houses. He writes that the men's house, therefore, can be
considered as the method of preserving the wider common
kinship among kindreds which had diverged from a single
kindred. [22] Even so, the fact that there were seven on Fakaofu supports the theory that there was a discreteness in kindred organization.

Regulatory functions were carried out by a chief and a
council in the village of each atoll. The chief of Fakaofu was
the head chief of the three atolls, but this arrangement dates
from the early nineteenth century at the earliest. [23] The head
chief of the village was called aliki or tupu. The method of
succession to this title has already been described. The
council of the village was composed of the village elders. [24]

---

22. Ibid., p. 48.

23. Ibid., p. 25.

24. In another context, MacGregor implies that there were
two councils, one of elders and one of kindred heads. Ibid.,
p. 43. But only one council in each village is described under the section called "Government." Ibid., pp. 49 f. On
page 53 MacGregor states that membership in the village
council was confined to heads of kindreds, but he does not
write that it was composed of all such heads.

225

On Fakaofu, these council members were "elected" by their men's houses, and one of the men's houses was also the meeting house of the council. This council of the elders was the major political force in the community. The emphasis on council is, of course, a descent-line characteristic.

The stratification structure was extremely simple. Two nonegalitarian status levels can be distinguished: an upper level consisting of the village chief and presumably, in earlier times, the village priest; and the remainder of the population in a lower level.[25]

Ontong Java.--There is evidence that the Ontong Javanese social organization as described by Hogbin had already undergone significant changes under European influence. However, as Hogbin did not carry out an historical analysis, the inferences about the precontact conditions will be made after the social system has been outlined as Hogbin describes it. Ontong Java has typological resemblances to both ramified and descent-line systems but is definitely committed to neither.

The basic kinship groups in Ontong Java were the household and what Hogbin calls the "joint family."[26] The household group to which Hogbin most often refers is a matrilocal extended family group. This "household" was actually only

_____

25. For additional principal sources, see also William Burrows, "Some Notes and Legends of a South Sea Island," Journal of the Polynesian Society, XXXII (1923), 143-73; J. J. Lister, "Notes on the Natives of Fakaofu (Bowditch Island)," Journal of the (Royal) Anthropological Institute, XXI (1891), 43-63.

Note: As this monograph goes to press, the author is reworking the Tokelau materials with what appears to be greater success. The results will be embodied in an article accepted for publication (probably in 1957) by the Journal of the Polynesian Society.

26. In an article postdating the publication of most of his data and after Firth had published We, the Tikopia, Hogbin termed the joint family a "ramage" because, "the notion of branching from a parent stem appears to be present in the minds of the natives themselves." As social groups almost universally grow by fission, and as people have some memory of the past, such evidence in itself would not justify

a unit during the small part of the year that villages were inhabited. In Hogbin's time (1927), there were two villages on the atoll. These were permanently inhabited, by most families, only for about one month a year, during the tribal ceremonies. For the rest of the year, most families lived on different islets of the atoll, which they cultivated. On the islets, people lived patrilocally, probably in patrilocal extended family groups, a number of which comprised a "joint family." Only those people, a definite minority, not allied with joint families having islet lands lived matrilocally all year around.

The joint family was composed of "all the persons who trace their descent through males back to a common ancestor who lived as a rule about six generations ago."[27] Most genealogies collected only do go back six generations; however, older people could trace relationship further back. The relatives descendent from remote ancestors were counted on for support in quarrels and for assistance in certain gift exchanges. But it is almost certain that the joint families were not integrated into an over-all ramified structure. In aboriginal times, there were about 150 joint families, in Hogbin's time, considerably less. The joint family of Hogbin's time (1927-1928) rarely exceeds fifteen members; a few had twenty-five. Formerly, there were as many as fifty people in a joint family. Each joint family had a head who was the oldest male in the group. Primogeniture was not a factor in succession to the headship. Quarrels over succession were on the basis of who was older, not who was senior in descent. The joint family was known by the same name as the islet on which most of its coconut lands were found, and which it resided on and exploited most of the year.

The joint families of Ontong Java were grouped into two "tribes," one in the north and one in the south. Each tribe centered in a village in which all the joint families resided

placing Ontong Java in a class with ramified societies. These "ramages" were, for the most part, discrete units, and seniority of descent was not an integral part of the social structure. H. Ian Hogbin, "'Polynesian' Colonies in Melanesia," Journal of the Polynesian Society, XLIX (1940), 204.

27. H. Ian Hogbin, "The Social Organization of Ontong Java," Oceania, I (1930-1931), 407-8.

during the annual tribal ceremonies. The tribe took the name of the village center (or vice versa). Each tribe had a number of officers (eight in one, five in the other) called maakua or aliki, whose primary functions were priestly. The maakua were headmen of powerful joint families of the tribe and, as such, succeeded to their titles on the basis of age.[28] It is proper to speak of various of the joint families as holding maakua titles. The tribal gods that the maakua worshiped were evidently the respective ancestors of the joint families they led. The maakua were divided into three groups corresponding to different religious roles but carrying differing status also. In fact, all maakua were ranked. One of them was the chief maakua. Each high maakua also had an executive officer, who principally functioned as food distributor. He was usually a sister's son.

In aboriginal times each village had several men's houses. In one of the tribes there were four, named after four of the islands or joint families. Information about the composition of these club houses, except what can be deduced from the names and the fact that a man belonged to his father's club, is nonexistent. The club houses were not associated with marriage rules. Marriage was prohibited within the joint family of either parent, that is, closer than fourth-cousin relationship. Each village also had a number of guards, polepole, who watched the village food reserves. The guards were, in early times, appointed by the maakua and were headed by a major maakua. There were about fifty of them; they served terms of duty.

Until about 1800, there were no paramount secular rulers in the politically independent tribes.[29] About that time a polepole head, who was also a maakua, became a despot. He shortly lost power to another maakua, who in turn lost it to someone else. Succession to this newly formed paramount chieftainship was, for some time, determined by military supremacy.[30] It was finally stabilized in one family in which the oldest male succeeded to the position. The power of the

---

28. In one case, two maakua came from one joint family.
29. Hogbin, "The Social Organization of Ontong Java," p. 423.
30. Hogbin calls this position "the kingship," and its holder, "the king."

paramount chief remained nil for some time. It was not until the advent of Uila, who "reigned" from 1878 to 1905, that this position actually carried any coercive authority. [31] Hogbin believes it entirely possible that the creation of the "kingship" was an autochthonous development. [32]

It is difficult to understand the development of the "kingship" as an internal evolution. It appears much more sensible, a priori, that the centralization of Ontong Javanese society at such a late date was a reaction to European influence. Especially the increase of power in 1878 would seem more intelligible in these terms. In actuality, the dates of the advent of Europeans substantiate such an interpretation. The precise dates of the earliest European contact are difficult to determine. [33] However, a few years before the reign of Uila, the crew of a European ship was massacred in the harbor. [34] Also, trading stations were established in the 1880's, in the early part of Uila's reign. [35] These facts make Hogbin's interpretation of the "kingship" highly suspect indeed. On the contrary, in Ontong Java, the rise of true chieftainship may well have been a result of acculturation processes.

European contact had another result which casts further doubt about the aboriginality of some other aspects of the social organization. The total population of Ontong Java at the time of Hogbin's study was 544 persons, yet estimates of aboriginal population figures run as high as 6,000--more conservatively 2,000 to 3,000. [36] It seems unlikely that the social organization described by Hogbin could be the same as when the population was five to ten times as large. A search of Hogbin's data confirms this. Besides the two present villages (centers of "tribes") which are called Luangiua

---

31. H. Ian Hogbin, Law and Order in Polynesia (New York, 1934), p. 224.

32. Ibid.; see also Hogbin, "The Social Organization of Ontong Java," p. 424.

33. Hogbin, Law and Order in Polynesia, p. 224.

34. Ibid.

35. H. Ian Hogbin, "The Problem of Depopulation in Melanesia as Applied to Ontong Java," Journal of the Polynesian Society, XXXIX (1930), 61.

36. Ibid., pp. 43-45.

and Pelau, he also mentions the former existence of other large villages, Keila, Kiloma, Kepae, Kemalu, and 'Avaha. [37] This suggests that formerly there were at least seven, rather than two, "tribes." Hogbin's list of the joint families which supply maakua titles in the present Luangiua tribe is of interest: Keila, Kiloma, Kepae, Kemalu, Oko, Akaha, and Keuolei. [38] The correspondence between this list and the list of villages is more than coincidental, especially when one considers that, as far as can be discerned from Hogbin's data, the headman of a joint family, the joint family, and the islet it occupied for most of the year were called by the same title. Furthermore, tribes were known by the same names as their village centers.

From this evidence the following deductions seem reasonable:

1. That there were more "tribes" in aboriginal times, each with a village center.

2. That the "tribes" were composed of a large extended family, perhaps one or more of the modern joint families (witness the four men's houses in Luangiua village, each with a joint family name).

3. That each "tribe" was headed by its oldest male who had a title (maakua).

The status levels were extremely simple. Since the title of maakua existed only in certain lines, the maakua are classified separately from the remainder of the populace, although it should be noted that age was the primary qualification for office within the line. [39]

Pukapuka. --The social organization in Pukapuka was the

37. Hogbin, Law and Order in Polynesia, p. 92.
38. Ibid., p. 166.
39. For additional principal sources, see also H. Ian Hogbin, "Tribal Ceremonies at Ontong Java (Solomon Islands)," Journal of the (Royal) Anthropological Institute, LXI (1931), 27-55; H. Ian Hogbin, "Coconuts and Coral Islands, "National Geographic Magazine, LXV (1934), 265-298; Charles M. Woodford, "Note on the Atoll of Ontong Java or Lord Howe's Group in the Western Pacific," Journal of the Royal Geographical Society, XXXIV (1909), 544-49; and Charles M. Woodford, "On Some Little-Known Polynesian Settlements in the Neighborhood of the Solomon Islands," Journal of the Royal Geographic Society, XLVIII (1916), 26-54.

most structurally complex, in the sense of having the most
different kinds of organizations, of all atolls considered
here. Every individual belonged to a household, a matrilin-
eage, a patrilineage, an age grade (for males, at any rate)
and a village organization.

The household was often based on the nuclear family, with
additions, most frequently of patrilineal relatives, and also
of matrilineal relatives. It was called ngatuwale and contained six to seven people on the average. A number of
households living together and tracing descent from a common ancestor comprised a yikuanga, a patrilocal extended
family.

The yikuanga was a unit of the po or kainga, a patrilineal
grouping. There were seven such groupings in Pukapuka;
they averaged less than one hundred members each. Each
po was divided into sublines which were further segmented
into smaller groups. Each subline had a chief or head, langatila, and the "lineage" as a whole had a chief who was either "chief" or "high chief," aliki or aliki wui. The division
of these lineages into branches and subbranches strongly
suggests a ramage system. The suggestion is strengthened
when we are told that succession to chieftainship passed from
father to son. Unfortunately, there is no reference to primogeniture, and the genealogies which indicate succession do
not clearly show primogeniture either. Only the succeeding
son is diagrammed in most cases. [40] However, primogeniture as well as an internal ranking structure in the lineage,
based on seniority of descent, are implied by the Beagleholes when they write of the succession pattern that "direct
male issue might be passed over in favor of someone from
a junior line of the lineage, who would be adopted into the
main line of descent before induction into office." [41] Stewardship over land by both lineage head and household head is
also reported--a ramified practice. It seems reasonable to
suppose that the patrilineage organizations were of the ramage type. The different lineages, however, do not fall into
an over-all ramage organization, since they trace their descent to fifteen different men who reputedly headed the fami-

---

40. Ernest and Pearl Beaglehole, Ethnology of Pukapuka (Bernice Pahau Bishop Museum Bulletin, No. 150 [1938]), p. 241.
    41. Ibid., p. 240.

lies left after a great tidal wave had depleted the population some 350 years ago.

Besides the ramified patrilineal structure, there was also a system of interconnected matrilineages called wua. Each wua was composed of several maternal sublines called keinanga. The maternal lines traced their descent through females to certain animal offspring of human beings--a suggestion of totemism. From a consideration of myths and traditions of the matrilineages, the Beagleholes suggest that the original division was into two maternal moieties which later subdivided. [42] At the time of study there were two maternal moieties, each subdivided into two lineages, each of the latter further subdivided into three to five exogamous sublines. Again there is a definite suggestion of ramification in this segmented organization. The suggestion is further stimulated by the fact that "Informants tended to visualize the matter in terms of a tree with spreading branches and limbs. "[43] As further proof of the process of ramification, one of the sublines in each lineage bears the same name as the lineage as a whole. The process is ramified certainly, and the various segments maintain their relationship of common descent. Yet the matrilineages lack one absolutely essential criterion of ramification, viz., seniority of descent and its implication for relative status. Succession to the headship of the matrilineages, and presumably to the sublines, was determined solely by age; they were headed by the oldest male or female in the group. Therefore, the maternal organization is not a ramage system. On the contrary, with the exogamy of the sublines and the emphasis on age, the whole gives more of the appearance of egalitarian clans, phratries, and moieties, as are found in many American Indian groups. [44]

There was also a system of age grades, primarily referring to males. The Pukapukans recognized eight different life periods, not all of which can be included in the age-grade system. [45] In actuality, the important feature of age

---

42. Ibid., p. 224.   43. Ibid., p. 225.

44. The sublines were, of course, much smaller in membership than American Indian clans. Their average numerical strength was between fourteen and fifteen persons.

45. MacGregor recognized five groups of ages that were

groupings was that they provided the young men's fishing group and the elders, the tupele. The young men's group included all those born in a six-month period and was led by the person first born in that period. They formed a deep-sea fishing organization and were replaced by a new group similarly constituted at periodic (usually six months, longer if the number in the new group was too small) intervals. The old men formed a council (see below), the most important regulatory body on Pukapuka.

The people lived in three villages. As residence was generally patrilocal, one was usually a member of one's father's village. A patrilineage was generally localized in one village. The village had a council composed of all the lineage chiefs, subchiefs, and adult males of the village. Operating in connection with the village council were a number of guards who watched over the village reserve lands. In one village the guards were old men. In the other two villages twenty-five men and fifty men, respectively, acted as guards each month, living in scattered guard houses. There were bachelor and spinster houses in the villages, but membership in them was not obligatory. Besides the village council there was also a council solely of chiefs which discussed island and interlineage matters, and a council of the tupele which also discussed island affairs. The interworkings of these councils have already been discussed.

The chief of one of the patrilineages was the chief of the island. According to traditions, chieftainship over the island was established through a consolidation of power after the great tidal wave of 350 years ago. Before that wave, four lineage chiefs competed for power. Only after the wave did real dominance arise, although "the other chiefly lineages, particularly those of Ngaki [village], have never completely acquiesced in either the political or religious dominance of I Tua [the high chief]."[46] Three of the lineages, perhaps remnants of the other powerful pre-tidal-wave lines, carried chiefly titles. The heads of the other lineages only bore

---

functionally significant: infants, boys, young men, married adult men, old men. Gordon MacGregor, Notes on the Ethnology of Pukapuka (Bernice Pahau Bishop Museum Occasional Papers, Vol. XI, No. 6 [1935]).

46. E. and P. Beaglehole, Ethnology of Pukapuka, p. 245.

langatila titles--comparable to the titles of the subchiefs in the former lineages. It was these chiefs and subchiefs who formed the upper, nonequalitarian status level. The remainder of the populace, including the powerful tupele, must be placed in the lower status level.

Interpretations

Variations in the forms of social organization and social stratification on the atolls, and the differences in these phenomena as they appeared in atolls as opposed to high islands, are intelligible in terms of the selective factors of atoll environment and the kinds of adaptation that the historically diverse cultures effected. The selective factors encountered on atolls and the methods of coping with these factors in terms of the organization of interpersonal relations were different from those found in high islands. Cultural adaptation and adaptive variations on the high islands were found to be related to the spatial distribution of resources and the degree of familial productive specialization. The essential adaptive problem met by the forms of social organization in the high islands (the ramified and descent-line systems) was that concerning the economic distribution of large amounts of surplus production. In low islands, by contrast, the selective factors did not so much involve the spatial distribution of resources, and the adaptive problem was not the distribution of surplus--more important was the problem of keeping a dense population alive in an area of sporadic or limited-surplus production.

The productivity data on the low islands considered here (see Appendix) reveal several factors relevant to an understanding of selective pressures, and hence sociocultural adaptive variation on the atolls. [47] First, every atoll is char-

---

47. See Appendix, XI, XII, and XIII. As Tongareva and Manihiki-Rakahanga were not considered in the chapters on the amount of stratification, they are not included in the Appendix. Relevant data on the technoenvironmental situations in these two atolls will be summarized in appropriate sections below. It is sufficient to note here that exploitative conditions in these islands do not differ in outline from conditions on the other atoll groups in the charts.

acterized by a lack of environmental diversity and opportunity. There are hardly any differing soils--really, hardly any soil--any water, any climatic variation, or other environmental variations on atolls. There is a paucity even of biological variation.[48] Coupled with this was a general limitation on the types of exploitation. Fishing and the cultivation of but a few crops at best were the major subsistence activities. Another feature was the often dense population. High density on atolls is directly attributable to the coconut which takes up little room, but, with fishing, is capable of providing a more or less continuous supply of food.[49] Little surplus is derived from coconuts, however, as the nuts ripen individually and, with the lack of other foods, must be consumed forthwith. There was, in fact, little and only sporadic surplus produced on atolls, a feature related to high-density populations living in areas of restricted exploitation; and the possibility of starvation through famines resulting from lack of rainfall, hurricanes, and the like was always imminent. It is postulated that limitation on surplus production is the crucial selective factor on atolls.

With sporadic and limited surpluses, organizational features of the atoll societies cannot be understood in the same terms as those on high islands. The adaptive problem is dif-

---

48. Elmer D. Merrill, Plant Life of the Pacific World (New York, 1945), pp. 207-08; see also Stanley J. Gardiner, Coral Reefs and Atolls (London, 1931).

49. The densities on Ontong Java, Tokelau, and Tongareva are difficult to estimate because of insufficient data on land area. Tokelau seems to fit into a range of 100-200 per square mile. On one of the Tokelau Islands, Atafu, the density was over 300, but this is the smallest atoll in the group. Other approximate densities per square mile are: Manihiki-Rakahanga, 190; Pukapuka, 200-300. The density of Tongareva, if Buck's areal estimate of 40,000 acres is accepted, is 32 per square mile. See Buck, Ethnology of Tongareva, p. 6. From a glance at a map, however, Buck's area figure would seem greatly overestimated. Bryan gives 6.2 square miles as the land area, exactly one-tenth of Buck's figure; this yields a density of 320 per square mile. See Edwin H. Bryan, Jr., "Central and Western Polynesia, " in O. W. Freeman (ed.), Geography of the Pacific (New York, 1951), p. 418.

ferent. Social groups are not intelligible as organizations adapted to the problems of distributing large surpluses. Instead of the development of stratified hierarchies for regulating surplus distribution, one would expect a trend toward egalitarianism. When surpluses are relatively small and deficiencies liable to arise in different localities, a premium is put on direct or reciprocal types of distribution, not types that travel up and down hierarchies. Kinship organization on an egalitarian basis would be of selective advantage. A direct relation between groups of people on an equal and reciprocal basis allows goods to be moved freely between any two points on the islet or atoll. Thus, associated with low productivity and sporadic surplus, an element of egalitarianism can be expected in the atoll groups. Such an element has already been demonstrated in chapter 5 of this work.

Also of significance here are other implications of production and distribution in an area of low productivity. Since every single type of productive endeavor would be vitally important to the entire society, one would expect the organization of personnel to be closely attuned to the productive demands of the environment and to the exploitative technology. A highly adaptive social organization in an area of limited and sporadic surplus production would be one in which there was a particular alignment of people exercising control over each production resource and engaging in particular productive operations--one particular organization for each task. Each type of resource or area of resources would then be exploited to the fullest, and everyone could share the fruits of the labor. However, with the limits on surplus production on the atolls, such organizational concentrations could not afford to specialize completely on one product or in one area. Specialization would mean starvation. But if each and every individual was connected by some alignment principle--descent, age grade, residence, and the like--to each and every type of socioeconomic group, then everyone might share in the distribution and consumption of what is produced. Adaptation in social organization would move toward a multiplicity of social groups, each connected with a given productive activity or exploitation of a particular area, and to each of which every individual belongs. Limited exploitative possibilities on the coral atolls place a premium on the organization of personnel--the more diversified these organizations become, the better adapted is the group. Other things being equal, coral atoll organization should show greater intricacy with respect to social alignment principles than high-island organization. [50]

Selective and historical factors are not always constant in the coral atolls; hence, the great diversity in organization among the atolls described. Crops and resource distribution, amount of available land, and the like vary from group to group. The atolls were settled from different places; thus it is reasonable to believe that different methods of social organization were present from the beginning. The atolls settled from Polynesian high islands can be expected to show elements of ramified or descent-line systems in their social structure. Even though such systems may be adapted to particular conditions of resource distribution and surplus production, their principles could be reworked on the atolls. And insofar as atoll environmental conditions do not depart markedly from those characteristic of high islands--Tongareva will be shown to be a case in point--total survival of high-island organization can be expected. Where atoll conditions approach what has been described as typical--small land area, high density, low productivity, etc.--the social organization, it is posited, should become quite different from high-island organization. This is especially true if the atoll has been long occupied and the social structure has had a chance to adapt to the new conditions. If this interpretation is correct, under typical atoll conditions, the greater the time of occupation, the greater the multiplicity of the social groupings and alignments, and the further removed from organizations formed on high islands. In this connection, relative isolation of the atoll is significant. Frequent and diverse contacts permit the introduction of social elements which can be used as principles of group formation perhaps more readily than such principles could be developed internally, and which are, almost certainly, of a different sort than internal development would produce.

Tongareva.--Tongarevan social organization was typical

---

50. The author is indebted to Dr. Andrew P. Vayda for many useful insights into this problem that he has contributed in the course of long and illuminating discussions on the matter.

of the ramage type. The only discernible aspect of Tongare-van social organization which conforms to the postulated, highly adaptive atoll type is the relatively small degree of social stratification.[51]

In some ecological features, Tongareva is unique among atolls, and these features apparently have bearing on the survival of ramage structure. For one thing, the total land area of the atoll is relatively large--6.2 square miles, if one takes Bryan's figure, 62 square miles according to Buck's undoubtedly exaggerated statement.[52] More impor-tant than that, the atoll is one of the largest in Polynesia, be-ing 108 miles in circumference and 40 miles in diameter. The atoll islets are long and thin, and planted throughout with coconuts, the most important food. Under such condi-tions, concentration of settlement is disadvantageous, and the population was dispersed in hamlets of about three houses (fifteen people) throughout the islets. Buck remarks, "The influence of the coconut trees in determining local res-idence cannot be overestimated."[53] Furthermore, "The ex-ploitation of fishing and shellfish grounds led some families to move away from the primary centers [i. e. , the areas of earliest occupation] and occupy other islands [i. e. , islets of the atoll] so as to be nearer the sources of sea food sup-ply."[54] Land shortage does not appear to have been a press-ing problem, as wide gaps in which no coconuts were planted were left to mark off district boundaries.[55] Relative abun-dance of land and dispersal of the sources of food supply on

---

51. The principal ethnographic materials on Tongareva are deficient in economic data; hence, Tongareva was ex-cluded from consideration in the early chapters of this work. However, the materials on stratification that do appear indi-cate a strong degree of egalitarianism. Tongareva would be roughly equivalent in stratification to those societies placed in Group III in the classification developed earlier (in chap-ter 5). See Buck, Ethnology of Tongareva.

52. See Bryan, Jr. , "Central and Western Polynesia, " p. 418; see also Buck, Ethnology of Tongareva, p. 6. Buck's figure might be a printer's error.

53. Buck, Ethnology of Tongareva, p. 69.

54. Ibid. , p. 68.

55. Ibid. , p. 70.

Tongareva parallel to some extent the ecological conditions in which ramages were found in higher islands.

The major portion of the Tongarevan population apparently stemmed from late immigrations from ramage-organized high islands. Although some traces of a previous population exist, the majority, if not the entire population, claim descent from immigrants whom Buck traces to such places as Tahiti and Aitutaki. [56] Judging from the length of genealogies--a method of chronological reckoning not above suspicion--the major settlement of Tongareva by these people did not occur much more than 300 years before the advent of Europeans, according to Buck. [57] The survival of the ramage organization may be partially attributed to the relatively short period of occupation, as well as to the rather unusual ecological conditions.

Manihiki-Rakahanga. --Manihiki-Rakahanga, like Tongareva, was essentially ramage-organized. The only additional social unit on these two small atolls--each less than two square miles in land area with lagoons under five miles in diameter--was village organization. It should be noted that the earliest settlement pattern was dispersed, as is usual with ramage organization. According to tradition, the scattered habitations were later fused into villages. [58] Nucleation of settlement may be related to the evidently localized and extensive puraka (like taro) pits. There was a marked degree of productive interdependence in the society, and this, too, may have had an influence in village formation. The two atolls were not continuously inhabited, rather the population occupied one at a time. When the supply of coconuts and taro ran out on one atoll, the entire populace undertook the hazardous twenty-five-mile journey to the other.

According to native traditions, the Manihiki-Rakahangans descended from a single biological family, without the addition of any other migrants. The family reputedly migrated

---

56. Aitutaki undoubtedly had ramage organization, as did other islands of the Cook Group. See Peter H. Buck, Arts and Crafts of the Cook Islands (Bernice Pahau Bishop Museum Bulletin, No. 179 [1944]).

57. Buck, Ethnology of Tongareva, p. 19. Buck calls this "fairly late."

58. Buck, Ethnology of Manihiki and Rakahanga, p. 59.

from Rarotonga where the ramified system of organization prevailed. [59] The genealogical record places the settlement period at twenty-two generations before 1929, or about the beginning of the fifteenth century. [60] Contact with European culture commenced in the first quarter of the nineteenth century making a total of about 425 years of native development. [61]

Tokelau. --The productive concentrates on Tokelau were the kindred and the village. The household group, which tended to be matrilocal and was composed of a matrilocally extended family rather than a patrilocal one, may have been a partially formed concentrate. Whereas residence centered in the village, the food plantations, especially coconut plantations, were found on the outlying islets, often six to eight miles from the village. The outlying plantations were controlled and exploited by the kindreds. Two or three times weekly the adult males and boys of the kindred visited the plantations to harvest coconuts. (Some coconuts growing near the village were picked daily for household use.)

Village life is partially an adjustment to fishing requirements, as the village is located, on each atoll, where canoe landing and access through the reef to the open sea is most advantageous. Males of the village often fish communally or in fleets, especially in the hazardous deep-sea expeditions. Villages provide the framework of this organization; islet occupation could not. Wells dug on the village islet also contributed to stabilizing village organization. Finally, the men's houses, serving as guard outposts, were another adjunct of village life as the guards watched over village reserve lands, periodically harvested by the group as a whole.

The matrilocally oriented household appears to be a partially formed productive concentrate. These groupings carried out important reciprocal exchanges with other similar groups during certain life-crisis rites. [62] This feature of or-

---

59. Although no detailed ethnography of Rarotonga is extant, scattered materials definitely indicate ramage organization. Buck, Arts and Crafts of the Cook Islands ; see also William Wyatt Gill, Rarotonga Records (New Plymouth, N. Z., 1916).

60. Buck, Ethnology of Manihiki and Rakahanga, p. 22.

61. Ibid., pp. 5 f.

62. MacGregor, Ethnology of the Tokelau Islands, pp. 39 f.

ganization may have been an adaptation to the introduction of certain food plants, principally taro, by Europeans. However, data on the production and control of the land used for these plants are not available. In Olosenga, now uninhabited, taro was grown aboriginally. It is noteworthy that the two productive concentrates, village and kindred, are based upon the two major types of resource exploitation, coconut and fishing. Unless other activities or techniques developed or were introduced, the formation of other productive concentrates would be decidedly inhibited.

Traditions as to the origin of the population are confusing. Most traditions attribute the settlement of Fakaofu to Samoans, although one account tracing the origin to Rarotonga is recorded. At the time Fakaofu was occupied, Atafu and Nukunono were already inhabited. However, these earlier inhabitants apparently did not contribute heavily to the formation of later generations, as they were driven off Atafu and Nukunono in the eighteenth century by Fakaofuans, and the atolls were repopulated from Fakaofu. Cultural influences from these early peoples may, of course, have been preserved in Fakaofuan life. The first settlement of Fakaofu took place, according to MacGregor's genealogical chronology, about the middle of the seventeenth century. "The history of the Fakaofu people of the Tokelau Islands then becomes a very recent event in the annals of the Polynesian peoples."[63] Frequent contacts with other islands are mentioned in the native traditions.[64] Contact with Europeans began in the mid-nineteenth century on Fakaofu.[65] MacGregor, after comparative study, concludes that the early, pre-Fakaofu culture was part of a Micronesian migration in the direction of eastern Polynesia, and contributed traits of material culture similar to those found in eastern Polynesia to the later culture of Tokelau. A survey of Micronesia would be necessary to establish whether or not Micronesian social elements were also preserved. The social groupings of village and kindred and the trace of matrilocal groupings are very similar (although perhaps not as crystallized) to those found in Ontong Java, a culture which was probably influenced by

---

63. Ibid., p. 26.
64. Ibid., pp. 26-28, 176.
65. Ibid., pp. 30-31.

Micronesia (see below). MacGregor's comparative distribution study corroborates a Samoan origin for the later population.[66]

Ontong Java. --The joint families, the matrilocal residence groups, and the village organizations were production concentrates. Every individual belonged to each type of organization. The joint family, especially the males thereof, formed fishing groups and also exploited islets of the atoll for coconuts. Taro gardens, however, were worked by women, and their use was matrilineally inherited. Most taro gardens were situated in the vicinity of the village. Therefore, the temporary matrilocal alignment in the village was associated with taro production and consumption. The village itself participated in periodic harvests of reserve lands. The village guards, an adjunct of this organization, were concerned with supervising the use of village reserves.

These distinctions in productive concentration were based not only on differing types of production but also on the spatial distribution of resources. Ontong Java is perhaps the largest atoll in the Pacific. The diameter of the ring of islands is between forty and fifty miles. Merely temporary residence in the village is intelligible in terms of the difficulty of constant exploitation of resources from a single center. But the location of most of the taro lands makes village residence also understandable. It was during this residence that the yearly festival, the sanga rites, was carried out, and the village reserves were exploited in conjunction with the ceremonies. It is also interesting that during the sanga festival a number of complex exchanges involving the products of the joint families and residential groups took place on a reciprocal basis.[67]

The maternal, paternal, and village groups are seen to be productive concentrates. The size of the islets has probably dictated the size of the paternal groups. The emphasis on the paternal organization as the groups from which the maakua were selected indicates the economic importance of the

66. Ibid. , p. 68.

67. "Each man presented fish to headman of his joint family, while the woman gave taro puddings to the headman of the joint families of their husbands. The headmen kept a portion for themselves and then distributed the fish amongst the

joint family. However, it is significant that the maakua operated in the village framework, and that the over-all organization was quite egalitarian.

The precise nature of the types of social grouping may be related to the origin of the Ontong Javanese population. It is now almost unquestionable that strong Micronesian elements occur in Ontong Java. Although the atoll has long been thought to be a Polynesian outlier in Melanesia, Shapiro shows a probable genetic relationship with Micronesian populations (specifically to certain of the Caroline Islands) rather than to Polynesia. [68] The relationship seems to have been cultural as well as physical, witness the unique appearance of the loom in Ontong Java and parts of western Micronesia. The Ontong Java social organization might be more fully understood if the Micronesian data were examined.

It is difficult to judge from the ethnographic data the length of time of occupation before Europeans. The assumption that it was several centuries seems not unwarranted. [69] Ontong

---

women to whom the members of their joint families were married. The pudding they divided between the members themselves. Each man took fish and brought back pudding, while each woman took puddings and brought back fish.

"Six days later there was another exchange. This time each man gave fish to the headman of his wife's joint family, while each woman presented a pudding to the headman of her own group." Hogbin, Law and Order in Polynesia, p. 196. See also Hogbin, "Tribal Ceremonies at Ontong Java (Solomon Islands)."

68. H. L. Shapiro, "The Physical Characteristics of the Ontong Javanese: A Contribution to the Study of the Non-Melanesian Elements in Melanesia," Anthropological Papers of the American Museum of Natural History, XXXIII (1933), 227-78. Woodford also hinted at Micronesian affinities. Charles M. Woodford, "On Some Little-Known Polynesian Settlements in the Neighborhood of the Solomon Islands," Journal of the Royal Geographical Society, XLVIII (1916), 26-54.

69. Samuel H. Elbert, "Internal Relationships of Polynesian Languages and Dialects," Southwestern Journal of Anthropology, IX (1953), 147-73. If Ontong Java was historically linked to Polynesia, such a guess would be corroborated linguistically by Elbert's data. However, with the evidence

Java was evidently not completely isolated, although not much intercourse occurred between Ontong Java and other islands. Traditions of canoes arriving with castaways from several Gilbert Islands are preserved. [70]

Pukapuka. --The patriramages, the matrilineages, the system of age grades, and the villages with their guards were productive concentrates on Pukapuka. The bachelor and spinster houses may have been adjuncts of the age-grade system.

The ramages controlled strips of land of indeterminate width across the islets. Most of these strips skirted the excavated taro beds and were used in the production of coconuts. It is noteworthy in this respect that the gathering of nuts was usually men's work.

Whereas the patrilineal descent groups held and worked strips of coconut land interspersed with a few taro plots, the matrilineages or segments thereof corporately controlled taro plots only. All the work of planting and harvesting taro, with the exception of excavating the beds, was done by women.

The age grades were primarily a male organization. The major productive function of the age-grade system was the deep-sea fishing done by the young men's group, the tangata. All the men born within a given period, usually six months, were organized into a deep-sea fishing group under the leadership of the first man born during that period. The system of age grades also involved a social and political division of labor, the tupele or elders being the primary regulatory group on the atoll.

The villages were organizations which provided the framework for certain communal activities, especially fishing. A village controlled a section of reserve lands exploited periodically for both cultivated and wild foods. The village guards supervised the use of reserve land for the benefit of all village members. The village was also the major organizational unit in a political sense.

---

now pointing to a Micronesian source, the linguistic comparisons with Polynesia are inconclusive on this point.

70. Charles M. Woodford, "Note on the Atoll of Ontong Java or Lord Howe's Group in the Western Pacific," Journal of the Royal Geographical Society, XXXIV (1909), 548.

Each of these productive concentrates was also a distributive unit. The goods produced, especially foods, were shared out among the membership and beyond, if possible. There were patriramage distributions, maternal lineage distributions, and village food divisions. The young men's group supplied the old men with fish, any surplus being widely distributed.

The Beagleholes place the origin of Pukapukan history about 600 years before 1938, making it possibly the longest continuously inhabited atoll considered. [71] European contact was not common before 1857, so the period of internal development was over 500 years long. [72] About 350 years ago, according to tradition, a catastrophic seismic wave reduced the population to fifteen families and the resources to almost nothing. [73] With such small population and limited resources, the development of intricate organizational alignments may have been accelerated. The myth of origin indicates Tonga as the Ursprung of Pukapukan settlement, but the myth may very well not be historically accurate. Pukapuka has not been isolated. [74] Native records report migrations and visitations from Tokelau, migrations from a place called Yayake, invaders from a place called Tongaleleva, contact with Nassau Island, migrants from Manihiki, and voyages made by Pukapukans to numerous places both east and, more frequently, west. The Tokelaus, Samoa, Tonga, and Niue were often reached, according to tradition.

Summary

The atolls have been shown to have organizations which sometimes widely depart from the descent-line and ramified systems of high islands. It was postulated that the development of a number of interlocking social groups, each dedicated to the exploitation of a particular resource or resource area, might be expected on atolls as a compensating adjustment to selective pressures limiting surplus production. By

---

71. E. and P. Beaglehole, Ethnology of Pukapuka, p. 378.
72. Ibid., p. 5.
73. Ibid., pp. 386 and passim.
74. Ibid., 375-78 f.·

this means, highly organized groups engaging in particular tasks and distributing strategic goods are created without necessitating specialization. Every member of the community, as a member of each type of group, automatically shares in the control, production, and distribution of every product. It was reasoned that, where "typical" atoll scarcity conditions prevail, and especially if the atoll had been long occupied and had frequent external contacts, structural complexity can be expected.

Even though it is not totally conclusive, the evidence accumulated appears to support these hypotheses. Pukapuka, for example, small, relatively long-settled, and frequently contacted, shows an intricacy of organization beyond that of the high islands. Each of the many types of cross-cutting social groups is associated with a specific productive and distributive activity. In Ontong Java, apparently also occupied for a long period, the social order was also intricate. A number of interlocking social groups are indicated, each concentrating in a particular type of production.

Tokelau, Manihiki-Rakahanga, and Tongareva were not as structurally complex as Ontong Java and Pukapuka. Correspondingly, they do not appear to have had as long a period of continuous settlement and development. Manihiki-Rakahanga, and particularly Tongareva, retained the ramage organization which had been introduced in the settlement of these atolls. In Tongareva, retention of ramage structure was evidently aided by the fact that ecological conditions there, more nearly than in other atolls, approached those in which high-island ramified systems are found. In Manihiki, survival of ramages may be due entirely to late settlement, although this explanation is perhaps not completely sufficient. But, admitting difficulties such as this, the hypothesis presented seems to account for and explain much of the diversity in social organization found in the Polynesian atolls.

246

12. Social Stratification and Adaptive Variation in Polynesia

ONE OF THE MOST engaging as well as pressing problems of anthropological studies is the explanation of cultural variations. The scientific aims of the study of culture are served by reducing the masses of heterogeneous materials on different cultures to general propositions, empirically verified, which illustrate variable relationships between differing sets or types of phenomena. Such a goal requires the development of concepts of cultural process which seek to make cultural variations intelligible. It has been posited in this work that the concept of adaptive variation is such a concept, one that can lead to statements of a general nature about the relationship between different aspects of culture.

A simple truism underlies the concept of adaptive variation, that exploitation of the energy resources of the natural world for the purpose of sustaining human life is a requirement which all cultures must meet. With this in mind, attention is focused on the environment in which a society is situated and the technology by means of which the culture is articulated with the natural world. The interaction of a particular technological system with a given environment is the basic adaptation of a culture. It is held that the basic adaptation effected by any culture will be reflected in the social structure, because of the organizational requirements of manipulating the technology and distributing life-sustaining goods. And, if cultures are in any way cohesive wholes, it is expectable that corresponding ideological sanctions of the prevailing social and technological conditions will be found. Thus, if variations occur in technology or environment, or both, concomitant, adaptive, variations should be found in other aspects of culture.

In this study, Polynesian cultures were chosen to illustrate the concept of adaptive variation. These cultures afford an example of a number of historically related groups found in environmentally diverse areas. They are members of a single cultural genus which has undergone adaptive differentiation. Indeed, in view of the historical process and the range of differences in Polynesian cultures, "adaptive radiation" would not be an inappropriate term. Differences in social stratification in the Polynesian islands have been of particular topical interest. It is this feature of culture, both in its formal aspects and in the degree to which it exists, which has been related to the types of adaptation present.

In this chapter, the major results of the study will be reviewed with the aim of formulating general statements about the relationship between the cultural phenomena considered.

Degrees of Stratification

Based on a lead provided by Kirchhoff's discussion of clanship in human societies, fourteen Polynesian cultures were ranked in a classification of the degree of stratification. [1] The criteria of classification were the degree to which there existed status differences between groups of individuals not based on age, sex, or personal attributes and the degree to which these status levels exercised differential privileges in the economic, social, and ceremonial realms of culture. Economic factors link social stratification and the technological adaptation to environment. It was found that a distinction existed in many of the societies between those who only produced need-serving goods, and those who regulated the distribution of such items. This distinction corresponded with the social difference, chief and nonchief. The predominant distribution process was that designated by Polanyi, "the redistributive form of economic integration." Strategic goods not consumed by the producers were often accumulated by chiefs and periodically redistributed among the pro-

---

1. Paul Kirchhoff, "The Principles of Clanship in Human Society," Davidson Anthropological Journal, I (1955), 1-11.

ducers of the goods, and as well among specialized and communal laborers. The distinction between chief and nonchief in distribution function further implies social differentiation in other aspects of the economy and society. It was suggested, therefore, that stratification is directly related to productivity, if productivity be considered to mean the ability of the wielders of the technology to produce strategic goods beyond their consumption needs. The greater the productivity, the greater the differentiation between distributors (chiefs) and producers (nonchiefs) and the greater the tendency for this distinction to extend itself into other aspects of culture.

The presence of a redistributive system was also of great value in solving the problem of measuring the productivity of the society for the purpose of comparison with the gradient of the amount of stratification. It was posited that in any given group, other factors being constant, the greater the surplus produceable by the producers the greater would be the range of distribution, and productivity was measured by considering the number of people embraced in the largest redistributive network of food and how frequently this overall network was utilized. As a check on productivity derived by this measure, the Polynesian groups were also examined with respect to the amount of non-food-producing specialists they contained and the particular types of technology and environment present. In the former case, it was assumed that the greater the productivity the greater the proportion of people who might be divorced from food production. The particular ecologies were rated according to other assumptions: e.g., other things being constant, agriculture is more productive than hunting and gathering; specialized techniques of domestication, such as irrigation agriculture and selection of crop varieties, are more productive than the lack of specialized techniques; the greater the diversity of environmental opportunities the more likely that productivity be greater; etc.

Although there is a lack of mathematical precision in the criteria of stratification and there are certain gaps in the data, the gradients of stratification and productivity show a remarkable correspondence. On the basis of the degree of stratification, the cultures were divided among four categories from more stratified to more egalitarian: I. Hawaii, Tahiti, Tonga, Samoa; IIa. Mangareva, Mangaia, Easter Island, Uvea; IIb. Futuna, Tikopia, Marquesas; III. Ontong

Java, Tokelau, Pukapuka. These groupings were found to correspond to productivity differences, and thus the Polynesian materials indicate that a high probability can be assigned to the first major generalization of this work: Other factors being constant, the greater the productivity, the greater the amount of stratification.

It should be stressed that the proviso, other factors being constant, is not to be taken lightly. The intimate relationship between productivity and stratification is intelligible in Polynesia because of the fact that a redistributive economic system prevailed in these islands. The redistributive system may be a necessary condition for the generalization. Furthermore, it is possible that in particular cultures alternative means may be found to cope with the problems of surplus production--means that may or may not lead to a high degree of social stratification. Therefore, cross-cultural comparisons of productivity and stratification may not lead to as significant results (in a statistical sense) as were obtained here.

The degree of stratification was also considered in light of the historical differences between western and eastern Polynesia. Although there is abundant evidence of cultural distinctions between western and eastern Polynesia due to historical exclusiveness of these areas, a greater degree of stratification was found not to be a part of either the eastern or the western Polynesian tradition. This does not exclude the possibility that in particular islands the amount of stratification in some aspects of culture was not on the same level of stratification as in other aspects. For example, ceremonial sanctification of chieftainship in Pukapuka and Tokelau was more elaborate than the economic and social role of the chief warranted. This can be interpreted as a survival of practices of stratification in a relatively nonadaptive domain of culture, ideology, as these islands were settled from high islands where stratification was probably greater.

Forms of Stratification

The systems of social organization and stratification in Polynesia can be divided into three types: ramage organization and descent-line organization on high islands, and the looser category, atoll organization. It was posited that these forms can be understood as adaptive variations.

The ramage organization was found in Hawaii, the Societies, Tonga, New Zealand, Marquesas, Tikopia, Easter Island, Mangareva, and Mangaia. The ramified system is a genealogical system. All the members of the society can be placed on one or a few genealogical trees. The rank of any individual is governed by his relative distance from the main line of descent in the group, the high chief being the direct descendant of the deified founder of the community. Primogenitural succession to positions of authority carries the implication of seniority which makes such a ranking system possible. Economic and social processes, such as distribution and the regulation of interpersonal affairs, are carried out along the lines of genealogy.

The descent-line system was found on Samoa, Futuna, and Uvea. In contrast to the ramified systems, descent-line societies are composed of local groupings of small, unrelated lineages, descent lines. Descent lines hold one or more titles on the territorial councils which govern the group. Primogeniture is not the succession rule; in fact, there is no definite rule of succession to the familial title. Rank implied by seniority of birth is absent or not significant; rather, rank is dependent on the traditional, mythological standing of the family title.

It was posited that the ramage and descent-line systems are alternative solutions to the problem of distributing surplus production, solutions related to the particular type of basic adaptation of the culture. It was reasoned that, other things being constant, a ramified system would tend to develop where there was familial specialization of production of surplus strategic goods. The kinship connection between households in the ramified system may be seen as a framework by which an equitable distribution of the different products might be obtained, as the kin ties could be utilized as a basis either of reciprocal exchanges or of redistributive, hierarchical distributions. It was deduced, therefore, that ramified systems would tend to develop where the spatial distribution of rich resource zones in the environment was one too scattered to be exploited by a single household, or where the range of crops was so large as to preclude effective exploitation of them by a single household, or both. By contrast, descent-line systems should be found where the spatial distribution of rich resource zones is clustered in a small area, or where the range of crops is small, or both.

251

Under these conditions, each family would produce the same strategic goods as every other, and the kinship connection between households which have split off from each other would tend to dissolve. Economic redistributions as well as social, political, and religious functions would therefore be carried out within a localized cluster of kin groups. As a corollary to the adaptational feature of resource distribution, one would expect to find ramage systems associated with scattered settlement patterns, whereas descent-line systems would probably be associated with nucleated or village settlements.

The available evidence largely, but not definitively, supports these deductions. In most cases a nearly perfect correlation was obtained: ramage systems were associated with scattered distribution of rich resource zones, a tendency toward familial specialization of production, and, usually, scattered settlement; descent-line systems were associated with clustered exploitation zones, familial self-sufficiency, and village settlement. In some cases, such as Tikopia and Easter Island, the selective factors were not pronounced--rather they tended toward indifference--yet ramages were found. A previous history of ramage organization may account for the presence of ramage systems in these areas of indifferent selective conditions. No explanation is forthcoming for Uvea which has a descent-line system, yet seemingly ramified adaptational features. However, the total weight of the evidence supports the generalization that: other factors constant, ramage organization tends to develop where highly productive resource zones are widely scattered; descent-line organization tends to develop where highly productive resource zones are concentrated.

The forms of organization on the coral atolls cannot be understood in the same terms as those on high islands. Familial specialization of production is prohibited by small surpluses and the consequent limitations on exchanges of strategic goods. Every type of resource is of vital importance to the continued existence of the society. It was postulated that effective exploitation of atolls can best be made, therefore, if there is a separate organization of people for exploiting each resource available. Without the possibility of producing large surpluses and hence of specialization, every person would have to be a member of each type of grouping. The result would be a particularly complex system of social groupings with each person--on the basis of different types of alignment principles--belonging to each type of organization. It was reasoned that if this postulate was valid, the longer the atoll was occupied and the more the ecological conditions differed from those of high islands, the more complex the organization. The particular form of stratification organization would depend on the previous history of the atoll.

Again, these deductions were in great measure borne out by the evidence. Pukapuka and Ontong Java were occupied for a longer period than most other atolls and had more complex, cross-cutting organizations than Tongareva, Manihiki-Rakahanga, and Tokelau. Pukapuka, for example, had both matrilineal and patrilineal descent groups, an age-grade system, and territorial (village and atoll) organizations. Tongareva had a simple ramage system, identical in principle to those found on high islands. This may be explained by the fact that the population derives, relatively recently, from ramage-organized areas, and that the ecological conditions on Tongareva, more than on any other atoll, most closely approach those with which ramages are associated on high islands. The evidence supports the conclusion that: other factors being constant, long occupation of a limited area under conditions of low productivity may result in a multiplicity of cross-cutting social groupings.

The data from Polynesia demonstrate the validity of a number of broad generalizations respecting the variable relationship between social stratification and organization and the technological adaptation of culture to the environment. Adaptation is thereby seen to be a major orienting factor in cultural evolution, as it is in biological evolution. It is hoped that the present work, whatever its limitations, will lead other students to utilize and test the concept of adaptation in their search for explanations of cultural differences.

APPENDIX

Appendix: Technology and Environment

I. HAWAIIAN ISLANDS[1]

Environmental opportunities

High (highest summit, 13,784') young volcanic islands. Eight inhabited islands have total area of 6,435 square miles.

Diversity of environments an important feature. Variations in altitude and seasonal trades and currents result in differentiation between
windward and leeward sides of islands, and between levels of land
above sea level. Large ecological differences because of these factors
and their effect on rainfall were found in relatively small areas. Soils
also contributed to the diversity. Several hundred are recognized. Red
kula (clay) soils, mostly upland, were suitable to certain crops, as
were alluvial soils on valley floors. Porosity of the young volcanic
soils and large areas of flat land were conducive to the development of
irrigation on a large scale. Furthermore, irrigation in a young volcanic area is exceedingly fruitful because of the high mineral content
dissolved in irrigation waters.[2]

Relief varies greatly. Radial drainage patterns from mountainous
centers are characteristic. On rainy slopes, valleys could be deeply
cut; in drier areas they were less incised. There were considerable
areas of rich coastal flats on some islands, as well as moderately
sloping upland lands suitable for horticulture. The deepest, most mature volcanic soils are found on moderately sloping old lava flows.

There was an abundance of permanent streams on most islands.

---

1. Major sources: Wendell Clark Bennett, Archaeology of Kauai,
(Bernice Pahau Bishop Museum Bulletin, No. 80 [1931]); William Alan-
son Bryan, Natural History of Hawaii (Honolulu, 1915); William E.
Ellis, Narrative of a Tour through Hawaii (2nd ed.; London, 1826);
Otis W. Freeman, "Hawaii and American Island-Outposts," in O. W.
Freeman (ed.), Geography of the Pacific (New York, 1951); E. S.
Craighill Handy, The Hawaiian Planter (Bernice Pahau Bishop Mu-
seum Bulletin, No. 161 [1940]).

2. Karl J. Pelzer, Pioneer Settlement in the Asiatic Tropics (New
York, 1945), p. 49.

Five vegetation zones are generally recognized: a coastal and low altitude zone; a lower forest belt; a middle forest zone; dense rain forests; upper forests--each characterized by a particular botanical complex.[3] Vegetation zones were also defined by the Hawaiians, a number extending from sea to mountain, characterized by the food plants, wild and cultivated, that grew in them.[4]

A number of wild edible plants were found, some offshoots of cultivated varieties: wild taro, wild banana, wild sugar cane, wild pandanus, fern roots of various sorts, and a number of different nuts. There was also edible seaweed.

Although the islands are usually devoid of reefs, and what there are, are fringing, there is and was an abundance of fish, both in variety and number.

There were no climatic factors which would make for large-scale famine.

Food supply

Source. --The great majority of food came from domesticated resources. Fishing was of considerable importance. Wild flora only a minor contribution to the diet.

Domesticated Food Resources	Special Techniques of Domestication	Zones Exploited by Domestication
1. Taro. The outstanding crop. A staple in many locales. Quite a number of varieties.[5]	1. There was a considerable use of irrigation in taro cultivation. Ditching, damming, terracing, for example, were used.[6] Also drainage of marsh lands. There was a selection of taro varieties for given locales. Fertilization to alleviate rot. Dry taro was constantly mulched. Some transplantation.	1. Wet taro widely distributed. Wet taro in valleys, maximum soil use. Terracing up valley sides to cliffs. Also along stream edges upland, marsh lands, and in sandy soils along coast. Dry taro was grown in upland forest zones. It was very adaptable. Primarily on leeward upper slopes.

---

3. Otis W. Freeman, "Geographic Setting of the Pacific," in O. W. Freeman (ed.), Geography of the Pacific (New York, 1951), pp. 338-40.

4. E. S. Craighill Handy and M. Pukui, "The Hawaiian Family System," Journal of the Polynesian Society, LIX (1950), 232-37.

5. E. S. Craighill Handy, The Hawaiian Planter. Handy lists 250 varieties.

6. Bennett, Archaeology of Kauai.

Domesticated Food Resources	Special Techniques of Domestication	Zones Exploited by Domestication
2. Sweet potato. In some areas, more important than taro. A considerable number of varieties.	2. Usually slash and burn. Special techniques developed for stony areas. Locally irrigated. Selection of varieties.	2. Widely spread. Highly adaptable in new and used soils. Grown mostly in coastal flats. Also in upland kula, small and dry valleys, even in extinct volcano craters and on terrace banks.
3. Banana. An important food; very plentiful in some districts.		3. In deep soil. Around dwellings on coast, lower and median forests. Hawaiian use of ecological niches seen in planting of bananas on irrigation banks.
4. Yam. Of importance in particular areas.		4. Inland gulches, high kula soils, rain forests. Considerable inland valley and forest tracts suitable.
5. Breadfruit. Of limited local importance.		5. In humus or red earth areas. Not grown in sand, cinders, or lava.
6. Sugar cane. Of limited importance.		6. On irrigation banks. Sporadically elsewhere.
7. Coconut. Not very important. Climate too harsh.		7. On protected lee slopes or sheltered valleys near sea level.
8. Pandanus. Of limited importance.		8. Near houses in lower valleys and near coasts.
9. Candlenut. Limited use.		9. In groves, in wet gulches, and in valleys.

Domesticated Food Resources	Special Techniques of Domestication	Zones Exploited by Domestication
10. Arrowroot. Little used.		10. On irrigation banks.
11. Ti. Little used.		11. On irrigation banks.
12. Fish. Not important from this source.	12. Raised in fish ponds in taro terraces.	
13. Chicken. Not important as a daily food.		
14. Pig. Not important as daily food.		
15. Dog. Not important as daily food.		

Natural biota exploited. --Fish and other sea life taken by a great variety of methods adapted for inshore, offshore, and open sea. More than 500 fish varieties known, almost all edible. Edible seaweed gathered in large quantities. A number of wild food plants gathered (as tree ferns). Wild fish stored in large offshore pools.

Shortages. --There were definite seasonal differences in type of food supply, but apparently no great decline in amount of food in any season. Cyclones were not usually a threat to large areas. The subsistence level was maintained at a high level year in and year out and from generation to generation, with some periods of surfeit, and localized famine, if any.

II. SOCIETY ISLANDS[7]

Environmental opportunities

A group of high (highest summit, 7,321'), relatively young volcanic islands. Total land area near 600 sq. miles. Islands generally circular in shape with streams radiating from central peak or peaks.

---

7. Major sources: Cyril Crossland, "The Island of Tahiti," The Geographical Journal, LXXI (1928), 561-85; William E. Ellis, Polynesian Researches (London, 1853); Kenneth P. Emory, Stone Remains in the Society Islands (Bernice Pahau Bishop Museum Bulletin, No. 116 [1933]); Otis W. Freeman, "Eastern Polynesia," in O. W. Freeman (ed.), Geography of the Pacific (New York, 1951); E. S. Craighill Handy, Houses, Boats, and Fishing in the Society Is-

Mountainous center often surrounded by maritime flat of rich alluvial
soil and swamps, often extending up low gradient valleys to depth of
four miles or more. This flat, because of soil and water, is extremely favorable to the growth of many types of crops.

Streams fall fairly rapidly. However, because of comparative
youth, the valleys are not as deeply cut as on some islands, the Marquesas, for example. There are often fertile flats in the upland valleys. Soils are numerous in type and generally fertile. The mountain
soils are thin. A red clay soil is found on the lower slopes. Irrigation is most practicable in inland valleys, but wet taro can also be
grown in swamps on maritime flats.

A heavy cover of bush and trees is found upland, the particular type
of vegetation varying with altitude and allied factors of rainfall, hu-
midity, and the like. The distribution of rainfall varies, in fact, with
altitude and windward vs. leeward sides of islands. The streams are
permanent. A two-season tropical climate prevails.

The islands have fringing and barrier reefs, the latter often one to
two miles out. The lagoon, the open sea, the reefs, fresh-water
lakes, and streams abound with water life.

A number of wild plants are edible including wild varieties of cultivated ones as well as Tahitian chestnut, candlenut, pandanus, Morinda citrifolia, various berries, fruits, etc. Edible plants are found in
lowland, valley, and upland regions.

There were quite a few edible birds.

Tropical storms and hurricanes are not frequent.

Food Supply

Source. --The great majority of food was domesticated food. Fish
were of importance, especially to coastal groups.

Domesticated Food Resources	Special Techniques of Domestication	Zones Exploited by Domestication
1. Breadfruit. Extensively used. A staple.		1. On maritime flats, and considerable distance up valleys.
2. Fei (upland banana). Very important.		2. On mountain slopes, and valley recesses.

lands (Bernice Pahau Bishop Museum Bulletin, No. 90 [1932]);
William Smith, Journal of a Voyage in the Missionary Ship Duff to
the Pacific Ocean in the Years 1796, 7, 8, 9, 1800, 1, 2, etc. (New
York, 1813); G. P. Wilder, The Breadfruit of Tahiti (Bernice
Pahau Bishop Museum Bulletin, No. 50 [1928]); Howel Williams, Ge-
ology of Tahiti, Moorea and Maiao (Bernice Pahau Bishop Museum
Bulletin, No. 105 [1933]).

Domesticated Food Resources	Special Techniques of Domestication	Zones Exploited by Domestication
2a. Meia (lowland banana). Very important.		2a. At lower altitudes. Generally on maritime flat.
3. Coconut. Of considerable importance.		3. In valley bottoms, banks of upland streams, mountains, and sea coast.
4. Taro. Of considerable importance.	4. Irrigation terraces are found in some places in interior. Swamps on maritime flats enclosed for wet taro. (Dry?)	4. Major portion evidently grown in swamps on maritime flat. Also in upland valley terraces.
4a. Kape (Alocasia indica). A plant related to taro. Of limited importance.		
5. Yam. Of importance locally.	5. Some terraces built for yams.	5. In mountains, especially, and on sides of lower slopes, along stream banks, and on maritime flat.
6. Sweet potato. Of importance.		6. Grown in rich mould, apparently in bottom lands.
7. Arrowroot. Limited importance.		7. In gardens, on maritime flat.
8. Ti (cultivation not certain). Of limited importance.		
9. Sugar cane. Of limited importance.		9. Evidently on maritime flat.
10. Pig. Little importance, a feast food.		
11. Chicken. As pig.		

Domesticated Food Resources	Special Techniques of Domestication	Zones Exploited by Domestication
12. Dog. As pig.		
13. Fish. Grown in ponds. Very little fish by this method.	13. In ponds in irrigation terraces.	

Natural biota exploited. --Inland wild plants such as banana, ginger, arrowroot, yams, and other foods--as ferns and various fruits and berries--sporadically gathered. Pandanus, candlenut, and Tahitian chestnut growing in the various zones are similarly exploited.

Fish of the lagoon, reef, and open sea taken by a number of methods as were other forms of sea life inhabiting these areas. The few fresh-water lakes and the rivers exploited for fish, eels, and the like.

Birds were not of great importance.

Shortages. --The maritime flats and lowlands being naturally irrigated, the staple bananas and breadfruit did not seriously suffer from drought.

Since the abundance of breadfruit, fish, yams, fei, and even taro was seasonal, there were marked food seasons and some dependence on wild resources at times and places. But there were no general serious famines, and the carrying level probably did not drop appreciably for any significant interval during the year. Occasional flash floods cause considerable crop damage in valleys, however.

III. SAMOA[8]

Environmental opportunities

A group of volcanic, high (up to 6,094' on Savaii) islands. Land area near 1,200 sq. miles. High temperatures and heavy rainfall with great variation in rain over given periods. Two seasons, a wet and a less wet.

Islands are of recent volcanic origin. Soils generally thin, but fertile--especially near coast.

Streams are not numerous. But few are permanent. There are inland and coastal springs.

The area around the coast offers the best exploitive possibilities. Hillside slopes are moderate here, and swamps are formed between the back of the beach and the interior hills. Further inland the mountains rapidly become very steep. Larger streams flowing to sea form wide valleys at their mouths.

The lagoon formed by the barrier reef contributes to the rich diversity of this coastal area as fish abound in the lagoon.

Hurricanes occur at regular intervals.

---

8. Major sources: Edwin H. Bryan, Jr., "Central and Western Polynesia," in Otis W. Freeman (ed.), Geography of the Pacific (New

There is much variation from island to island, but as a general rule, ecological opportunities are limited to the coastal area and its environs. Diversity of ecological zones seems more restricted than in Hawaii, or at least the zones have not been exploited by native or European and thus not noticed in the literature.

A dense, tropical-forest cover over most of the islands. Edible wild flora include: wild taro, wild yam, Tahitian chestnut, tree fern, and seaweed. There were also wild birds.

Food supply

Source.--There was a marked dependence on horticulture. But the sea was much used as a resource area. Fish were important in the diet.

Domesticated Food Resources	Special Techniques of Domestication	Zones Exploited by Domestication
1. Taro. Probably the most important food.	1. Grown wet, and dry by slash and burn. Trunks girdled. No fertilizer. Wet taro grown in swamps on elevated beds drained by ditches. Mulched.	1. More dry taro than wet. Dry grown in patches of inland forests on mountain slopes up to elevations of 1,000 ft., higher than any other crops. Could be grown on slopes of 60°. Left fallow after two years for recuperation of soil. Wet taro grown in swamps between beaches and mountains. Taro plots grow smaller farther inland. At two miles plot can be only 0.1 acre.

York, 1951); Peter H. Buck, Samoan Material Culture (Bernice Pahau Bishop Museum Bulletin, No. 75 [1930]); John Wesley Coulter, Land Utilization in American Samoa (Bernice Pahau Bishop Museum Bulletin, No. 170 [1941]); Reginald A. Daly, "The Geology of American Samoa," Papers from the Department of Marine Biology of the Carnegie Institution of Washington, XIX (1923), 93-143 (Carnegie Institution of Washington, No. 340); Felix M. Keesing, Modern Samoa (London, 1934); Margaret Mead, The Social Organization of Manua (Bernice Pahau Bishop Museum Bulletin, No. 76 [1930]); William A. Setchell, American Samoa. Papers from the Department of Marine Biology of the Carnegie Institution, Vol. XX (1924) (Carnegie Institute of Washington, No. 341). Part 2, "Ethnobotany of the Samoans," pp. 189-224.

Domesticated Food Resources	Special Techniques of Domestication	Zones Exploited by Domestication
2. Banana. An important food.		2. Up mountain slopes; not as high as taro. Some also planted around houses near coast, presumably in coral sand soil.
3. Breadfruit. An important food.		3. Same as banana.
4. Coconut. Used for food and drink, less important than 1-3.		4. Seems adapted to all zones from sandy beach up to mountain slopes. Usually within a mile of shoreline, however.
5. Yam. Opinions vary as to aboriginal importance.	5. Same as dry taro except require more attention. Replanting practiced.	5. On inland, mountain plots; in forest. Sometimes same plot as taro.
6. Sweet potato. Of limited, local importance.		6. Seen growing on sandy beach soil.
7. Sugar cane. Limited use, mostly for sweets.		7. Near houses on sandy soil near shore.
8. Pandanus. Of very limited importance as food.		8. Near coast.
9. Ti. Of little importance as food.		9. Near coast on sandy zone.
10. Arrowroot. Of little food importance.		
11. Fowl. Used in feasts.		
12. Pig. Used in feasts.		

Natural biota exploited. --Wild fauna, especially birds, were hunted and fowling was of some significance.

Fish caught in the lagoon and the deep sea. The reef was combed daily. A great variety of techniques used. Other sea food also appropriated.

Wild flora were not extensively utilized.

Shortages. --Because of the impressive range of crops and the constant supply of fish, there was probably little seasonal variation in the food supply level.

Mead writes, "In Samoa there is no winter, no lean season, no period when scrimping and saving are necessary."[9] However, famines could follow hurricanes.

IV. MANGAREVA[10]

Environmental opportunities

Four small (altogether, 11 sq. miles) volcanic islands surrounded by reef. Highest summit 1,427 feet. The encircling reef contains some coral islets valuable as access points to reefs and fishing grounds.

Each main island traversed by a razorback ridge along its long axis. Secondary ridges run perpendicularly to coast where they end in steep promontories. Between them are bays forming valley mouths. The valleys extend inward from sea with a varying, usually small, amount of flat land, sometimes swampy. These valleys are the most cultivable parts of the islands, given the native techniques.

The climate is rainy, but there are no permanent streams, although there are various springs and seepages on high and low land.

The soil is often rocky. Forest cover consists mainly of clumps at valley heads and cliff bases, and cane growth on the ends of main ridges.

The lagoon, reefs, and open sea abound in fish, shellfish, and other sea life.

Edible wild flora include: Morinda citrifolia, Cucimus sp., Portulaca iutea, Telephrosia purpurea, and others.

Food supply

Source. --There was a marked emphasis on domesticated resources, but fish were extremely important. Laval's estimate that fish provide half the diet, however, seems to us exaggerated.

---

9. Margaret Mead, The Social Organization of Manua, p. 65.

10. Major sources: Peter H. Buck, Ethnology of Mangareva (Bernice Pahau Bishop Museum Bulletin, No. 157 [1938]); Otis W. Freeman, "Eastern Polynesia"; Honoré Laval, Mangareva: L'Histoire Ancienne d'un Peuple Polynésien (Braine-le-Comte, 1938).

Domesticated Food Resources	Special Techniques of Domestication	Zones Exploited by Domestication
1. Breadfruit. The most important vegetable.		1. Mostly in the valleys.
2. Coconut. Of considerable importance.		2. As breadfruit (?).
3. Taro. Of some importance.	3. Small scale irrigation in narrow strips below rock outcrops or cliffs below seepages. Terraces only a few feet wide. Soil had to be replaced at times.	3. Irrigation in uplands. Every trickle utilized. Some taro grown in swamps of flatlands without irrigation. Some on dry land.
3a. Kape. A taro variety.		3a. In moist soil near springs (incomplete).
4. Banana. Of some importance.		4. Apparently on flat lands.
4a. Plantain. Of some importance.		4a. ?
5. Sugar cane. Of some importance.		5. Probably flat lands (incomplete distribution).
6. Sweet potato. Of some importance.		6. In dry soil. (Where?)
7. Ti. Of very limited importance.		7. ?
8. Arrowroot. Of very limited importance.		8. ?
9. Yam. Of very limited importance.		9. ?
10. Turmeric. Of limited importance.		10. ?

Domesticated Food Resources	Special Techniques of Domestication	Zones Exploited by Domestication
11. Pandanus and 12. Mountain apple? The description of these is included with cultivated plants by Buck.[11] However, it is not certain that they were cultivated, as pandanus abounds in a natural state in these islands. Both were of some importance as foods.		11. ? 12. ?

Natural biota exploited. --Fish abound, especially in the inner lagoon. The coral islets were used as camps for easy access to fishing grounds. The reefs provide shellfish. Besides fish, oysters, turtles, limpets, octopus, and land crabs taken. Fishing resources were heavily exploited.

Various edible plants were locally and seasonally valued.

Birds were unimportant.

Shortages. --There is mention of wild foods used in scarcities. But such scarcities might refer to those occurring locally because of defeat in war. Métraux, however, writes that food was frequently a problem.[12]

Some harvested breadfruit and ti were stored for use at other times of the year.

V. EASTER ISLAND [13]

Environmental opportunities

Volcanic island, about 62 sq. miles. Highest summit, 1,730 feet. Triangular in shape with three volcanoes at angles.

The island lacks permanent rivers, is therefore not rugged or deeply eroded. Rainfall averages about 50" per annum, falls heaviest during the Mar.-Oct. period of the two-season tropical climate. The soil is fertile, especially when deep. However, it is generally porous and rain runs rapidly through. Much of the interior is a plain com-

---

11. Buck, Ethnology of Mangareva.

12. Alfred Métraux, "Une Féodalité Cannibale en Polynésie Française," Revue de Paris, V (1937), 639. (Based on Laval's manuscript.)

13. Major sources: Alfred Métraux, Ethnology of Easter Island (Bernice Pahau Bishop Museum Bulletin, No. 160 [1940]); Foreign Office (British), Historical Section, "Malpelo, Cocos and Easter Islands"

posed of soil of varying depth and rock outcrop. Evidently much of the deep soil is near the coast, affording the best agricultural land. The only interior water supply is in three crater lakes.

The coast itself is jagged, in some places abutted by an escarpment of 50-100 feet. Sandy beaches are few.

There is no barrier reef and fishing opportunities are, in consequence, limited.

Grass is the most common cover on the island. Forests were very limited, occurring mostly near crater lakes. Indigenous flora was on the whole, extremely limited in variety. Edible plants were few.

Aside from fish and water life, sea birds and rats were exploitable fauna.

Short droughts occurred. The water supply was limited. Wells were necessary. The crater lakes are largely inaccessible.

Thomson estimates that about 32 square miles are suitable for cultivation. It should be mentioned that there is a great deal of variability in early accounts as to the fertility at Easter Island.[14]

Food supply
  Source.--The great majority of the food supply was domesticated. Fish evidently of significance only seasonally.

Domesticated Food Resources	Special Techniques of Domestication	Zones Exploited by Domestication
1. Sweet potato. The staple.	Information is not specific for certain crops, except that ta-	Information is not specific for particular crops. Most cultiva-
2. Banana. Of extensive use.	ro is cultivated in stony places in enclosures.	tion was near the coast but there is evidence of inland planta-
3. Yam. One of the most used foods.	Mulching and burning of grass for fertilizer practiced.	tions and of cultivation on the mountain slopes. Since sweet
4. Taro. Of some significance.	Banana plantations 1/4 and 1/8 leagues have been described.	potato thrives in well-drained soil, porosity was an advantage.
5. Arrowroot. Of some significance.		Bananas were grown in deep soil, taro in

(Peace Handbooks, Vol. XXII, Nos. 141, 142 [1920]); Mrs. Scoresby Routledge, The Mystery of Easter Island (London, 1919); C. Skottsberg, "Notes on a Visit to Easter Island," in The Natural History of Juan Fernandez and Easter Island, Vol. I, No. 1 (Uppsala, Sweden, 1920); William J. Thomson, "Te Pito Te Henua, or Easter Island," United States National Museum, Annual Report (1889), 447-552.

    14. Alfred Métraux, Ethnology of Easter Island, pp. 12-14. See also Thomson, "Te Pito Te Henua, or Easter Island," pp. 455 f.

Domesticated Food Resources	Special Techniques of Domestication	Zones Exploited by Domestication
6. Sugar cane. Of some significance.		stony places with thin soil as these could be made to retain moisture.
7. Ti. Not extensively used for food.		
8. Fowl. Of limited importance.		

Natural biota exploited. --Sea birds, especially their eggs, were extensively hunted.

Some rats were taken.

Wild flora were only of limited value.

Fish were taken in abundance only seasonally and locally. Other forms of sea life, as shellfish, octopus, and turtles, were taken also in fair quantity.

Shortages. --The droughts were evidently too short to influence vegetation.

Certain wild foods are alluded to as being used during scarcity, but the nature of scarcity periods is unknown. Scarcities may refer to the situation of groups defeated in war, but may also have been more general due to water conditions.

VI. UVEA[15]

Environmental opportunities

Volcanic island, but height only 400-500 feet. (Area about 37 square miles.) There was a lack of permanent streams, precluding irrigation and necessitating dependence on coconut for drink. Streamlets at base of bluff on inland side of shore strip. Soil evidently quite fertile. Much of interior arable. Tall rain forest in north becoming scrub in south. There was a small unarable desert in the center of the island.

A fringing and a barrier reef resulting in rich supply of lagoon fish. Islets on reef useful as access to fishing resources.

Wild biota otherwise limited.

Two-season climate varying with trade winds.

Occasional hurricanes.

Food supply

Source. --A good proportion of food supply comes from cultivated plants. But fishing is very important also.

---

15. Major sources: Edwin G. Burrows, Ethnology of Uvea (Bernice Pahau Bishop Museum Bulletin, No. 145 [1937]); Edwin G. Burrows, "Topography and Culture on Two Polynesian Islands," Geographical Review, XXVIII (1938), 214-23.

Domesticated Food Resources	Special Techniques of Domestication	Zones Exploited by Domestication
1. Yam. A staple.	1. Slash and burn. Large trees girdled. No fertilization except ash left from burning.	1. Grown in interior except in desert and tall-forest regions. Plots abandoned after 2-3 crops and left fallow 15-20 years.
2. Banana. An important food at certain times of the year.	2. Same as yams on interior plantations.	2. On interior plots. Some also along coast.
3. Taro. Not abundant.	3. Wet land taro in marshes drained by ditches, but not irrigated. Mulched. Dry land taro as yams.	3. Wet taro on shore strip where there is a streamlet or seepage from the interior. Dry taro inland.
3a. Kape. Important in certain seasons.	3a. As yams.	3a. As yams.
4. Coconut. Not as much used for food as for liquid.		4. All along the shore. Across the island only on N. and S. ends.
5. Breadfruit. An important item.		5. Along shore, mainly.
6. Arrowroot. Not important.		6. ?
7. Sugar cane. Limited importance.		7. ?
8. Pig. Used for feasts.		
9. Chicken. Used for feasts. Eggs not used to any extent.		

Natural biota exploited. -- Wild vegetables such as pandanus, wild arrowroot and yams important only during famine.
Birds, coconut crabs, and flying foxes were delicacies.
A great variety of fish from the sea, especially the lagoon. They

were very abundant and important percentagewise in the diet. Reef islets used for fishing and gathering.

Crustaceans, mollusks, seaweed, and turtles important sea foods
also. A number of techniques used for capturing sea foods.

Shortages. --Definite lean seasons of about two-month duration occurred because of a gap in the crop cycle and lack of adequate storage
techniques.

Taro, kape, and bananas were year round food plants but taro not
abundant and kape most plentiful only in August. Although yams and
breadfruit occurred for most of the year, there were only two main
harvests of each, approximately the same. During Sept. -Oct., bananas the only plant food.

Furthermore, famines may have occurred because of hurricanes
or plant disease which considerably limit the carrying capacity.

VII. MANGAIA[16]

Environmental opportunities

Small (17,500 acres), relatively low (554') volcanic island.

A narrow coast running against a raised coral limestone shelf,
makatea, which encircles the island. The shelf, several hundred
yards to 1 1/2 miles wide, terminates abruptly at its interior border,
dropping about 150 feet. At inner foot of the makatea lie swamps up
to 500 yards wide wherever streams, running off a central plateau,
abut and eventually seep through the shelf. This swamp land is called
puna and is immensely valuable for the growing of taro. Small pockets
of friable soil are also found on the makatea and are useful for certain crops. Besides the makatea abounds with edible candlenut.

The upper reaches of the streams cut narrow valleys upland suitable for some crops. The relatively low height results in a definite
dry season, July to December, in which streams are apt to be impermanent, and the puna lands unsuitable for taro.

There is a surrounding fringing reef, 80 to 300 yards wide. Fish
fairly abundant seasonally.

The volcanic slopes are covered with dense fern and casauria.
Thickets of trees and scrub in stream valleys. Besides candlenut,
pandanus, and a number of other edible, uncultivated fruits and berries found, and native chestnut.

Hurricanes were rare, about once every 20 years.

Food supply

Source. --Majority of food domesticated. Fish, however, are as
important in diet during certain seasons. And wild flora were sometimes depended upon.

16. Major sources: Peter H. Buck, Mangaian Society (Bernice Pa-
hau Bishop Museum Bulletin, No. 122 [1934]); William Wyatt Gill, From
Darkness to Light in Polynesia (London, 1894); P. Marshall, Geology of
Mangaia (Bernice Pahau Bishop Museum Bulletin, No. 36 [1927]).

Domesticated Food Resources	Special Techniques of Domestication	Zones Exploited by Domestication
1. Taro. The staple.	1. Grown wet (and dry?). Terraces constructed on puna land and water diverted.	1. Grown extensively on puna land and up the slopes for about 1/2 mile. Also in patches in upland valleys.
2. Yam. Importance undocumented.		
3. Banana. Both plantain and banana grown. Importance undocumented.		
4. Sweet potato. An important food.		4. On makatea and in upland valleys.
5. Coconut. Seasonally important.		5. At base of hills above taro flats and near houses. Also on shore strip.
6. Ti.		6. Near houses, some in upland valleys.
7. Arrowroot, and 8. Pandanus. Not certain if cultivated. Important locally and seasonally.		7. In upland valleys.

Natural biota exploited. --Fish and sea life taken in "lagoon" and open sea whenever possible.

Wild foods were rather well exploited.

Shortages. --Floods coming down the hills can wreak havoc among crops at base. During the dry season, July to December, taro was scarce and there was a dependence on coconut, wild yam, and ti. The last was stored for use at this time.

Environmental opportunities

High volcanic islands. Summits of Nukuhiva and Hiva Oa over 4,000'. Total land area of inhabited islands is about 375 square miles.

Islands relatively old, deeply eroded with deep-cut valleys of canyon and amphitheater shape and sharp ridges (upland) or plateaus (lower) between them. Valley walls are steep.

Coast is formed by rugged cliffs punctured by embayments at the valley mouths. There is no maritime flat, the absence of which is a definite hamper to agriculture.

There are few beaches and no barrier reef, which limits fishing to the deep-sea variety and cuts down the relative abundance of fish.

Most streams are intermittent at their lower reaches and may go dry in periods of drought.

Rainfall usually varies little seasonally, but varies much with altitude and windward or leeward sides of islands. High altitudes are wetter, and leeward sides of islands are dry, often exceedingly so. Furthermore, rainfall may vary from year to year, with the result that cycles of drought and plenty occur within a human generation. The drought years are hard on vegetation and may produce severe famine.

The soil is generally porous and fertile, but it is limited in agricultural possibilities. A lack of level ground hampers the development of large-scale irrigation, even where water supply is adequate.

Three zones of vegetation can be described, altitude being the delimiting factor. The uppermost areas are cloaked in rain forest; the other areas also have thick indigenous cover except on the leeward side, which may be desiccated.

No severe storms occur, but tidal waves can flood valleys up to 1/2 mile inland.

Useful food plants (wild) include pandanus and Tahitian chestnut.

Food supply

Source. --The lack of a barrier reef and the consequent limitation of sea-food supply necessitated dependence on agriculture wherever possible.

---

17. Major sources: A. M. Adamson, Marquesan Insects: Environment (Bernice Pahau Bishop Museum Bulletin, No. 139 [1936]); Lawrence John Chubb, Geology of the Marquesas Islands (Bernice Pahau Bishop Museum Bulletin, No. 68 [1930]); Otis W. Freeman, "Eastern Polynesia"; E. S. Craighill Handy, The Native Culture in the Marquesas (Bernice Pahau Bishop Museum Bulletin, No. 9 [1923]); Ralph Linton, The Material Culture of the Marquesas Islands (Bernice Pahau Bishop Museum Memoir, Vol. VII, No. 5 [1923]); Ralph Linton, Archaeology of the Marquesas (Bernice Pahau Bishop Museum Bulletin, No. 23 [1925]).

Domesticated Food Resources	Special Techniques of Domestication	Zones Exploited by Domestication
1. Breadfruit. By far the staple. Quite a few varieties.		1. Apparently largely grown up to 1,500' wherever possible in valleys, usually valley floors.
2. Coconut. Of considerable importance.		2. By and large as breadfruit.
3. Banana. Of considerable importance.		3. Some grown in uplands (incomplete).
4. Taro. Of limited importance.	4. In stone-bordered patches near streams or in irrigated terraces above stream banks or on valley floors.	4. As indicated, irrigation was limited due to lack of level land and uncertainty of water supply. Not numerous anywhere. Mostly on stream borders and valley floors.
4a. Kape. As taro proper.		
5. Sugar cane. Limited importance.		5. Near houses (in lower vegetation zone?).
6. Sweet potato. Limited importance.		6. ?
7. Yam. Of only limited importance.		7. ?
8. Pig. Of limited importance.		
9. Chicken. As pig.		

Natural biota exploited. --Lack of barrier reef limits food supply. Deep sea fish taken as were crab, lobster, shrimp, and octopus.
   Birds and wild flora locally important.
   Shortages. --Although breadfruit was stored in pits for indefinite periods and some fish dried for short periods, the long droughts caused frequent and prolonged famines. ("Famine was a constant and

entirely unpredictable threat."[18] One would presume that during these droughts (occurring periodically over an interval of years), the carrying capacity of the area would be lowered to that provided by stored breadfruit and nondomesticated foods. The latter were limited here.

IX. FUTUNA[19]

Environmental opportunities

Two volcanic islands, Futuna, 25 sq. miles; Alofi, 11 sq. miles. Highest peak, 2,500', on Futuna.

Alofi has no streams, a bowl-shaped interior plateau holding water and forest vegetation. It is otherwise like Futuna but was not permanently inhabited, and was exploited only in the interior at the time of ethnographic study.

From the central heights of Futuna, streams flow down to the sea cutting deep gorges. The interior upland area has a dense forest only in the mountains and upper valleys. Otherwise, the red dense soil spills off moisture and the cover of vegetation is stunted. This area is not promising for agriculture.

The mountain land of Futuna ends with an abrupt ridge near the sea. The coastal flat is relatively narrow and coral in composition except where streams flooding down from the mountains have built up alluvial deposits. These streams, because of high mountains and a trade-wind season and the resultant rainfall, are very rarely dry. Water also seeps through the seaward ridge. It is this area of coastal flat and valley bottom with the adjoining ridge tips that is the most promising for agriculture.

However, a barrier reef is lacking and the result is a relatively poor fish and other sea-food supply.

Several sorts of wild plants, mostly of the interior, are edible. There are also edible birds.

Hurricanes may occur at the end of the wet season.

Food supply

Source. --The use of cultivated foods is overwhelmingly greater than the use of undomesticated foods. Fish a flavoring, not a staple.

---

18. Ralph Linton, "Marquesan Culture," in Ralph Linton and A. Kardiner, The Individual and His Society (New York, 1939), p. 143.
19. Major sources: Edwin G. Burrows, Ethnology of Futuna (Bernice Pahau Bishop Museum Bulletin, No. 138 [1936]); Edwin G. Burrows, "Topography and Culture on Two Polynesian Islands," pp. 214-23.

Domesticated Food Resources	Special Techniques of Domestication	Zones Exploited by Domestication
1. Taro. The staple.	1. Irrigation at valley mouth. Water dammed and led into upper terraces by ditches and from here to lower terraces. Water frequently changed and silt redistributed. Ditches kept clear. Dry land slash and burn also used. Trees cut down but not dragged away. No deliberate fertilization. No mulching. Sites usually changed yearly.	1. Wet taro at valley mouths and below the ridges. Dry taro on lower slopes above ridges.
1a. Kape. A taro variety.	1a. As dry taro.	1a. Kape grown in dry plantations.
2. Yam. Of importance, especially where streams are lacking.	2. Slash and burn as dry taro.	2. As dry taro. Also in interior Alofi.
3. Coconut. Of considerable use.		3. Mostly on shore strips, also on ridge tips, valley bottoms, upland groves, and interior Alofi.
4. Breadfruit. Of considerable use.		4. Usually on shore strips.
5. Banana. Of limited use.	5. Some slash and burn as dry taro.	5. Usually on shore strip. Some on upland plantations on ridge tip and interior Alofi.
6. Arrowroot. Of limited use.		6. On shore strip.
7. Sugar cane. Of limited use.		7. On shore strip.
8. Pig. Use limited.		

Domesticated Food Resources	Special Techniques of Domestication	Zones Exploited by Domestication
9. Dog. Use as food limited.		
10. Chicken. Use limited.		

Natural biota exploited. --Wild fruits and nuts not heavily exploited. A variety of sea foods but limited in quantity. Lack of lagoon limited supply of fish and development of techniques. Shore fish usually 1/2 to 3" long. Some deep-sea bonito taken in aboriginal times. Shortages. --Hurricanes, occurring at the end of the wet season, probably seriously limited population possibilities.

X. TIKOPIA[20]

Environmental opportunities
Small (3 sq. mi.) volcanic island. Island composed of ancient crater rim, with highest point 2,000 ft., enclosing a crater lake. On the southwest, a flat plain about 1/2 mile at widest points, with a large natural swamp. A narrow strip of beach and a fringing reef.

Land on the sides and crest of the old crater is primarily composed of volcanic rock with areas of soil, especially on the crest, which is worn flat at places. The flat-land plain is composed of alluvial soils near mountain, sandier soils near coast. The soil is fertile. Springs and pools run down slopes from the crater lake.

Vegetation is sparse on coast, but it increases further inland. Several wild plants (i.e., not found in plantations or gardens) are of some value as food, including arrowroot, Cordyline terminalis and pandanus.

The interior crater lake, the fringing reef (especially in south, it is narrow in north), and the open sea abound in fish life seasonally. But, "the absence of any extensive reef system prevents any large constant supply from being obtained. In a period of rough weather the people may taste no fish for several weeks at a time, and then live enentirely on vegetable food."[21] Birds of a number of species occur, as do eels.

A two-season climate prevails. Severe gales occur in the early monsoon, sometimes becoming hurricanes. Droughts occur on occasion.

---

20. Major sources: Raymond Firth, "Report on Research in Tikopia," Oceania, I (1930-31), 105-17; Raymond Firth, We, the Tikopia (London, 1936); Raymond Firth, Primitive Polynesian Economy (New York, 1950).
21. Raymond Firth, "Report on Research in Tikopia," p. 107.

Food supply

Source. --Marked dependence on domesticated vegetables although fish of considerable importance, especially during certain seasons.

Domesticated Food Resources	Special Techniques of Domestication	Zones Exploited by Domestication
1. Taro. The staple.	1. Brush cut, but rarely burned. Mulching. Two-three weedings. Fallowing 2-3 years after each crop.	1. 1/5 to 1/7 of island given over to taro. Fairly well distributed. Grown on flat lands, plateaus on crater rim, and slopes of mountains almost to peak. Swamp lands are not used because they cannot be drained.
1a. Pulaka (Alocasia sp.). Of limited importance.	1a. ?	1a. Grown on wet, level land mostly near lake at low altitude.
2. Coconut. Of considerable importance.		2. On coastal flat lands and lower slopes.
3. Breadfruit. Of considerable importance.		3. Widely distributed, but less than taro and mostly lower land.
4. Sago. Of limited importance.	4. Self-propagating, but in plantations.	4. On flats and lower slopes, mostly near lake.
5. Banana. Of considerable importance now, but less importance before Europeans.		5. Fairly wide distribution, but less than taro.
6. Yam. Of limited importance. Some varieties introduced.	6. As taro.	6. As taro, but more limited distribution.
7. Tahitian chestnut. Grown in gardens. Of limited importance.		7. Fairly wide distribution, but less area than taro.

Domesticated Food Resources	Special Techniques of Domestication	Zones Exploited by Domestication
8. Turmeric. Of little importance as food.		
9. Sugar cane. Of little importance.		

Natural biota exploited. --Fringing reef extensively utilized for food. Several edible fish of crater lake taken. Open sea also exploited. Fishing was a seasonally variable activity. Eels not taken. But few birds hunted. Wild plants sporadically utilized.

Shortages. --Periodic droughts often severe. Pests reduce taro supply. For about 3 1/2 months a year, taro relatively scarce and carrying capacity is reduced to limits of coconut, sago, and forest fruits.

Gales occurring during monsoon can turn into hurricanes whose devastation reduces food supply for months.

There is a marked scarcity of every kind of food supply in May and June which storage of breadfruit, taro, and banana does not entirely alleviate.

XI. ONTONG JAVA[22]

Environmental opportunities

Coral atoll, 40-50 miles in diameter, composed of large number of islands. Islands are low and small, largest being 4-5 miles long by 300 yards wide.

Typical atoll with little environmental variety, and usual limitations on agricultural development. Soil consists of sand and coral detritus mixed with decayed vegetation. The native vegetation is luxuriant, but limited in variety and exploitative possibilities. There are no streams; wells and coconuts supply liquid. There are two seasons, trade wind and monsoon, the latter being wetter, but there is little climatic variation seasonally, and evidently no seasonal rhythm of occupations.

Aside from coral beach and soil, there are some swamps on the larger islands. These swamps are suitable for taro growth.

Fish abound in the lagoon and open sea.

Hurricanes not frequent.

---

22. Major sources: H. Ian Hogbin, "The Social Organization of Ontong Java," Oceania, I (1930-31), 399-425; H. Ian Hogbin, Law and Order in Polynesia (New York, 1934); H. Ian Hogbin, "Coconuts and Coral Islands," National Geographic Magazine, LXV (1934), 265-98; H. Ian Hogbin, "'Polynesian' Colonies in Melanesia," Journal of the Polynesian Society, XLIX (1940), 199-220.

Food supply

Source.--Nondomesticated resources, fish, evidently approached domesticated resources in significance in diet.

Domesticated Food Resources	Special Techniques of Domestication	Zones Exploited by Domestication
1. Coconut. Ranked with fish as the principal food source.		1. Evidently on most parts of the islands.
2. Taro. An important food.	2. Grown in swamps; require attention. Have banks thrown up to retain water.	2. Grown in swamps on the larger islands.
3. Banana (Aboriginal?). A few grown.		3. ?

Natural biota exploited.--Fish abundant, especially in the lagoon. The open sea also exploited. Fishing undertaken daily by a variety of methods.

Shortages.--There is no information about shortage. Since there is a lack of climatic variation and the cropping of taro and coconut is continuous, it is evident that any shortages which would occur would be caused by such things as cyclones, and these are relatively rare.

XII. PUKAPUKA[23]

Environmental opportunities

Three small coral islets (1,250 acres) forming a triangular atoll. Highest point 40 feet.

Typical coral atoll environment with coral gravel and sand soil and limited variety of vegetation, often sparse with bush in a few areas. Only restricted agriculture possible.

Two-season climate, dry May-Sept., wetter Nov.-April. Deep-sea fish during dry season abundant, but difficult in wet season. Taro, however, is limited by the dry season.

Occasional hurricanes, droughts, and tidal waves.

Fish are abundant in the interior lagoon and the deep sea. The reef provides other sea life.

A variety of sea birds.

---

23. Major sources: Ernest Beaglehole, Islands of Danger (Wellington, N.Z., 1944); Ernest and Pearl Beaglehole, Ethnology of Pukapuka (Bernice Pahau Bishop Museum Bulletin, No. 150 [1938]); Gordon MacGregor, Notes on the Ethnology of Pukapuka (Bernice Pahau Bishop Museum Occasional Papers, Vol. XI, No. 6 [1935]).

Food supply

Source.--Fish approach domesticated resources in importance in diet.

Domesticated Food Resources	Special Techniques of Domestication	Zones Exploited by Domestication
1. Coconut. The vegetable staple.		1. Apparently fairly generally distributed on islets.
2. Taro. Of less significance than coconut.	2. Grown in excavated pits which allow seepage, filled with vegetable matter. Mulched twice yearly, weeded once a month. Some dry taro once grown.	2. Pits may have been in center parts of atoll islet, as these usually have depression.
2a. Pulaka. Evidently a variety of taro.	2a. Pulaka as taro.	2a. As taro.
3. Banana. Of limited importance.	3. As taro.	3. As taro.
4. Pandanus (cultivated?). Of limited importance.		

Natural biota exploited.--An imposing list of fish utilized both from lagoon and seasonally from the open sea. Lagoon fished daily. Reefs combed for sea life.

Birds were taken seasonally.

Shortages.--During the dry months, May-Sept., no taro reaches maturity, the carrying level being reduced in consequence. The taro crop was subject to other vicissitudes also. In dry years the beds could dry up entirely. New tubers planted afterward would require 6-12 months to reach maturity. A rain flooding the beds followed by a period of brilliant sunshine will kill the taro by heat.

A complete taro loss might be even more serious since deep-sea fishing is hard during taro season because of rough seas.

Hurricanes and tidal waves could also cause considerable damage that would result in famine and depopulation, despite some storage of coconuts.

In summary, considerable lowering of carrying capacity may occur seasonally or at times over a number of years.

Environmental opportunities

Four typical coral atolls with paucity of environmental variety, low elevation, shortage of water supply, and small land area.

During trade-wind season, Óct.-July, rainfall heavy. However, drought may set in, in drier Nov.-Feb. period. Some hurricanes reported.

There is a lack of fertile soil on all atolls, although Olosenga, now uninhabited, evidently has somewhat greater soil potentialities. On all the atolls, soil is composed of coral, sand, and loose rubble through which rain drains quickly carrying decaying vegetable matter, which makes agriculture "almost impossible."

Fish abound in the inner lagoon and the open sea, although the fact that the reefs are not broad precludes large-scale communal fishing. Shellfish are also present.

Two of the native floral products are edible.

Wild birds are present.

Food supply

Source.--Fish compare favorably with domesticated products as the mainstay of the diet.

Domesticated Food Resources	Special Techniques of Domestication	Zones Exploited by Domestication
1. Coconut. The staple vegetable.		1. All over the islets of the atoll, even near houses on the islets with villages.
2. Pandanus. Of considerable importance.		2. Scattered over atolls.
3. Taro. Evidence of its former cultivation on Olosenga.		3. On Olosenga on areas bordering western shore of lagoon.
4. Yam (aboriginal?). Reported by Lister.		4. ?

24. Major sources: J. J. Lister, "Notes on the Natives of Fakaofu (Bowditch Island)," Journal of the (Royal) Anthropological Institute, XXI (1891), 43-63; Gordon MacGregor, Ethnology of the Tokelau Islands (Bernice Pahau Bishop Museum Bulletin, No. 146 [1937]).

Natural biota exploited. --Fish extensively taken, largely in the lagoon, but also on the open sea. Fishing a daily occupation of adult males. Turtles, crabs, and other sea life also utilized.

Birds and their eggs a minor contribution to the food supply, as were the fruit of two wild types of trees.

Shortages. --Coconuts harvested continuously, and there were preservation methods for pandanus and certain fish. There does not seem to be any gap in the consumption cycle during a normal year. The effect of drought on carrying capacity is not documented, however.

Famines and hurricanes are mentioned in the traditional history and in passing by MacGregor. Olosenga's population was wiped out by famine.

Glossary

The following Polynesian terms are frequently used in this book. Glottal stops are omitted in the transcription of these terms because of inconsistencies in the sources.

ainga. A localized Samoan descent line.

alii. A person of chiefly status in Hawaii; in Samoa, a chief as opposed to a talking chief (tulafale), both of these being of the highest status. (Alii is a cognate of ariki, arii, aliki, etc., see below.).

alii nui. The paramount chief of an Hawaiian island.

aliki. A Pukapukan high chief (cognate of ariki, alii, arii, etc.).

api. An Uvean household.

arii. A person of chiefly status in the Society Islands (cognate of ariki, alii, eike, etc.).

ariki. A Tikopian chief; a Mangaian chief; a Tongarevan chief; a Manihiki chief (cognate of aliki, arii, etc.).

ariki mau. Paramount priest-chief of Easter Island.

ariori society. A traveling entertainment group in the Society Islands.

aumaga. The nontitled males of a Samoan village.

eike. A person of chiefly status in Tonga (cognate of alii, arii, ariki, etc.).

falefa. A Tongan of chiefly status; ceremonial attendant of a very high chief.

fono. A council in Samoa and Tonga.

haa. Ramage of highest order in Tonga.

hakaiki. The paramount chief of a Marquesan "tribe" or maximal ramage.

hapu. A ramage of intermediate order among the Maori of New Zealand, usually corresponds to a village.

iatoai. Junior relatives of a Society Island chief, themselves of chiefly status.

ivi. A maximal ramage among the Maori of New Zealand.

kainanga. A Tikopian maximal ramage.

kainga. A localized descent line in Uvea.

kalaimoku. The chief adviser of a Hawaiian paramount chief.

kava. A Polynesian drink prepared from the root of Piper methysticum reputedly having slight intoxicating qualities.

kio. A member of a group defeated in war in Mangareva and Easter Island.

konohiki. Persons of intermediate status in Hawaii.

kutunga. A localized common-descent group (descent-line) in Futuna.

maakua. A priest-chief in Ontong Java.

makaainana. A person of commoner status in Hawaii.

mana. Sacred power accruing to persons of rank throughout Polynesia.

manahune. A person of commoner status in the Society Islands.

marae. A platform temple in Central Polynesia.

matai. A person holding a political title in Samoa.

matapule. A person of intermediate status in Tonga, an attendant of a chief.

matatoa. A renowned warrior in Easter Island.

ohana. A multihousehold ramage in Hawaii.

paito. A Tikopian ramage composed of several households.

pakaora. A member of a group victorious in battle in Mangareva.

raatira. A person of intermediate status in the Society Islands (cognate, rangatira).

rangatira. A person of chiefly status among the Maori of New Zealand (cognate, raatira).

sa. A Samoan common-descent group having similarly designated branches in various villages.

tapa. Polynesian bark cloth manufactured from the bark of the paper mulberry tree.

taupo. The ceremonial maid of a Samoan village.

toa. A powerful warrior in Mangaia.

tofia. A large tract of land in Tonga utilized by members of a maximal ramage (haa).

togoiti. A person of chiefly status in Mangareva.

tohunga. A Polynesian expert or craftsman (cognates tahuna, tafunga, etc.).

tua. A person of commoner status in Tonga.

Tui Haa Takalaua (abbr. THT)--the second ranking chief of Tonga.

Tui Kanokupolu (abbr. TK)--the third ranking chief of Tonga.

Tui Tonga. The paramount chief of Tonga.

tulafale. A Samoan talking chief.

tupele. An elder of Pukapuka.

urumanu. Mangarevan commoner.

whanau. The ramage of minimal order among the Maori of New Zealand.

Bibliography

Adamson, A. M. Marquesan Insects: Environment. (Bernice
Pahau Bishop Museum Bulletin, No. 139.) Honolulu, 1936.

Aitken, Robert T. Ethnology of Tubuai. (Bernice Pahau
Bishop Museum Bulletin, No. 70.) Honolulu, 1930.

Anderson, Charles Robert, Melville in the South Seas. New
York: Columbia University Press, 1939.

Arii Taimai E. Tahiti, ed. Henry Adams. New York: R. E.
Spiller, 1947. (Facsimile.)

Barrett, Otis Warren. TheTropical Crops. New York: Macmillan Co., 1928.

Bartholomew, George A., and Joseph B. Birdsell. "Ecology
and the Protohominids," American Anthropologist, LV
(1953), 481-98.

Beaglehole, Ernest. Islands of Danger. Wellington, New
Zealand: Progressive Publishing Society, 1944.

-------, and Pearl Beaglehole. Ethnology of Pukapuka.(Bernice Pahau Bishop Museum Bulletin, No. 150.) Honolulu,
1938.

-------, and Pearl Beaglehole. Pangai: Village in Tonga.
(Memoirs of the Polynesian Society, Vol. XVIII.) Wellington, N. Z., 1941.

Beckwith, Martha W. (ed.). Kepelino's Traditions of Hawaii.
(Bernice Pahau Bishop Museum Bulletin, No. 95.) Honolulu, 1932.

Bennett, Wendell Clark. Archaeology of Kauai. (Bernice
Pahau Bishop Museum Bulletin, No. 80.) Honolulu, 1931.

Best, Eldson. "Food Products of Tuhoeland," New Zealand
Institute Transactions, XXXV (1902), 45-111.

--------. The Maori. (Memoirs of the Polynesian Society, Vol. V.) 2 vols. Wellington, N. Z., 1924.

--------. Maori Agriculture. (Dominion Museum Bulletin, Vol. IX.) Wellington, N. Z.: Whitcombe and Tombs, Ltd., 1925.

--------. Forest Lore of the Maori. (Dominion Museum Bulletin, No. 14, and Polynesian Society Memoir, No. 19.) Wellington, N. Z., 1942.

Bryan, Edwin H., Jr. Ancient Hawaiian Life. Honolulu: Advertiser Publishing Co., reprint, 1950.

--------. "Central and Western Polynesia," in Geography of the Pacific, ed. O. W. Freeman. New York: John Wiley, and Sons, Inc., 1951.

Bryan, William Alanson. Natural History of Hawaii. Honolulu: Hawaiian Gazette Co., 1915.

Buck, Sir Peter H. (Te Rangi Hiroa). Samoan Material Culture. (Bernice Pahau Bishop Museum Bulletin, No. 75.) Honolulu, 1930.

--------. Ethnology of Tongareva. (Bernice Pahau Bishop Museum Bulletin, No. 92.) Honolulu, 1930.

--------. Ethnology of Manihiki and Rakahanga. (Bernice Pahau Bishop Museum Bulletin, No. 99.) Honolulu, 1932.

--------. Mangaian Society. (Bernice Pahau Bishop Museum Bulletin, No. 122.) Honolulu, 1934.

--------. Ethnology of Mangareva. (Bernice Pahau Bishop Museum Bulletin, No. 157.) Honolulu, 1938.

--------. Vikings of the Sunrise. Philadelphia: Frederick A. Stokes Co., 1938.

--------. Arts and Crafts of the Cook Islands. (Bernice Pahau Bishop Museum Bulletin, No. 179.) Honolulu, 1944.

--------. The Coming of the Maori. Wellington, N. Z.: Whitcombe and Tombs, Ltd., 1949.

Bülow, Wilhelm von. "Der Landbesitz der Eingeboren auf der Insel Savaii," Globus, LXXXI (1902), 85-87.

Burrows, Edwin G. Ethnology of Futuna. (Bernice Pahau Bishop Museum Bulletin, No. 138.) Honolulu, 1936.

--------. Ethnology of Uvea. (Bernice Pahau Bishop Museum Bulletin, No. 145.) Honolulu, 1936.

--------. "Topography and Culture on Two Polynesian Islands," Geographical Review, XXVIII (1938), 214-23.

--------. "Western Polynesia: A Study in Cultural Differentiation," Etnologiska Studier, VII (1938), 1-192.

-------. "Breed and Border in Polynesia," American An-
thropologist, XLI (1939), 1-21.
-------. "Culture Areas in Polynesia," Journal of the Pol-
ynesian Society, XLIX (1940), 349-63.
Burrows, William. "Some Notes and Legends of a South Sea
Island," Journal of the Polynesian Society, XXXII (1923),
143-73.
Chubb, Lawrence John. Geology of the Marquesas Islands.
(Bernice Pahau Bishop Museum Bulletin, No. 68.) Honolu-
lu, 1930.
Cook, James. A Voyage to the Pacific Ocean . . . in the
Years 1776, 1777, 1778, 1779, and 1780. 2 vols. London:
G. Nicol and T. Cadell, 1784.
Coulter, John Wesley. Land Utilization in American Samoa.
(Bernice Pahau Bishop Museum Bulletin, No. 170.) Hono-
lulu, 1941.
Crossland, Cyril. "The Island of Tahiti," Geographical
Journal, LXXI (1928), 561-85.
Daly, Reginald A. "The Geology of American Samoa," Pa-
pers from the Department of Marine Biology of the Car-
negie Institution of Washington, XIX (1923), 93-143.(Car-
negie Institution of Washington, No. 340.)
Dole, Sanford B. "Evolution of Hawaiian Land Tenure," Ha-
waiian Historical Society Papers, III (1892), 1-18.
Drioult-Gerard, R. H. La Civilisation des Iles Marquises.
Paris: Rodstein, 1940.
Drucker, Phillip. "Rank, Wealth and Kinship in Northwest
Coast Society," American Anthropologist, XLI (1939),
pp. 55-65.
Elbert, Samuel H. "Internal Relationships of Polynesian
Languages and Dialects," Southwestern Journal of Anthro-
pology, IX (1953), 147-73.
Ellis, William E. A Journal of a Tour around Hawaii. Bos-
ton: Crocker and Brewster, 1825.
-------. Narrative of a Tour through Hawaii. 2nd ed.; Lon-
don: H. Fisher, Son, and P. Jackson, 1826.
-------. Polynesian Researches. 4 vols. 2nd ed.; London:
Bohn Press, 1853.
Emerson, N. B. "The Bird-Hunters of Ancient Hawaii,"
Hawaiian Annual, XXI (1895), 101-11.
Emory, Kenneth P. "Warfare," in Ancient Hawaiian Civili-
zation, ed. E. S. Craighill Handy. Honolulu: Kamehameha
Schools, 1933.

-------. Stone Remains in the Society Islands. (Bernice Pahau Bishop Museum Bulletin, No. 116.) Honolulu, 1933.

Firth, Raymond. Primitive Economics of the New Zealand Maori. New York: E. P. Dutton and Co., Inc., 1929.

-------. "Report on Research in Tikopia," Oceania, I (1930-31), 105-17.

-------. "Totemism in Polynesia," Oceania, I (1930-31), 291-321, 377-98.

-------. We, the Tikopia. London: George Allen and Unwin, Ltd., 1936.

-------. The Work of the Gods in Tikopia. (Monographs I and II, London School of Economics.) London, 1940.

-------. "Authority and Public Opinion in Tikopia," in Social Structure, ed. M. Fortes. Oxford: Clarendon Press, 1949.

-------. Primitive Polynesian Economy. New York: Humanities Press, 1950.

Foreign Office (British), Historical Section. "Malpelo, Cocos and Easter Islands," (Nos. 141, 142); "French Possessions in Oceania" (No. 145); "Former German Possessions in Oceania" (No. 146) (Peace Handbooks, Vol. XXII.) London: H. M. Stationery Office, 1920.

Fornander, Abraham. An Account of the Polynesian Race, Its Origin and Migrations and the Ancient History of the Hawaiian People to the Times of Kamehameha I. 2 vols. London, 1880.

Freeman, Otis W. "Geographic Setting of the Pacific," "Hawaii and American Island-Outposts," and "Eastern Polynesia," in Geography of the Pacific, ed. O. W. Freeman. New York: John Wiley and Sons, Inc., 1951.

Gardiner, J. Stanley. Coral Reefs and Atolls. London: Macmillan and Co., 1931.

Gifford, Edward Winslow. Tongan Society. (Bernice Pahau Bishop Museum Bulletin, No. 61.) Honolulu, 1929.

Gill, William Wyatt. Life in the Southern Isles. London: Religious Tract Society, 1876.

-------. From Darkness to Light in Polynesia. London: Religious Tract Society, 1894.

-------. Rarotonga Records. New Plymouth, N. Z.: Polynesian Society, 1916.

Goldman, Irving. "Status Rivalry and Cultural Evolution in Polynesia," American Anthropologist, LVII (1955), 680-97.

Goodenough, Ward H. "A Problem in Malayo-Polynesian Social Organization," American Anthropologist, LVII (1955), 71-83.

Handy, E. S. Craighill. The Native Culture in the Marquesas. (Bernice Pahau Bishop Museum Bulletin, No. 9.) Honolulu, 1923.

——————. History and Culture in the Society Islands. (Bernice Pahau Bishop Museum Bulletin, No. 79.) Honolulu, 1930.

——————. Houses, Boats, and Fishing in the Society Islands. (Bernice Pahau Bishop Museum Bulletin, No. 90.) Honolulu, 1932.

——————. "Government and Society," "Religion and Education," "Feasts and Holidays," and "Houses and Villages," in Ancient Hawaiian Civilization, ed. E. S. Craighill Handy. Honolulu: Kamehameha Schools, 1933.

——————. The Hawaiian Planter. (Bernice Pahau Bishop Museum Bulletin, No. 161.) Honolulu, 1940.

——————, and M. Pukui, "The Hawaiian Family System," Journal of the Polynesian Society, LIX (1950), 170-90; 232-40; LX (1951), 66-79, 187-222; LXI (1952), 243-82.

Hawthorn, H. B. The Maori: A Study in Acculturation. (Memoir Series of the American Anthropological Association, No. 64.) Menasha, Wis., 1944.

Henry, Teuira. Ancient Tahiti. (Bernice Pahau Bishop Museum Bulletin, No. 48.) Honolulu, 1928.

Hobbs, Jean. "The Land Title in Hawaii," Hawaiian Historical Society Annual Report, XL (1931), 26-33.

Hogbin, H. Ian. "The Problem of Depopulation in Melanesia as Applied to Ontong Java," Journal of the Polynesian Society, XXXIX (1930), 43-66.

——————. "The Social Organization of Ontong Java," Oceania, I (1930-31), 399-425.

——————. "Tribal Ceremonies at Ontong Java (Solomon Islands)," Journal of the (Royal) Anthropological Institute, LXI (1931), 27-55.

——————. "Polynesian Ceremonial Gift Exchanges," Oceania, III (1932), 13-39.

——————. Law and Order in Polynesia. New York: Harcourt, Brace and Co., 1934.

——————. "Coconuts and Coral Islands," National Geographic Magazine, LXV (1934), 265-98.

-------. "'Polynesian' Colonies in Melanesia," Journal of the Polynesian Society, XLIX (1940), 199-220.

Keesing, Felix M. Modern Samoa. London: George Allen and Unwin, Ltd., 1934.

Kirchhoff, Paul. "The Principles of Clanship in Human Society," Davidson Anthropological Journal, I (1955), 1-11.

Krämer, Augustin. Die Samoa-Inseln. 2 vols. Stuttgart: Schweizerbart, 1902.

Kuykendall, Ralph S. The Hawaiian Kingdom 1778-1854. Honolulu: University of Hawaii, 1938.

Lambert, Sylvester M. The Depopulation of Pacific Races. (Bernice Pahau Bishop Museum Special Publication, No. 23.) Honolulu, 1934.

Lamont, E. H. Wild Life among the Pacific Islanders. London: Hurst and Blackett, Ltd., 1867.

Landtman, Gunnar. The Origin of the Inequality of the Social Classes. Chicago: University of Chicago Press, 1938.

Laval, Honoré. Mangareva: L'Histoire Ancienne d'un Peuple Polynésien. Braine-le-Comte: Maison des Pères de Sacrés-Cœurs, 1938.

Linton, Ralph. The Material Culture of the Marquesas Islands. (Bernice Pahau Bishop Museum Memoir, Vol. VIII, No. 5.) Honolulu, 1923.

-------. Archaeology of the Marquesas. (Bernice Pahau Bishop Museum Bulletin, No. 23.) Honolulu, 1925.

-------. "Marquesan Culture," in Ralph Linton and A. Kardiner, The Individual and His Society. New York: Columbia University Press, 1939.

Lister, J. J. "Notes on the Natives of Fakaofu (Bowditch Island)," Journal of the (Royal) Anthropological Institute, XXI (1891), 43-63.

Loeb, Edwin M. History and Traditions of Niue. (Bernice Pahau Bishop Museum Bulletin, No. 32.) Honolulu, 1926.

Luomala, Katharine. The Menehune of Polynesia and Other Mythical Little People of Oceania. (Bernice Pahau Bishop Museum Bulletin, No. 203.) Honolulu, 1951.

MacGregor, Gordon. Notes on the Ethnology of Pukapuka. (Bernice Pahau Bishop Museum Occasional Papers, Vol. XI, No. 6.) Honolulu, 1935.

-------. Ethnology of the Tokelau Islands. (Bernice Pahau Bishop Museum Bulletin, No. 146.) Honolulu, 1937.

Malinowski, Bronislaw. Argonauts of the Western Pacific. London: George Routledge, 1932.

-------. "Anthropology as the Basis of Social Science," in Human Affairs, eds. R. B. Cattell, J. Cohen, and R. Trabers. London: Macmillan and Co., 1937.

Malo, David. Hawaiian Antiquities. (Bernice Pahau Bishop Museum Special Publication, No. 2.) 2nd ed.; Honolulu, 1951.

Mariner, William. An Account of the Tongan Islands in the South Pacific Ocean, ed. John Martin. 2 vols. 3rd ed.; Edinburgh: Constable Press, 1827.

Marshall, P. Geology of Mangaia. (Bernice Pahau Bishop Museum Bulletin, No. 36.) Honolulu, 1927.

McKern, W. C. Archaeology of Tonga. (Bernice Pahau Bishop Museum Bulletin, No. 60.) Honolulu, 1929.

Mead, Margaret. "The Role of the Individual in Samoan Culture," Journal of the (Royal) Anthropological Institute, LVIII (1928), 481-95.

-------. The Social Organization of Manua. (Bernice Pahau Bishop Museum Bulletin, No. 76.) Honolulu, 1930.

-------. Coming of Age in Samoa. New York: Mentor Books, 1950.

Meek, C. K. Land, Law and Custom in the Colonies. London: Oxford University Press, 1946.

Melville, Herman. Typee. New York: Aventine Press, 1931.

Merrill, Elmer D. Plant Life of the Pacific World. New York: Macmillan Co., 1945.

Métraux, Alfred. "Une Féodalité Cannibale en Polynesie Française," Revue de Paris, V (1937), 636-61.

-------. "The Kings of Easter Island," Journal of the Polynesian Society, XLVI (1937), 41-62.

-------. Ethnology of Easter Island. (Bernice Pahau Bishop Museum Bulletin, No. 160.) Honolulu, 1940.

Mishkin, Bernard. "The Maori of New Zealand," in Cooperation and Competition among Primitive Peoples, ed. Margaret Mead. New York: McGraw-Hill Book Co., 1937.

Morrison, James. The Journal of James Morrison. London: Golden Cockerel Press, 1935.

Murdock, George P. Social Structure. New York: Macmillan Co., 1949.

Nakuina, Emma M. "Ancient Hawaiian Water Rights and Some of the Customs Pertaining to Them," Hawaiian Annual, XX (1894), 79-84.

Nicholls, Sir Henry A., and John H. Holland. A Text-book

of Tropical Agriculture. London: Macmillan and Co., Ltd., 1929.

Nichols, John T., and Paul Bartsch. Fishes and Shells of the Pacific World. New York: Macmillan Co., 1945.

Pelzer, Karl J. Pioneer Settlement in the Asiatic Tropics. New York: American Geographical Society, 1945.

Perry, Antonio. "Hawaiian Water Rights," Hawaiian Annual, XXXIX (1913), 90-99.

Polanyi, Karl. The Great Transformation. New York: Farrar and Rinehart, 1944.

--------. "Semantics of General Economic History" (Mimeographed, rev. ed., 1953)

Popenoe, Wilson. Manual of Tropical and Subtropical Fruits. New York: Macmillan Co., 1920.

Pukui, M. K. (trans.) "The Canoe Making Profession of Ancient Times," Hawaiian Historical Society Papers, XX (1939), 27-37.

Rivers, W. H. R. The History of Melanesian Society. 2 vols. Cambridge, Eng.: University Press, 1914.

Rollin, Louis. Les Iles Marquises. Paris: Société d'Editions Géographiques, Maritimes et Coloniales, 1929.

Routledge, Mrs. Scoresby. The Mystery of Easter Island. London: Hazel, Watson and Vinney, 1919.

Schultz, E. "The Most Important Principles of Samoan Family Law, and the Laws of Inheritance," Journal of the Polynesian Society, XX (1911), 43-53.

Schultz-Ewerth, Erich. "Samoa," in Das Eingeborenenrecht, ed. E. Schultz-Ewerth and Leonhard Adam. 2 vols. Stuttgart: Strecker und Schröder, 1929-30. Vol. II.

Setchell, William A. American Samoa. Papers from the Department of Marine Biology of the Carnegie Institution of Washington, Vol. XX (1924). (Carnegie Institution of Washington, No. 341.) Part 2, "Ethnobotany of the Samoans," pp. 189-224.

Shapiro, H. L. "The Physical Characteristics of the Ontong Javanese: A Contribution to the Study of the Non-Melanesian Elements in Melanesia," Anthropological Papers of the American Museum of Natural History, XXXIII (1933), 227-78.

Skottsberg, C. "Notes on a Visit to Easter Island" in The Natural History of Juan Fernandez and Easter Island. Vol. I, No. 1. Uppsala, Sweden, 1920.

Smith, S. Percy. "Tongarewa, or Penryhn Island, and Its People," New Zealand Institute Transactions, XXII (1889), 85-103.

————. "Futuna, or Horne Island and Its People," Journal of the Polynesian Society, I (2nd ed.; 1909), 33-53.

————. "Uea, or Wallis Island, and Its People," Journal of the Polynesian Society, I (2nd ed.; 1909), 107-17.

————. "Notes on the Mangareva or Gambier Group of Islands, Eastern Polynesia," Journal of the Polynesian Society, XXVII (1918), 115-31.

Smith, William. Journal of a Voyage in the Missionary Ship Duff to the Pacific Ocean in the Years 1796, 7, 8, 9, 1800, 1, 2, etc. New York: Collins and Co., 1813.

Stair, Reverend John B. Old Samoa. London: Religious Tract Society, 1897.

Steinen, Diether von den. "Das Stande-wesen der Polynesier in seiner wirtschaftlichen Bedeutung," Zeitschrift fur vergleichende Rechtswissenshaft, XLII (1926), 146-94.

Thomson, William J. "Te Pito Te Henua, or Easter Island," United States National Museum, Annual Report (1889), pp. 447-552.

Thurnwald, Richard. Economics in Primitive Communities. London: Oxford University Press, 1932.

Tregear, Edward. The Maori Race. Wanganui, N.Z.: A. D. Willis, 1926.

Turner, George. Samoa: A Hundred Years Ago and Long Before. London: Macmillan and Co., 1884.

White, Leslie A. "Energy and the Evolution of Culture," American Anthropologist, XLV (1943), 335-56.

————. The Science of Culture. New York: Farrar, Straus and Young, Inc., 1949.

Wilcox, Earley V. Tropical Agriculture. New York: D. Appleton and Co., 1924.

Wilder, G. P. The Breadfruit of Tahiti. (Bernice Pahau Bishop Museum Bulletin, No. 50.) Honolulu, 1928.

Williams, Howel. Geology of Tahiti, Moorea and Maiao. (Bernice Pahau Bishop Museum Bulletin, No. 105.) Honolulu, 1933.

Williamson, Robert W. The Social and Political Systems of Central Polynesia. 3 vols. Cambridge, Eng.: University Press, 1924.

————. Religion and Social Organization in Polynesia, ed.

R. Piddington, with an introduction by Raymond Firth.
Cambridge, Eng.: University Press, 1937.

-------. Essays in Polynesian Ethnology, ed. R. Piddington.
Cambridge, Eng.: University Press, 1939.

Wise, John H. "The History of Land Ownership in Hawaii,"
in Ancient Hawaiian Civilization, ed. E. S. Craighill
Handy. Honolulu: Kamehameha Schools, 1933.

Woodford, Charles M. "Note on the Atoll of Ontong Java or
Lord Howe's Group in the Western Pacific," Journal of the
Royal Geographical Society, XXXIV (1909), 544-49.

-------. "On Some Little-Known Polynesian Settlements in
the Neighborhood of the Solomon Islands," Journal of the
Royal Geographical Society, XLVIII (1916), 26-54.

Index

District organization: in Tahiti, 113, 133, 164-65; in Samoa, 113, 133-34, 181-89 passim; in Mangaia, 172, 174-75; in Futuna, 189-91 passim; in Uvea, 191-94 passim. See also Territoriality

Divine descent of chiefs: in Polynesia, 9, 151; in Hawaii, 21; in Samoa, 36, 185; in Society Islands, 44; in Mangareva, 53; in ramage systems, 142, 146. See also Divinity of chiefs; Mana

Divinity of chiefs: in Society Islands, 44; in Easter Island, 58, 169; in Tokelau, 104.

Domesticated animals: in Hawaii, 260; in Society Islands, 262-63; in Samoa, 265; in Easter Island, 270; in Uvea, 271; in Marquesas, 275; in Futuna, 277-78

Dual chieftainship: in Easter Island, 54, 158-59, 169-71; in Mangaia, 59-60, 158-59, 171, 173-74; in ramage organization, 146, 179-80; in Tonga, 158-59; absent in Mangareva, 176-77

Easter Island: social stratification in, 11, 54-59, 68-71; ecology of, 211-12, 268-70; social structure of, 167-71

Ecology: relative productivities of in Polynesia, 125-29. See also Environment; Technology

Egalitarian society: defined, 1; statuses in, 1-2; traits of, 7-9; traits of in Uvea, 64, 65; traits of in Marquesas, 76; traits of in Futuna, 86, 87-88; traits of in Pukapuka, 92; traits of in Tokelau, 102-3, 225; elements of in atolls, 236; strong indication of in Tongareva, 283n. See also Elders

Elders: rule by as egalitarian trait, 8; position in Uvea, 64; right to wear insignia in Uvea, 65; role in Marquesan polity, 76; authority of in Futuna, 86, 87-88; powers of in Pukapuka, 92, 94-95, 233; council of in Tokelau, 101-2, 225-26; powers of in Tokelau, 101-2

Endogamy, rules of: in New Zealand, 155; Tonga, 157; in Marquesas, 160; in Hawaii, 163; in Easter Island, 168. See also Marriage, intrastatus; Status endogamy

Environment: variable productivities of, 123; diversity on high islands, 123; limitations of on atolls, 123, 234-35; of Hawaii, 126, 207-8, 257-58; of Society Islands, 126, 206-7, 260-61; of Samoa, 126-27, 213-14, 263-64; of Tonga, 204; of Marquesas, 204-5, 274; of Mangaia, 205-6, 272; of Mangareva, 208-9, 266; of Tikopia, 209-10, 277; of New Zealand, 210-11; of Easter Island, 211-12, 268-69; of Futuna, 212-

13, 276; of Ontong Java, 280; of Pukapuka, 281; of Tokelau, 283. See also Atolls; Ecology

European influences: on Uvean chieftainship, 66; on Uvean legal procedure, 67; strengthen Futuna councils, 88; on Ontong Java chieftainship, 97, 100, 229; on Mangaian district organization, 174-75; on Uvean district organization, 193

Exchange: reciprocal in Pukapuka, 93, 245; reciprocal in Tokelau, 102, 240; reciprocal kin form in Polynesia, 149-50;

--coastal-inland: in Tonga, 204; Marquesas, 205; Tahiti, 206; Hawaii, 208; Mangareva, 208-9; Easter Island, 212; Samoa, 213, 214

Exogamy, rules of: in Mangareva, 53; not characteristic of Tikopian "clan," 139; in ramage systems, 142; in Tikopia, 153; in New Zealand, 155; in Tonga, 157; in Marquesas, 160; in Hawaii, 163; in Easter Island, 168; of Mangaian tribes, 172; in Tongareva, 219; in Ontong Java, 228; in Pukapuka, 232. See also Marriage, intrastatus

Familial production, supervision by chiefs: as index of stratification, 7; in Hawaii, 16; in Tonga, 24; in Samoan council, 31; no evidence for in Society Islands, 39; absent in Mangareva, 50; absent in Easter Island, 55; absent in Mangaia, 60; lacking in Uvea, 65; absent in Marquesas, 73; absent in Tikopia, 81; absent in Futuna, 86; lacking in Pukapuka, 93; absent in Ontong Java, 98; absent in Tokelau, 101

--specialization of: in Tonga, 204; in Marquesas, 204; in Mangaia, 205; in Society Islands, 206; in Hawaii, 208; limited in Tikopia, 209-10; among New Zealand Maori, 211; absent in Futuna, 213; absent in Samoa, 214; no evidence regarding in Uvea, 215; impossible in atolls, 236. See also Production, specialized

Famine: productivity implications of, 124; in Uvea, 128; in Futuna, 128; in Marquesas, 128; in atolls, 218, 235. See also Food shortage

Fertility, associated with chiefs: in Tikopia, 84, 153; in Ontong Java, 100; in Polynesia, 142

Feud: in Tonga, 28; ended by Samoan village council, 35. See also collective retaliation in disputes; Disputes, settlement of

Feudalism, 54n, 148, 150

First fruits: given to Tongan chiefs, 24; given to Society Islands chiefs, 39;

waii, 14-15; in Tonga, 23; in Society
Islands, 38n, 39n; in Mangareva, 49;
in Mangaia, 60; in Marquesas, 72-73;
free use in Tikopia, 79; in Futuna, 86;
in Pukapuka, 92-93; in Ontong Java,
97-98; in Tokelau, 101. See also Communal lands; Land rights of chiefs
Law: "code" of in Society Islands, 43;
distinguished from collective retaliation, 150. See also Collective retaliation; Disputes, settlement of; Retaliatory powers of chiefs
Life-crisis rites, rank differences in: in
Hawaii, 21-22; in Tonga, 29; in Samoa,
37; in Society Islands, 45; in Mangareva, 53; in Easter Island, 59; in Mangaia, 63; in Uvea, 68; in Marquesas,
77; in Tikopia, 85; in Futuna, 89; in
Pukapuka, 96; in Tokelau, 104; of
senior sons, 141

Malinowski, Bronislaw: on distribution
and cheiftainship, 3
Mana: and Polynesian chieftainship, 9;
of Hawaiian chiefs, 21; of Society Islands chiefs, 44; of Easter Islands
chiefs, 58; of Tikopian chiefs, 84; of
Marquesan chiefs, 77; and descent,
142; of ramage heads, 151. See also
Divine descent of chiefs; Divinity of
chiefs
Mangareva: social stratification in, 11,
48-54, 68-71; social structure of, 175-
78; ecology of, 208-9, 266-68
Mangaia: social stratification in, 11,
59-64, 68-71; social structure of, 171-
75; ecology of, 205-6, 272-73
Manihiki-Rakahanga: history of settlement of, 220-21, 239-40; social structure of, 220-22; ecology of, 239-40
Marquesas: social stratification in, 11-
12, 72-77, 89-91; social structure of,
159-61; ecology of, 204-5, 274-76
Marriage, intrastatus: as measure of
stratification, 9; in Hawaii, 20, 163;
Tonga, 28, 157; Samoa, 36; Society
Islands, 43; Mangareva, 53; Easter
Island, 58; Mangaia, 63; not recorded
for Uvea, 68; Marquesas, 76, 161;
Tikopia, 84; not recorded for Futuna,
88; Pukapuka, 96; Ontong Java, 100;
Tokelau, 104. See also Endogamy;
Exogamy
Matrilineal descent: so-called in Polynesia, 146; in Pukapuka, 232
Matrilocal extended family: in Ontong
Java, 226-27
Matrilocal residence: so-called in Polynesia, 146; in Tokelau, 240
Mead, Margaret: on Samoan social
structure, 30-37 passim, 181-89 passim

Melville, Herman: on Marquesas, 74-75,
75n, 111
Menials: in Society Islands, 38n; so-
called, in Mangareva, 48, 49, 178; in
Mangaia, 60; in New Zealand, 156; in
Easter Island, 171. See also "Ser-
vants"; "Slaves"
Men's clubhouses: in Tokelau, 225, 240;
in Ontong Java, 228
Moieties: in Pukapuka, 232
Murder, punishment of: in Samoa, 35; in
Mangareva, 52; in Mangaia, 62; in Uvea,
67-68; in Marquesas, 76; in Pukapuka,
95; in Ontong Java, 99

New Zealand Maori: variations in culture
of, xii; social structure of, 154-56;
ecology of, 210-11
Niue, xii
Nonunilinear descent groups: defined by
Goodenough, 217; in Tokelau, 222n

Offenses against the community, punishment of: in Samoa, 33, 35, 36; in Futuna, 88; in Pukapuka, 95; in Ontong
Java, 99
--against persons. See Disputes, settlement of
Ohana family group, Hawaii: 162, 208
Ontong Java: social stratification in, 12,
97-100, 104-6; social structure of, 226-
30; ecology of, 242-44, 280-81; history
of, 243-44
"Outcastes": in Hawaii, 14. See also Menials; "Slaves"

Pandanus cultivation: in Hawaii, 259; in
Samoa, 265; in Mangareva, 268; in Mangaia, 273; in Pukapuka, 282; in Tokelau,
283
Patrilineal descent: in ramages, 140,
146; in Samoa, 181; in Futuna, 189; in
Uvea, 192; in Tokelau, 222; in Pukapuka, 231-32. See also Ramage organization
Patrilocal extended family: in New Zealand, 155; in Tonga, 157; in Marquesas,
159; in Hawaii, 161; in Easter Island,
168; in Mangaia, 171; in Mangareva,
175; in Samoa, 182; in Futuna, 189; in
Uvea, 191-92; in Tongareva, 219; in
Manihiki-Rakahanga, 221; in Ontong
Java, 227; in Pukapuka, 231
Patrilocal residence: in Polynesia, 146;
in Tokelau, 223-24; in Pukapuka, 233
Population, aboriginal: materials for estimating Polynesian, 112; of Hawaii, 132-
33, 161; of Tonga, 133; of Tahiti, 133,165;
of Samoa, 133-34, 184-85; of Mangareva,
134; of Easter Island, 168; of Uvea,
134; of Futuna, 134-35, 189; of Tikopia,
135; of Marquesan "tribes," 134; of

Law and Status among the Kiowa Indians. Jane Richardson. (Monograph I) 1940. 142 pages, bibliography. Out of print

Rank and Warfare among the Plains Indians. Bernard Mishkin. (Monograph III) 1940. 73 pages, bibliography. Out of print

Disease, Religion and Society in the Fiji Islands. Dorothy M. Spencer. (Monograph II) 1941. 92 pages, chart. Out of print

An Analysis of Inca Militarism. Joseph Bram. (Monograph IV) 1941. 93 pages, bibliography. $1.50

A Primitive Mexican Economy. George M. Foster. (Monograph V) 1942. 123 pages, plates, maps, bibliography. Out of print

The Effects of White Contact upon Blackfoot Culture, with Special Reference to the Role of the Fur Trade. Oscar Lewis. (Monograph VI) 1942. 79 pages, maps, bibliography. $1.50

Arapesh. R. F. Fortune. (Publication XIX) 1942. 243 pages. $5.00

Prayer: The Compulsive Word. Gladys A. Reichard. (Monograph VII) 1944. 121 pages, figures, bibliography. $2.50

Changing Configurations in the Social Organization of a Blackfoot Tribe during the Reserve Period (The Blood of Alberta, Canada). Esther S. Goldfrank. (Monograph VIII, bound with IX) 1945. 81 pages, plates, bibliography. $2.50

Observations on Northern Blackfoot Kinship. L. M. Hanks, Jr., and Jane Richardson. (Monograph IX, bound with VIII) 1945. 37 pages, figures. $2.50

Map of North American Indian Languages. Compiled and drawn by C. F. Voegelin and E. W. Voegelin. (Publication XX) 1945. Wall size, color. $2.00

The Influence of Islam on a Sudanese Religion. Joseph Greenberg. (Monograph X) 1946. 83 pages, figures, map, bibliography. $2.50

Alaskan Eskimo Ceremonialism. Margaret Lantis. (Monograph XI) 1947. 143 pages, maps, bibliography. $2.75

Economics of the Mount Hagen Tribes, New Guinea. Abraham L. Gitlow. (Monograph XII) 1947. 122 pages, plates, figures, maps, bibliography. $2.75

Ceremonial Patterns in the Greater Southwest. Ruth M. Underhill. (Monograph XIII, bound with XIV) 1948. 74 pages, bibliography, index. $2.50

Factionalism in Isleta Pueblo. David H. French. (Monograph XIV, bound with XIII) 1948. 54 pages, bibliography. $2.50

The Negro in Northern Brazil: A Study in Acculturation. Octavio da Costa Eduardo. (Monograph XV) 1948. 139 pages, map, bibliography. $2.75

Bali: Rangda and Barong. Jane Belo. (Monograph XVI) 1949. 71 pages, plates, figures, bibliography. $2.75

The Rubber-Ball Games of the Americas. Theodore Stern. (Monograph XVII) 1950. 129 pages, plate, maps, bibliography. $2.50

Fighting with Property: A Study of Kwakiutl Potlatching and Warfare 1792-1930. Helen Codere. With Tribal and Linguistic Map of Vancouver Island and Adjacent Territory, drawn and compiled by Vincent F. Kotschar. (Monograph XVIII) 1950. 143 pages, figures, maps, charts, bibliography. $3.00

The Cheyenne in Plains Indian Trade Relations 1795-1840. Joseph Jablow. (Monograph XIX) 1951. 110 pages, maps, bibliography, index. $2.50

The Tsimshian: Their Arts and Music. The Tsimshian and Their Neighbors, by Viola E. Garfield; Tsimshian Sculpture, by Paul S. Wingert; Tsimshian Songs, by Marius Barbeau. (Publication XVIII) 1951. 302 pages, plates, figures, maps, music, bibliography, index. $6.00

Navaho Grammar. Gladys A. Reichard. (Publication XXI) 1951. 407 pages, bibliography. $7.00

Buzios Island: A Caiçara Community in Southern Brazil. Emilio Willems in cooperation with Gioconda Mussolini. (Monograph XX) 1952. 124 pages, figures, maps, bibliography. $2.75

Chichicastenango: A Guatemalan Village. Ruth Bunzel. (Publication XXII) 1952. 464 pages, figures, bibliography. $7.00

Changing Military Patterns on the Great Plains (17th Century through Early 19th Century). Frank Raymond Secoy. (Monograph XXI) 1953. 120 pages, maps, bibliography. $2.75

Bali: Temple Festival. Jane Belo. (Monograph XXII) 1953. 78 pages, plates, chart, bibliography. $2.75

Hungarian and Vogul Mythology. Géza Róheim. With appendixes by John Lotz. (Monograph XXIII) 1954. 96 pages, map, bibliography. $2.75

The Trumaí Indians of Central Brazil. Robert F. Murphy and Buell Quain. (Monograph XXIV) 1955. 120 pages, plates, map, bibliography. $2.75

The Deeply Rooted: A Study of a Drents Community in the Netherlands. John Y. Keur and Dorothy L. Keur. (Monograph XXV) 1955. 208 pages, plates, maps, bibliography. $3.00

The Tlingit Indians: Results of a Trip to the Northwest Coast of America and the Bering Straits. Aurel Krause. Translated by Erna Gunther. 1956. 320 pages, plates, figures, map, bibliography, index. $4.50

Village and Plantation Life in Northeastern Brazil. Harry William Hutchinson. 1957. 209 pages, plates, maps, charts, bibliography, index. $4.50

Malaya. Norton Ginsburg and Chester F. Roberts, Jr. 1958. 547 pages, maps, charts, bibliography, index. $6.00

Social Stratification in Polynesia. Marshall D. Sahlins. 1958. 306 pages, figures, bibliography. $4.50

Status Terminology and the Social Structure of North American Indians. Munro S. Edmonson. 1958. 92 pages, charts, bibliography. $3.00